# Higher Ground

# Higher Ground

## Morality and Humanity in the Evolving Politics of Race

Brian P. Tilley

LEXINGTON BOOKS
*Lanham • Boulder • New York • London*

Published by Lexington Books
An imprint of The Rowman & Littlefield Publishing Group, Inc.
4501 Forbes Boulevard, Suite 200, Lanham, Maryland 20706
www.rowman.com

86-90 Paul Street, London EC2A 4NE

British Library Cataloguing in Publication Information Available

**Library of Congress Cataloging-in-Publication Data**

Names: Tilley, Brian P., 1978- author.
Title: Higher ground: morality and humanity in the evolving politics of race / Brian P. Tilley.
Description: Lanham: Lexington Books, [2023] | Includes bibliographical references and index.
Identifiers: LCCN 2023003594 (print) | LCCN 2023003595 (ebook) | ISBN 9781666907537 (cloth; alk. paper) | ISBN 9781666907544 (epub)
Subjects: LCSH: United States—Race relations—Moral and ethical aspects. | Racism—Moral and ethical aspects—United States.
Classification: LCC E185.615 .T5755 2023 (print) | LCC E185.615 (ebook) | DDC 305.800973—dc23/eng/20230203
LC record available at https://lccn.loc.gov/2023003594
LC ebook record available at https://lccn.loc.gov/2023003595

# Contents

*For Joshua, Adrian, Leo, Lucia, and for Maggie.*
*Always for Maggie.*

# Acknowledgments

I am perpetually grateful to my family, especially my wonderful wife, Maggie, for their patience with me as I wrote this book. Maggie loaded the whole family on her back while I wrote on weekends, while I read and edited in late hours, while the home office we built during the COVID-19 pandemic probably felt as far away as my prior office thirty minutes up the freeway. As they say in *The Notebook*, that's my sweetheart.

I plan to make up for the time I missed playing with my curious, indefatigable twins, Adrian and Joshua, and their brother, my little buddy, Leo. When I think of this book, I will always remember Lucia, my little angel, sitting next to me on the couch as I read or by my feet as I typed. My wife and children inspired me more than they know, and if there's anything in here that stays with you, it's because of them. I gave this as much of me as I could for a year, and now I go back to giving them all of me. I love you all to the moon and back.

To my parents, Ellen and Pat, incredible people without a bunch of degrees on the walls, people who fought for everything in life to make our childhoods happier, people who sacrificed for us, people who love and protect me unconditionally, I owe more than I can say. If this book reflects any moral values, they are the values they instilled in me from day one. I love you both.

Thank you to my colleagues and mentors over the years, who pushed me to grow as an academic and grow into adulthood. I wrote this book bearing in mind the high standards set by Lisa Larson, my major professor in graduate school. She pushed me to challenge myself as an academic and a young adult. I hope this work verifies the faith senior faculty placed in me when recommending me for my first academic job, helping me on each step up the ladder, and preparing me for where I am today. I thank my valued colleagues at National University, especially in the old psychology department and in the JFK School of Psychology and Social Sciences for believing in me and fostering an environment that encourages creativity and a thirst for justice.

Special thanks to the estate of Audre Lorde for granting permission to use her words in this text. This quote is from page 139 of *Sister Outsider* (New York, NY: Ten Speed Press), a collection of essays and speeches containing Lorde's talk "Learning from the 60s." That talk was given on Malcom X Weekend at Harvard University in February 1982. The copyright (© 1984, 2007) belongs to the estate of Audre Lorde.

H.L. Mencken is quoted from a periodical, *The Free Lance*, published on October 23, 1915. Marcus Aurelius is quoted from his journal, *Meditations*, written circa 171–175 CE. (This date is based on estimates in the *Internet Encyclopedia of Philosophy*, https://iep.utm.edu/marcus-aurelius/.) Marcel Proust is quoted from *À la recherche du temps perdu*, which we know in English as *In Search of Lost Time*. The quote used here is from the first part of his master work, Du côté de chez Swann, known in English as *Swann's Way*, which was self-published in 1913.

Richard Nixon is quoted from what are known as the Nixon White House Tapes, which were released by the U.S. government and are part of the public domain. (For more, please see the Richard Nixon Presidential Library and Museum at nixonlibrary.gov.) Justice Clarence Thomas is quoted from the public record of a speech given at the Heritage Foundation on August 1, 1987. (For more, please see https://www.blackpast.org/african-american-history /1987-clarence-thomas-why-black-americans-should-look-conservative -politics/.) Donald Trump is quoted based on multiple reports from aides present at a bipartisan meeting held on January 11, 2018, in the Oval Office. The report was first made by the *Washington Post*'s Josh Dawsey. (Dawsey, Josh. January 12, 2018. "Trump Derides Protections for Immigrants from 'Shithole' Countries." *Washington Post.* https://www.washingtonpost.com /politics/trump-attacks-protections-for-immigrants-from-shithole-countries -in-oval-office-meeting/2018/01/11/bfc0725c-f711-11e7-91af-31ac729add94 _story.html.)

Lyndon Johnson is quoted from a special message to Congress introducing what is commonly known as the Voting Rights Act, on March 15, 1965. Rev. Jesse Jackson is quoted from an interview hosted by the Public Broadcasting Systems on their program *Frontline*. The interview was held in 1997, and the episode aired in 1998 (*Frontline*. 1998. Season 16, Episode 9, "The Two Nations of Black America." Public Broadcasting Systems. Aired February 10, 1998). President Biden is quoted from public remarks made shortly after the Buffalo shooting, in which the shooter was linked to the Great Replacement conspiracy theory, on May 17, 2022.

# Introduction

"It is a terrible, an inexorable, law that one cannot deny the humanity of another without diminishing one's own: in the face of one's victim, one sees one's self."

That was written by James Baldwin, in an essay called "Fifth Avenue, Uptown" about the false, seemingly inescapable boundaries of a racial system. Boundaries that get re-created no matter where a Black American lives because they are easier to create than acknowledging one another's humanity. Baldwin wrote those words in 1960. He wrote them, in part, to break through the comfortable defenses of White Americans accustomed to granting a relative sort of humanity: it could be worse. Then things got worse.

What happened next in the United States was a so-called racial reckoning. When it is time for one of these, it isn't determined by great deliberation, nor is it initiated by politicians. It is the result of a groundswell: people outraged, pained, insulted, marginalized, threatened, drained, shocked, and fed up coalesce around a moment or a goal. The effort builds until, like a wave, it crests and rushes forward, flowing over and around all who stand before it.

Just as in the 1960s, that time is now.

In the current racial reckoning, there are debates in legislatures—but also on podcasts, social media, cable news, and around dinner tables—about wokeness, so-called cancel culture, and critical race theory. Each of these discussions is related to race in America, and each of these discussions prominently features people talking right past one another, making counterarguments without discussing *why* there is so little common understanding in an area that profoundly impacts American life. More importantly, what does that common understanding look like?

\*\*\*

In May 1963, Bull Connor ordered policemen to shoot fire hoses and sic police dogs on civil rights demonstrators, many of them children. It just so happened that cameras captured these actions and broadcast them to the nation on the nightly news (Bryant 2015; PBS 2016).

1

In May 2020, George Floyd was killed when a police officer trying to restrain him knelt on the back of his neck for over nine minutes. It just so happened that a bystander recorded and then uploaded online, thereby distributing to the world, the last minutes of Floyd's life (Williams 2021).

It was clear to many who saw these events that something truly repugnant was going on. In both cases, the event captured on camera was not a clash of racial ideologies. It was simply another event in a controversial conflict that most of the country felt more comfortable ignoring. It was the shock of seeing images of the event that was enough to awaken a racial reckoning, for whatever that is worth (Hassan and O'Grady 2020).

The most important element shared by these events is the motivational power they represent. It is an adage in political science that people vote in their self-interest (Downs 1957). If that is true, then, in 1964, why did many White[1] people who previously ignored or even disagreed with the civil rights movement (Converse, Clausen and Miller 1965; Hoffman 2015) vote, in a thunderous landslide, for a president who loudly promoted his support for a Civil Rights Act? In 2020, why did many relatively affluent and privileged White people risk their safety amid a pandemic to march in solidarity against racism (Demby 2020; Washington 2020)? Why did these White people choose to leave the relative comfort of their houses for a cause unlikely to personally affect them? Why change now?

In some cases, such as Rosa Parks's role in the Montgomery Bus Boycott and the anti-segregation demonstrations that provoked Connor's ire, the showdown was part of a larger strategy. In others, such as George Floyd's awful fate and Rodney King's relentless beating by the Los Angeles Police Department, the event was spontaneous, revelatory, and meant to be hidden from public view. No matter the prologue, the record of those events spoke volumes.

Those videos made unavoidable what was previously avoidable: these scenes were so ugly that they went beyond the constructed defenses and politics of the mainstream and tapped into a sense of shared humanity. Those children, those protesters—George Floyd, Breonna Taylor, Atatiana Jefferson, Stephon Clark, Botham Jean, Philando Castile, Eric Garner, Daunte Wright—and countless others are human beings. When we see other human beings treated in a manner so egregious that we call it inhuman, when we feel compassion, a natural reaction is to be moved to help in some way (Eisenberg et al. 1989; Stevens and Taber 2021).

Due to the work of various grassroots movements with lengthy histories in America, one way to push back against inhumanity is to publicly protest. The mid-twentieth-century civil rights movement memorably proclaimed "I AM A MAN" for the world to see. That was not a choice, but an imperative, followed at the cost of one's safety, job, freedom, or, even, life. Today's protesters rarely face the same consequences as these pioneers, who paved the ground with their sacrifices. Today, we walk that road when we see no other option than to speak up, to stand up.

Black lives *should* matter because Black people are people.

And so, since Floyd's death and the summer 2020 protests, we find ourselves experiencing this racial reckoning. But the consensus that motivated a thousand #BlackLivesMatter tweets from corporations is gone. The movement itself is just as popular (or unpopular) as it was before the nation was shocked and angered by unavoidable video evidence of the snuffing out of a human life (Ghosh 2021; Tesler 2020). I cannot walk out my front door for more than four blocks in any direction without seeing a picket in a front yard reading "We Believe . . . " followed by numerous inclusive slogans closing with, "Be Kind to All."

There is no marching on those streets, though.

***

May 1963 wasn't the end of the story. The president at the time, who said civil rights was a "moral" issue, had to be murdered and a country had to mourn before his successor signed the Civil Rights Act and the Voting Rights Act. We know too well that May 2020 wasn't the end of the story. The humanity that inspired solidarity marches is part of the same human character that feeds on skepticism and fear, which pitted valuing Black Lives against "Blue Lives." What more destruction and pain is coming? What good can come of this?

It is taken for granted that we live in a polarized country where we live in our own bubbles of information (Spohr 2017). Human experience tells us that the truth is more complicated than that. We shared a purpose in the paralyzing early days of the COVID-19 pandemic just as we shared a purpose in the wake of the destruction of September 11, 2001. Yet the current racial conversation operates like a debate that pits one person's statistics against another's, one's experience against another's, ideology versus ideology, identity versus identity. We can discuss the thorny issues of race, not across any socially imposed lines, but within humanity, person to person.

By nature, race is a personal issue. It is made personal by people around you, maybe in your family, your neighborhood, your city, your workplace, or your society. Psychological research shows us that how you see yourself is partially a reflection of how others see you (Cooley 1902; Henriques 2011; Lent, Brown and Hackett 1994). It's part of being social animals. No matter our ethnic backgrounds, by virtue of our American status we participate in how White Americans feel about being White, to the extent that they think about it, just like we participate in how Black Americans feel about being

Black. As such, we are all part of this discussion on racial issues and racism, whether we are fed up with hearing about it or just plain fed up.

I believe in the power of communication and shared humanity because this is my background. I was trained as a counseling psychologist, and for almost a decade I served as director of a master's program that trains potential therapists. I was taught to see the fifty minutes a therapist spends with each client as the most important fifty minutes of that person's week, even if you have five other appointments that day. I learned that whatever is going on in my life needs to be left outside the door of the counseling room so I can deeply engage with the other person.

This mindset is necessary to develop a major element of modern counseling, empathy. Empathizing is attempting to sense the inner world of the other person as if it were your own. Everyday empathy is the equivalent of "walking a mile in another person's shoes." Empathy shows the other person that you can be trusted with valuable or sensitive information, that you want to know more about that person's experience because you care.

Why am I talking about empathy? Because, at some point, if this reckoning is to mean something it can't just be a small portion of the country saying something with everyone else ignoring or talking over it. It can't be people being dragged to progress. It doesn't take much of any of this before some people decide, well, why would I listen to someone else if they've shown themselves unwilling to listen to me? Why would I share my experience and relive that pain or frustration if my vulnerability is going to be hand-waved off or disputed?

Empathy builds trust; trust leads to vulnerability. Your guard begins to lower. Vulnerability and trust, when embraced in a conversation, engender more vulnerability and more trust. This cycle deepens a relationship between people. That relationship is a crucial ingredient in producing the incredible changes people experience in therapy (McClintock, Anderson, Patterson and Wing 2018; Rosenzweig 1936; Wampold 2015).

When I think about this supposedly unbreachable divide on race I am often reminded of a story *This American Life* did on an episode entitled "The Incredible Rarity of Changing Your Mind." The story was about marriage equality advocates changing people's minds about this then-divisive issue. They did it by going door-to-door to speak with voters who were opposed to legalizing marriage for gay and lesbian couples. When this phenomenon was tested scientifically, using transgender canvassers approaching voters in Florida about laws targeting antitransgender prejudice, the results showed lasting effects: the people reached weren't just being nice to the canvassers' faces, follow-up three months later showed they really had changed their minds (Broockman and Kalla 2016).

Why did this work? The human connection. It's the reason for the change in politicians like Rob Portman, an Ohio Republican opposed to gay rights until his son came out as gay. It's the same reason why self-segregating in the Fox bubble or the MSNBC bubble is a problem. The less you see and hear from the "other side," the easier it is to mischaracterize or demonize them (Kteiley and Bruneau 2017; Kteily, Hodson and Bruneau 2016; Said 1997). You don't want them living in the same neighborhood as you (Bishop 2008), and you sure as hell aren't interested in building any connections with them. In fact, Americans are even becoming more opposed to their children marrying someone from the opposite political party (Pew 2014; Vavreck 2017).

Unfortunately, there is evidence that this disconnection is mirrored in issues of race in a phenomenon called *racialization* (Sides, Tesler and Vavreck 2016). When politics are racialized, discussion of racial issues is prey to political divisions. Hence the former public consensus around racial civil rights issues has split in political directions: White Democrats believe civil rights should be expanded speedily; White Republicans believe they should only expand slowly, not at all, or even be rolled back. These views tend to get more extreme the stronger one's partisan attachment is. Issues attached to prominent politicians of color get racialized in a *racial spillover effect* in which associating the issue with them makes the issue a racial one, meaning it now reflects your racial values. Social scientist Michael Tesler (2016a) found that even President Obama's dog, Bo, was subject to this effect.

There is no rule of humanity that says we must behave this way about racial issues.

\*\*\*

The following chapters lay out how the politics of race function in the United States and each gives us indicators how we can choose a different path than the one we have been on. I draw from research in social psychology, political science, and law as well as my background in counseling psychology to support my contentions throughout the book. I approach this analysis from a humanistic viewpoint.

There are issues of personal morality—the fundamental sense of what is right and what is wrong—at stake in American discussions of racism and racial issues. As such, there is a moral imperative to do right, or what I refer to as a *moral weight,* that I prioritize in evaluating the various viewpoints that have developed on racism. For example, the moral weight was on the side of the protesters in 1963. The work of civil rights protesters made it so that enough people, a critical mass, were able to see that the actions of Bull Connor and the like were so despicable that the civil rights movement transformed pain into progress.

It is important that we preserve the status of racism as a moral issue. This is crucial because of the successes throughout history of mobilizing public support for meaningful change on issues of race and racism. That support, as is support of many political issues, is an emotional matter (e.g., Haidt 2012; Neuman, Marcus, Crigler and MacKuen 2007).

When racism is limited to only the most egregious violations of human dignity, or when it is so ambiguously defined as to be safely explained away, we lose that critical mass. Either the power it implies is too narrow and nearly impossible to activate or it cannot be assembled due to apathy or confusion. Consider the high bar for interpersonal violations that result in widespread condemnation; consider racial conservatives' propensity to offer alternate explanations for disproportionate treatment of Black people (Azerrad 2022; McCarthy 2020; Pearce 2020). George Floyd's grisly and public death barely cleared that bar, and even then, there were prominent voices criminalizing him postmortem (Best 2021; Carlson 2021; Shapiro 2021a).

We, those of us who believe in the value of every human, must be clear *why* disparate treatment is wrong. Why the epithet "racist" applies, why it is unjust that a system that helps many still can hold down many others. Why these are violations not of a political creed but a golden rule and our fundamental sense of humanity.

Why must the antiracist forces justify themselves? Isn't this unfair to ask? Maybe. But first, it is imperative in racial issues to conduct oneself morally, to know and be able to explain your indignation. And second, the forces enabling racism and discrimination are entrenched: they have the home field advantage (as you'll see in Chapters 2 and 3). If we are to create lasting change, we must be able to build a strong enough coalition to do so and do so in a way that relies on common humanity rather than political gimmickry.

As a country, we can have the conversation about race by seeking a *higher* ground: one supported by a strong moral mandate against racism and a robust sense of shared humanity.

Each chapter is focused on one facet of racism, though taken together they contain the roadmap leading to a common, higher ground on addressing racism in America. I believe that the key to fighting racism lay in its moral nature. History has shown us that successful antiracist movements including abolitionism and the Student Nonviolent Coordinating Committee gained sympathies and commitment from White Americans by highlighting the morality and humanity of their cause. This strategy has been borrowed in statements like "women's rights are human rights" and the humanization at the heart of Harvey Milk's crusade for gay equality. I demonstrate how agreement on a moral imperative against racism is threatened today by polarization. It must be protected. The chapters focus on areas where there is space for agreement on the moral violations of racism, as they are where Americans of disparate views could begin to build toward that higher ground.

The book is divided into three sections. The first section, A Change Is Gonna Come, is about how the history of racism informs our present and our potential solutions to it. I start with the role of morality in American opposition to racism. I examine how morality and religiosity have historically interacted to both perpetuate and oppose racial discrimination. I also cover how morality influences our decision making, underlining the importance of moral weight in fighting racism.

I continue with analysis of how the political parties realigned around racial issues during the twentieth century. Where once the Republicans proclaimed themselves the Party of Lincoln, with a reliable hold on the Black vote, the Democrats—former party of the Ku Klux Klan and Southern plantation class—have become the party most Black Americans support. I give special attention to how politicians use racism to appeal to voters, sometimes below voters' conscious awareness.

I end the first section by covering the current controversy over Critical Race Theory as an example of how a racialized discussion reflects dynamics that have roots throughout American history. I present how the term has evolved and why the controversy is really about the American story.

Next, in a section called What's Going On, I examine the realities of racism. I begin with racism's real-world impacts. The discussion is grounded in the experiences of Black Americans today in several areas, including psychological stress and difficulties receiving appropriate therapeutic treatment. I prioritize research with persuasive findings that hold the moral weight discussed throughout the book. Thus, the chapter is not a source of statistics to be argued and counter-argued, but a case that something very wrong is going on in the country.

I then move on to the ongoing disagreement in modern politics about what constitutes racism: is racism the bigoted views and actions of individuals or is it anti-Black bias embedded in American systems? Furthermore, I explore how defining racism in modern times has presented problems for sociologists and political scientists. There have been various attempts to measure racism in study participants, though much of the debate can be reduced to whether one can show the expression of racism has substantially changed since the Civil Rights Era.

Throughout these sections, the primary focus of the book is on racism directed at Black Americans,[2] though I certainly draw from research on racism toward other groups. The reason for this is, not only that racism toward different groups takes on a different character and requires extensive exploration, but also that racism toward Black Americans has been the focus of the recent racial reckoning. Additionally, racism toward Black Americans has the second-longest history on this continent, except for anti-Indigenous racism, and slavery has had a unique impact on American society throughout our history. It is my intention that focusing mostly on anti-Black racism will add cohesiveness to my argument.

In the book's final section, Think, I examine the main solutions to racism being offered by today's political parties and the extent to which they hold moral weight. I start with a case study of the 2016 election and how racial politics can shed light on Donald Trump's victory. This includes research findings illuminating the holes in "economic anxiety" narrative. I also discuss the problematic nature of the discourse around Trump voters, such as how their humanity is represented.

I then move on to how political parties have approached racism using prominent party representatives as examples. How much does the Republican party's recent appeal to people of color align with their messages on race? And how has the strong anti-racist bent of the Democrats' progressive wing been applied and mis-applied to racial issues? This critique again focuses on the humanity of each party's proposed solutions to racism.

The book ends with a potential path forward for dialogue on race and racial issues. I close with a call to recognize the value of taking interpersonal risks in reaching higher ground for the national conversation on race.

If the current racial reckoning is a wave, we are the wind. We determine whether that wave has crested, how hard the crash will be after it tips, and how fast and far it will flow. It only remains for us to seize this power and use it to channel the racial reckoning toward lasting change that embraces and ensures the humanity of all people in this country.

## NOTES

1. Throughout the book, I capitalize usage of all racial groups. Traditionally this has been done for all racial groups except Black and White. Recently, writers have more consistently capitalized Black. I agree with the reasoning for doing so. I understand the rationale in capitalizing Black but not "white," as an inversion of the power differential throughout the history of this country. White, as it is discussed in the book and in much modern literature on race, is a racial group. As such, it is only fair to the people identified with that group to capitalize White as well.

2. Please note that the book is about racism, which necessarily centers the views of White people in several chapters and multiple ways throughout the volume. I do not propose to encapsulate or otherwise represent the Black experience, which is too expansive to cover here without giving it short shrift.

# PART I

# History

*A Change Is Gonna Come*

# Chapter 1

# Moral Implications of Racism

*To the woman he said:*
*I will intensify your toil in childbearing; in pain you shall bring forth chil-*
*dren. Yet your urge shall be for your husband, and he shall rule over you.*

*To the man he said:*
*Because you listened to your wife and ate from the tree about which I*
*commanded you, you shall not eat from it. Cursed is the ground because*
*of you! In toil you shall eat its yield all the days of your life.*

—Genesis 3:16–17

In this chapter, I discuss why racism is seen as a moral issue, and I introduce the problem of colorblindness. Using examples drawn from history, I
analyze how religion has been perverted to further racism and the role of
humanity and morality in opposing it. A moral opposition to racism is rooted
in fundamental concepts of humanity; I present the evidence for why viewing racism as a moral issue is crucial to building an antiracist consensus.
Finally, in analysis of a recent controversy, I show how racism can operate at
unconscious levels, how psychologists account for this, and how empathy is
valuable in fighting racism.

\*\*\*

In the first book of the Torah and the Christian Old Testament, there are
two creation stories. One is of God creating the heavens, the earth, and its
creatures. The other is a specific tale of how humanity came to be: the story
of Adam and Eve. Most of those reading recall that the latter creation story
explains why there is evil in the world. The first man and woman disobey
God and are banished from the harmony and abundance of the Garden of

Eden. The remnant of that banishment is passed down to Adam and Eve's descendants—all of humanity—through the concept of *original sin*.

This chapter is not about religion; it is about morality. But the language of religion is often used when discussing morality. Take, for example, this concept of original sin. In the second creation story, the actions of Adam and Eve bring an end to their peaceful coexistence, replacing it with the traditional male dominance of the female. Harmony has been replaced with hierarchy,[1] bringing pain and toil.

The barbaric practice of chattel slavery is often referred to as America's *original sin*. Because of slavery, its related justifications, and reverberations, American society is stained. Instead of a nation in which all people live in (relative) harmony, a racial hierarchy was introduced that, like the Judeo-Christian concept of original sin, has been inherited by every American generation since. Slavery is gone, but the beliefs that scaffolded and fueled it, including a system that draws societal lines based on the color of one's skin, lives on.

Our morality is part of the human condition. Morality evolved, according to ecologist Garrett Hardin, to solve what is known as the Tragedy of the Commons: if everyone acted in self-interest, the areas we share would erode. As Joshua Greene (2013) puts it in his excellent book on the subject, morality is a psychological adaptation that allows naturally selfish beings to benefit from cooperation.

In this chapter and those that follow, I write a great deal about humanity. Please do not confuse this with the common defense of, "we're all humans; we're all the same." Yes, we are all human beings. But unfortunately, we are not all the same in terms of how we are treated. Assuming we all must have the same reaction to an event, a work of art, a specific word, is actually the opposite of humanity. This misunderstanding often comes in a particular form, which is the form I analyze and discuss here: the insertion of a judgmental mindset we call "colorblindness."

For instance, if I expect a Mexican American to ignore being called a "beaner" or being asked about tacos every day because it's "just a joke" and "I wouldn't care what you call me," then I am allowing colorblindness to block me from seeing why a person from that background may react differently. If I ask why poor Black people get "special treatment I didn't get" in college admissions, I allow colorblindness to block me from considering hindrances they may have encountered due to racial bias. Colorblindness, then, becomes the opposite of prizing each person's humanity: it is self-centered. It excuses racism by conflating equality in my mind with equality in how the world works.

On the other hand, I want to be careful not to err in the other direction. Black people, Mexican Americans, Korean Americans, Indigenous

Americans, and so many other "racial groups" are not a monolith. Stereotypes are hurtful for a reason. For example, not all Mexican Americans want to increase immigration or access to Spanish-speaking public services. This reduces a diverse group of people to their country of origin. Not all Black people are poor, downtrodden, or in need of rescuing. This mindset discounts the humanity of Black people, their resilience, and their abilities.

So, racism isn't everything, but it isn't nothing, either. This is where some fold their hands and walk away. But think first about humanity. When I teach counseling students about the initial therapy appointment with someone from a different background, I want them to be able to create a connection with that mental health consumer. I ask them to address the difference directly, but without assumption, by asking the client, "Can you tell me a little bit about how you identify yourself?" A lesbian Black woman may see herself as a feminist first, or Black first, or as a lesbian, or a Black woman, or any combination of those forms of identity. Or she may just see herself as a poet. Allow the client to fill in that blank.

Just as importantly, we want to know how living in America has affected this person. If we stopped with the first question, it would give us some information, but allow us to skirt racial identity, which many people of color are aware of. Research (Meyer and Zane 2013) on client-therapist relationships found that clients of color are more likely to care about racial issues than White therapists. Their outcomes were better when these elements are included in their care. Research (Burkard and Knox 2004) also shows that ignoring racial identity can make clients of color feel invisible or that their therapist is not responsive to the client's therapeutic needs.

I ask my students to consider asking a second question, "How do you think others see you?" This opens the conversation to how socially constructed categories such as race can impact the sort of treatment people receive, the expectations placed on them, and what meaning they make of their place in the world. In this way, we recognize the full humanity of each person without ignoring their social context. Who we are is a reflection of how we are treated, which may include racist discrimination. Such treatment influences how we view ourselves and can provide a window into the suffering that impels a person to seek therapy.

Race operates in a public and a private way. In private, we have our own feelings about how integral our race is to our identity, how we conceptualize our race, how authentic we feel, and so on. In public, how we are treated can reflect our race. This phenomenon produces what W. E. B. Du Bois (1903) famously called a "double consciousness." My mother is a mixed-race woman whose biological father was a Black man. She would be considered "White-passing," because her olive complexion does not identify her immediately as Black. She also was adopted as a young child and did not know her heritage until much later in life. She often was asked about her racial background by her classmates and others in her life. This question, without an easy answer,[2] can affect how you view yourself.

At the same time, since she presents as White, many people do not discriminate against her. Her *public* racial identity, therefore, may be markedly different from that of her half-sister, who has darker skin. As such, the two have different experiences with racial identity.[3] Racism publicly impairs people of color throughout this country, as detailed in Chapters 4 and 5. It also privately hurts those who share kinship, identity, and empathy with those discriminated against. There is no rule that empathy and kinship must be limited to a socially constructed group. The bridge to this higher ground is a common moral imperative against racism.

Seeing racism as a moral issue gives it particular standing: how we feel about being racist, how we feel about others who display racist behaviors, what we do in response to racism, these all become important matters. Morality, too, is rooted in our humanity. There are things we see as immoral that offend our sense of shared humanity: stealing, murder, and for many of us, racism. It is immoral to steal because it hurts another human being unfairly and degrades the human being doing the stealing. In the same way, it is immoral to be racist because it dehumanizes fellow human beings and betrays the racist's lack of belief in their own humanity.

## CHRISTIANITY, WHITENESS, AND MORAL ANTIRACISM

Historically, contextualizing racial issues within morality has not always been to the benefit of humanity. Theologian Willie James Jennings (2010), a Baptist preacher and faculty member at the Yale Divinity School, writes that Christianity initially worked against the slave trade. After all, how could worshipers of a God who sent his only Son to preach to the poor and uplift the outcasts not be disturbed by the torture and inhumanity visited on enslaved people? But over time, slavery began to be justified as spreading the Word of God to "heathen" people—unironically and antithetically "saving" them—as ordered by divinely appointed kings. What began as a social justification gained immeasurable power: the White Savior deservedly reigning over the darker-skinned, lesser people.

What imperialism did, according to interreligious researcher Rebecca Cohen (2020), was create a "cult of purity." She draws this terminology from Second Temple Judaism, which concerned itself with purity rituals.[4] Cohen draws this connection based on the complementary binaries of "sacred/profane" and "pure/impure." Though the early Christians began to disregard the purity concerns of their forebears, they retained a belief that the sacred must be kept separate from the polluting influence of the profane.

To imperialistic gain, purity was reinterpreted as Whiteness. Whiteness, in the guise of Christianity, was coming to save—but keep separate—inhabitants of coveted lands. As Cohen puts it, salvation was offered, but on the condition of racialization. Racialization resulted in the tragic loss of one's nationhood, resources, and individual identity. This is the cult of purity, which idolatrized Whiteness.

The effect of this cult is visible throughout the last five hundred years of colonization and Westernization throughout the world. Racialized American society was built in a way that spread this idolatry. One cannot help but think as Cohen does of the one-drop rule later to become part of American society. There was no need for calculation of Blackness or Whiteness of one's genealogy: one "impure" drop of Black genetic blood was enough to make a person Black.

During American slavery, Christianity was used to keep enslaved people from rebelling against White "masters." The plantation owners worked to convert enslaved people to Christianity by reading them the teachings of Jesus Christ from the gospels and Saint Paul's letters. Enslaved people were to remain weak and poor and seek comfort in the next life.[5] Though part of the appeal of early Christianity was that it promised equality in the face of a vastly unequal society, that faith was manipulated to maintain inequality through selective quoting of verses reminding the enslaved to "obey your human masters."[6]

Thus, morality was inverted, with moral Christian behavior purportedly including enslaving people, attempting to pacify them with warped religious teaching, and profiting from their labor.

The second Great Awakening in the 1830s encouraged a religious rededication to morals. This activated a strain of morally righteous antagonism toward racism, which inspired early abolitionists such as William Lloyd Garrison to a more active campaign to end slavery. Garrison called his method "moral suasion."

When an issue is described in moral terms, it becomes harder to see it in shades of moderation. If it is morally wrong to cheat on my spouse, what difference is it if cheating, say, helped me get a promotion? Cheating is just as morally impermissible, regardless of any ancillary benefit. The numerous political evasions of the antebellum period, such as the Compromise of 1850, kept a shaky peace but did not resolve the moral wrong. On the contrary, they extended the life of slavery, thus contributing to said wrong. It is heartbreaking but not unthinkable that a bloody Civil War was the resolution to this condition.

A century later, what was known as the Civil Rights Era dawned. Historian Manning Marable (2007) termed this era yet another Great Awakening. This time, the awakening was rooted in the activism and leadership of Black churches throughout the country. As Marable puts it, "Black ministers were at the very center of the struggle." There is a long history of the cultural significance of Black churches, much too long to summarize here. Notably, it was Black churches that were targeted[7] during some of the worst terrorism of the Jim Crow era. The leadership for a new Awakening to fight a moral battle, including a charismatic preacher named Martin Luther King Jr., was drawn from the ranks of the religious.

The moderate, media-attracting approach of the Southern Christian Leadership Conference occasionally clashed with the grassroots-active Student Nonviolent Coordinating Committee. What helped unite the two groups for their pivotal year of 1963 was their message. By this time their appeal to White consciences, to morality, slowly began to spread. King had been arrested protesting Alabama Governor George Wallace's verbal gauntlet, "segregation now, segregation tomorrow, segregation forever." While imprisoned, King (1963) wrote the moving *Letter from a Birmingham Jail*, which elucidated the rationale for nonviolent resistance: breaking unjust laws "lovingly, openly" was necessary to "arouse the conscience" of others to injustice.

This moral appeal, along with some vintage arm-twisting from President Johnson on the political side, resulted in the passage of the Civil Rights Act and the Voting Rights Act. This was moral conviction channeled into public demonstration, translated into legislative action that directly improved the lives of Black Americans.

The coalition that engineered social change in the 1960s was chipped apart by politics. The Republican Party successfully absorbed the demonstrative wing of fundamentalist Christians during the 1970s, splitting the pull of morality for these voters between equality and the newly relevant issue of abortion. The success of Richard Nixon's Southern Strategy scared Democrats away from focusing on racial issues, putting them on the defensive about racial justice throughout much of the 1980s and 1990s while welfare, Medicaid, and other domestic programs that traditionally benefit Americans of color were cut.

With the goal of racial equality, defined by the freedom sought by the end of Jim Crow, having been "achieved," the consciences of White Americans were freed to consider whether what Americans of color were asking for was too much. A period of relative racial conservatism from both parties followed with occasional hints of possible moral appeal. The utopian promise of Jesse Jackson's Rainbow Coalition, the justified anguish in response to the Rodney King verdict, and the steady work of criminal justice activists throughout the 1990s carried moral weight, but the message seemed always to be fighting upstream. Paradoxically, the fastest-growing musical genre of the time, Black-created hip-hop, graphically illuminated social inequality and discrimination, often for the first time, to mass audiences of White American teens.

One reading of this development is that it laid the foundation among Generation Xers already skeptical of tradition and authority[8] for a future coalition to fight inequality on moral grounds. This generation would be instrumental in sweeping the first Black president into power in 2008. Barack Obama's embodiment of hope extended beyond an economic turnaround. Whatever one thinks about President Obama, by his mere existence as a Black man on the cusp of the presidency, he symbolized the ideals[9] that once aroused American consciences, as Dr. King might have put it, to seek a better way.

And now, following disappointment and backlash, we find ourselves at another moral crossroads.

## THE IMPORTANCE OF MORAL CONVICTION

Most people see racism as a moral wrong. I say this not with a stack of surveys or sociological studies at my side, but as a lifelong American. Consider that every so often there is an event that is a clear-cut case of racism. The common response to events such as these is widespread disapproval, usually tapped into by political and social leaders' public statements. Sometimes these statements use the words *morality* or *moral values*, and other times, even without the word *moral*, the language is strong enough to imply that the racism in question violated some fundamental shared sense of right and wrong.

Take the example of the 2017 "Unite the Right" march of White supremacists and neo-Nazis on Charlottesville, Virginia. Republican Senate Majority Leader Mitch McConnell tweeted that the protesters did not "reflect American values." Democratic fundraisers sent emails questioning the "moral clarity" of those who did not forcefully condemn the actions of the protesters. Independent senator and sometime aspirant for the Democratic presidential nomination Bernie Sanders called them "reprehensible" and representative of "hatred that has no place in our society."

Sanders's comment cuts straight to the value of labeling racism a moral evil: once something is deemed immoral, assuming we agree, we are motivated to remove it from our society. Murder, long considered a moral evil, is punishable by death in some instances. We reserve this most extreme of punishments for the murderer, the person who has transgressed our moral values so flagrantly that taking their life via state action is an option.

Likewise, designating racism as immoral serves as a deterrent to the racist: your views are not acceptable in our society, and if you share them, you will be punished.[10]

Joshua Glasgow (2009), a professor of philosophy and ethics, states racism is immoral because it not only harms people of color, but it also encourages indifference to their fate. Such indifference denies the humanity of fellow people. When we ignore or mistreat a person because of their racialized group, they are no longer autonomous, independent, sensitive, morally significant individuals. They become different and diminished. Chapter 5 presents why condoning a system's racism, too, is a moral violation.

Morality is not merely theoretical. It is essential that racism, however it is defined, be viewed as a moral issue. This is because when issues are held with moral conviction, or "moralized," they are much more likely to inspire us to persistence and meaningful action on behalf of the belief. This has been found in a wide range of psychological studies on moralization (e.g., De Cristofaro et al. 2021; Garrett and Bankert 2020; Tagar, Morgan, Halperin and Skitka 2014; van Zomeren, Postmes and Spears 2010).

When psychologists study the effects of holding a belief with moral conviction, they mean the belief reflects our fundamental sense of what is right and wrong. Moral conviction has been found to predict strong, emotional responses to those who disagree with our view (Cole Wright, Cullum and Schwab 2008; Ryan 2014; Zaal et al. 2017), believing the end justifies the means regarding our conviction (Mullen and Nadler 2008; Napier and Tyler 2008) and issue-based activism (Bloom 2013; Skitka and Wisneski 2011).

A group of psychologists have developed what they call the Moral Conviction Measure (Brandt, Wisneski and Skitka 2015; Skitka and Morgan 2014) to assess how "moralized" a person's belief is. Throughout the book, I use their scale to assess how strongly people feel about racial issues and racism. Research using the measure (Brandt et al. 2015) has found moral convictions both influenced by emotions and influential on emotions. Enthusiasm increases moral conviction for an issue, and hostility increases moral conviction against an issue. We might be even more strongly convicted against racism, for example, when seeing something like the George Floyd video creates feelings of hostility in us. The measure has also predicted whether we are willing to go outside the law to protect our sense of right and wrong (Skitka and Morgan 2014).

According to analysis by a group of clinical psychologists (Danzer, Rieger, Schubmehl and Cort 2016), racism is a historical trauma inherited by people of color. The events of the antebellum period, Reconstruction and Redemption, Jim Crow, and the post–Civil Rights Era resounded through the American population, creating a shared traumatic experience for people of color, specifically Black Americans. Racism reproduces some of the worst features of trauma, such as inadequate socioeconomic resources, a vulnerability to being retraumatized, the stress of hypervigilance, feelings of helplessness, and intrusive reexperiencing of the trauma. On a positive note, the psychologists believe that engaging with the core strengths of Black culture help people recover. These include a tradition of resistance, a resilience mindset, positive ethnic identification, spirituality, hope, and meaningful connections to family and community.

It is critical that racism continues to be deemed a moral issue; this draws our attention to how racism violates our fundamental concept of humanity. A moral imperative against racism unites right and left in politics, discourages its blatant forms, and places social pressure on individuals to question, contradict, or suppress racist ideas. Seeing racism cast in this way thus motivates action against it—not window-dressing gestures, but actions that alleviate the suffering caused by racism.

For further illustration of the power of morality when it comes to racial issues, consider the concept of counterfactual transgressions. A counterfactual transgression is an avoided misdeed from one's past. If I am feeling down about myself, I could cheer myself up by thinking back to a time when I could have done something bad, but I didn't. For example, many places I shop have a self-checkout stand. If I am having a bad day, I can think back to my last trip to the grocery store and remind myself, *At least I scanned everything in my cart. I could have chosen not to ring up the expensive bag of avocados I bought. No one would have been any wiser. But I paid for them all the same.*

Researchers have used this mode of thinking to study the influence of moral values, particularly when our status as moral beings is being threatened. In one study, psychologists Daniel Effron, Dale Miller, and Benoit Monîn (2012) examined immoral counterfactual transgressions. Participants in their study, all of whom were White, were asked to evaluate two suspects in an imaginary crime. One suspect is clearly guilty while the other has a strong alibi and appears to be innocent. For one group of participants, both suspects were White. For the other, the innocent suspect was Black.

The participants in the second group had access to an immoral counterfactual: they could have acted in a racist manner by accusing the Black suspect, but they did not. After evaluating the suspects, the participants were asked to consider five ambiguous behaviors and determine whether they were racist. The example the authors give is a White woman walking alone at night crossing the street after seeing a Black man walking toward her. The group that had "saved" the innocent Black suspect rated significantly fewer of the ambiguous behaviors as racist. Why?

Again, the moral injunction against racism is strong. We might imagine it as creating a bit of pressure for White people: give people of color a fair chance, consider your motives when faced with matters even obliquely

involving race, and so forth. When these participants could point to a counterfactual immoral transgression, the pressure was relieved. As a result, they
felt emboldened to express less racial sensitivity.

Another study (Merritt et al. 2012) tested the effect in the opposite direction. They had participants, all of whom were White, read a brief article about
the Implicit Association Test (IAT), discussed in detail in the following section. For one group (called High Threat), the article characterized the IAT as
able to detect racial prejudice such that most White people who take it find
out they tended to hold biases against Black faces. For another (Low Threat),
the article continued to state that some psychologists believe the IAT merely
measures awareness of racial stereotypes. Then all participants were told they
will take the IAT later. We would assume the Low Threat group, compared
to the High Threat group, is less concerned with taking the IAT because they
have learned there are alternative interpretations of the results.

Before taking the IAT, the participants were asked to rate eight potential
job candidates from most to least qualified. Only one of the candidates was
Black. The High Threat group, concerned about taking the IAT later, rated the
Black candidate about two slots higher than the Low Threat group.[11] In this
case, participants' anticipation of getting a morally upsetting news induced
them to earn some moral credentials ahead of time; they could "prove" they
were not racist by rating the Black candidate higher than average.

As the researchers (Effron, Miller and Monin 2012, 928) put it, "when
people can easily point to an immoral road not taken, they feel that they can
act in morally questionable ways without fear of discrediting themselves."
On the other side of the coin, Anna Merritt and colleagues (2012, 776) conclude, when anticipating that behaviors will impact one's moral track record
"people can actively shape their track record to shield future behavior from
others'—or their own—reproach." When we feel moral weight, it can change
our behavior.

## EMPATHY AND BIAS:
## THE CASE OF THE NATIONAL
## FOOTBALL LEAGUE

At the end of the 2021 NFL season, the Miami Dolphins fired their head
coach, Brian Flores. Flores, an Afro-Latino, had taken what was a moribund
franchise[12] to winning records his final two of three years there, finishing
with a 24–25 record. Even as team management debated what to do with the
quarterback drafted on Flores' watch (former Alabama star Tua Tagovailoa),
in his final season he led the team to wins in eight of the final nine games.

Normally in the NFL, this would be interpreted as a positive sign. Instead, Flores was fired. Flores sued the NFL, citing discrimination.

The NFL has a Black coaches problem (Borges 2022; Braddock and Piquero 2022; Pereira 2022). The NFL is about 70 percent Black men, yet it is rare that the NFL hires a Black head coach. The pattern alone was disturbing enough for the NFL to take action in the form of 2003's Rooney Rule. The policy requires each team to interview at least one or more candidates of color for coaching vacancies. (This was later expanded to administrative vacancies.) As Andscape's Jason Reid (2022) notes, the Flores firing was a major setback to the NFL's diversity commitment right at the start of the traditional coaching hire cycle.

The problem, as Flores's suit alleges, is that the Rooney Rule is being adhered to in form, but not in spirit. Black coaches have spoken about the comparatively slim margin for error they are given to keep their jobs and the tendency for teams to fly them to an interview but never give them serious consideration. Flores alleges the latter is exactly what happened following his departure from Miami. What tipped Flores off was a previous colleague accidentally texting him congratulations before his interview. The kicker is that text was intended for another Brian, Brian Daboll, who was hired by the New York Giants. Flores was scheduled to interview with the Giants three days later, which meant the Giants had communicated their decision on Daboll (who is White) *before* interviewing Flores.

Starting in 2020, the NFL made a ten-year, $250 million commitment to social justice initiatives. The league stenciled "End Racism" in the end zone of their football stadiums. Players were encouraged to wear antiracist helmet decals. The league also announced the performance of a song widely known as the Black National Anthem, "Lift Every Voice and Sing," before the start of each team's first game of the season.

So, wait, is the NFL a terrible racist organization willing to commit hundreds of millions of dollars to cover up their lying about a commitment to end racism to make money? Or are they really a financially committed, progressive, antiracist organization that happens to make racist mistakes?

The truth is probably somewhere in between. Psychologists have studied contradictory behavior around race. The concept that it is possible to reject bias explicitly yet behave in biased ways is called implicit bias. We can see Brian Flores's firing as another case of an unconscious bias on the part of Stephen Ross, the individual who fired him. Or we can look at it in the context of the NFL and see systemic racism at work. Much like a good deal of the action that results in negative outcomes for Americans of color, it is hard to tell. Such ambiguity fuels systemic racism and complicates attempts to address these negative outcomes.

Behaviors incongruent with stated intentions, especially in situations involving race, are not uncommon. Scientists have found one reason for this, which is that decision-making involves an element of emotion. Maybe we keep things longer than they are necessary because of sentimental value or we keep accepting a person who hurts us because we still love them. These logic-defying decisions highlight the influence of "emotional attitudes" (Alfano 2016).

We can measure emotional attitudes using a test called the Implicit Association Test (IAT). The IAT asks participants to quickly sort words into categories. The speed of the sort indicates how closely the category and the word are connected within the participant's mind.

We know, via psychological neurobiology, that the more connections we make between things, the easier it is for one thing to help us recall another thing. That's why something like hearing the number-one song from our senior year in high school seems to bring back a flood of faces, names, events, and feelings. Associating an idea, a person, a food, or an experience with something else like a song, over and over, connects the two. If I hear that Mariah Carey "Fantasy" remix, boom, I'm back to high school, eating cheese fries with Wild Cherry Pepsi, or goofing around on the team bus after our football game, or playing cards with my friends Dan and Tony, or lying on the beach trying to look cool. Our brain builds these connections because they help us remember important things without having to work from scratch each time.

The IAT is an attempt to measure how well connected two concepts are in your mind: maybe you did it through experience, maybe the connections were drawn for you by the media you consume or the messages you got from your parents. The IAT is useful in assessing connections you wouldn't automatically share. In the case of racial attitudes, it has become less socially acceptable for White people, especially, to share critical views of people of color for fear of being labeled racist, which would put them in the moral wrong. We know what we do about implicit bias because of the IAT's skill at uncovering emotional attitudes.

Implicit bias researchers and a group of researchers called social intuitionists believe that implicit attitudes, via emotion, lead our behavior and cognitive explanations follow. Jonathan Haidt (2012), a prominent researcher of moral psychology, describes this relationship as the rider and the elephant. Our logical, cognitive self is the rider on the emotional elephant. We provide some guidance, but we really are at the mercy of the elephant. Emotion matters when it comes to racism because racism is fundamentally irrational and, given the chance, most White people reject the sort of cognitive beliefs classified as racist. Even when an image-conscious megacorporation like the NFL tells us to our face, painted in grass in ten-foot-long letters, that it wants to end racism, it still gives us a pattern of hiring behavior that is discriminatory.

Neuroimaging studies consistently indicate that moral judgments are grounded in emotion (Decety and Wheatley 2015). Even though emotion can overwhelm what society tells us is right and result in racially biased behavior, it also helps us recognize what is morally correct, assuming an option resonates with an important emotional attitude. One of the emotions that is an important ingredient in morality is empathy.

Empathy has three components: affective, motivational, and cognitive. Affective resonance means that another's emotions resonate with us and arouse a connection between us. Motivational empathy moves us to care for another person. Cognitive empathy encourages us to take the perspective of someone else. Empathy might play a role in feelings of shared pain and healing among people whose ancestral lands were colonized, motivation to march against injustice, or considering how someone who isn't like us might feel if they heard a racial slur or joke.

Empathy is often a fundamental part of morality, and with good reason: motivational empathy has been found to be deeply rooted in biology (Decety and Wheatley 2015). The key, however, is engaging that empathy. The cognitive exercise of perspective-taking has been found by many studies to lower prejudice and bias. Empathy was aroused by the George Floyd video because so many saw what happened as heartbreaking: it affectively resonated with them. They were motivated to seek change for many reasons that could be boiled down to care for the fate of fellow human beings.

Empathy is part of appeals to end racism. The people who already see the unfairness of racism know they are witnessing a moral violation. Convincing people—the same work the civil rights activists undertook to end Jim Crow—requires showing the difference between right and wrong as starkly as possible. It is saying, if you feel for us because something is broken here, come fight for what is morally right.

When I talk about empathy, though, I admit I am making an assumption. That assumption gets to the root of how morality and racism intersect. Empathy starts with establishing commonality. The assumption, then, is that White people see people of color as sharing something with them, as part of their group. Empathy can either move White people to recognizing inequality (thus, helping people of color) or reinforcing identification with their group (White people). White Americans are caught at an empathetic crossroads, then: do I empathize with my fellow Americans of color who are suffering, or do I empathize with my fellow White people who likely would have to sacrifice something to change this situation?

This dilemma, though, is based on an artificial distinction. There is nothing neurologically different between the "races." There is nothing of significance that is biologically different between the "races." Race is a social construct. As such, it can be deconstructed. For us in the United States, this starts with building a bridge between these manufactured groups based on a common human identity. (Some may find it more persuasive to pursue a common American identity.) This empathetic bridge can give us the moral conviction to do something meaningful about racism.

\*\*\*

It is clear, via our own native feelings about the word and the scientific studies on how we think about it to the way our society reacts to it, that racism is a moral issue. But racism has grown as a concept, as we social scientists have studied it more, and as previously marginalized and voiceless folks have begun to share their experiences. For some, this growth has outpaced their understanding, leaving them feeling ambivalent about their moral commitment to opposing all things racist. The issue becomes, how do we make sense of disagreements about racism's scope while maintaining agreement that it is wrong?

The following chapters lay out the case that racism is about what injures the humanity of people of color, mainly using the example of Black Americans. It should be clear that many of these cases, if not all of them, amount to a *morally objectionable state of affairs* that underlines the American norm opposing racism. However we define *racism*, we must be careful to keep its moral weight. The fight against racism has degenerated into yet another area in which proposed approaches in America sharply diverge. If we are going to be turned back onto the trajectory set in the mid-twentieth century, the moral imperative against racism must remain intact.

Research, history, and human intuition tell us *we are better equipped to fight racism when we are supported by a moral mandate* and *empathy can lead to this moral inclusion.* My intent is that the remainder of this volume clearly illustrates racism's realities and makes a persuasive case for a robust humanitarian response from each of us—a response sprouting from our deeply held sense of right and wrong.

## NOTES

1. My thanks go to the writing of Rebecca Cohen (2020) for reminding me of the hierarchical repercussions of original sin, according to Catholic theology.
2. Her adoptive parents, the people I knew and loved as my maternal grandparents, probably did not know she was Black. My mom had her suspicions, though, if for

no other reason than to the pains she had to take to straighten and re-curl her hair in high school to fit in.

3. For that matter, my experiences differ as well. Though I often have been asked the famous question posed to many mixed-race people ("What are you?") and I share my mother's olive skin, I have not received much bigotry or experienced significant discrimination. On the contrary, I frequently have been in spaces where those behaviors are condoned.

4. The purity rituals encompass food laws (food considered unclean, proper food preparation, cleaning oneself before eating, etc.), ritual purity, moral purity, and other forms of seeking to separate the clean from the unclean.

5. The concept of escaping slavery through death was a common theme of field songs and spirituals such as "Swing Low, Sweet Chariot" and "Wade in the Water." The hymns were a powerful coping mechanism for enslaved people and arguably founded the American musical tradition.

6. Saint Paul's Letter to the Colossians 3:22; Ephesians 6:5.

7. This pattern stretches back before even the bombing of Black Wall Street Church in Tulsa and forward through an unfathomably long list of bombings in the 1990s to the mass shooting at Emanuel AME Church in Charleston in 2015, and beyond.

8. Concurrently, there was an evolution of punk music and eventually the birth of "grunge" rock. Both grew in popularity alongside hip-hop. While grunge despaired and raged against a world that didn't seem to make sense, punk, especially, echoed hip-hop's frustration with inequality via the music of groups like Bad Religion. Not coincidentally, many punk groups of the era credit roots reggae music as an inspiration.

9. There is a good deal of literature supporting Obama's exceptional worth, apart from his humanity, as a symbol of anything from racial equality to the promise of a better America. Political scientist Andreja Zevnik (2017) wrote from a psychodynamic perspective about "Obama-Trump" voters who idealized Obama and had the rug pulled out from under them by a reality that could hardly have lived up to those expectations. Michael Tesler (2016a) has published a wide swath of articles and research papers about voters' strong reactions to Obama, best summarized in his book on the subject. As his presidency ended, an article in Obama's adopted hometown newspaper, the *Chicago Tribune* (Koeske 2017), surveyed historians and scholars about Obama as a symbol of hope specifically for Black Americans, but also of White expectations for Black Americans. Obama himself (2006) embraced the concept of hope but wrote with ambivalence on the limitations of his position and his desire for transformational change. Later, he acknowledged (2020) how this image helped and hindered his first term as president.

10. This is not to say that all racist behavior is punished equally.

11. Both groups' ratings were contrasted with a control group that only rated the applicants. The average rating there ($M$=5.08) was about the same as the average for the Low Threat group ($M$=5.09) and significantly different from the High Threat group's average ($M$=3.00).

12. As any longtime fan of the NFL, let alone a Dolphins fan, knows, "moribund franchise" is an entirely fair way to describe the post–Dan Marino, pre-Flores state of the Miami Dolphins.

## Chapter 2

# How We Got Here

## *The Politics of Racism and Identity*

*Within each of us there is some piece of humanness that knows we are not being served by the machine which orchestrates crisis after crisis and is griding all our futures into dust.*

—Audre Lorde, *Sister Outsider*

In this chapter I describe how American politics have become intertwined with racial issues and how the political landscape regarding race has evolved. Why are today's discussions about race so easily and often derailed into shouting matches? In exploring the answer, I trace the history of the two main American political parties, the Republicans and the Democrats, and their role in suppressing or advocating for racial justice. During this history, I pause for interludes on the human cost of racism, identity politics, how political tribalism cripples meaningful dialogue about race, and how racial issues are manipulated by politicians to gain power.

\*\*\*

On April 10, 2013, Republican Kentucky Senator Rand Paul spoke to an audience at one of the top historically Black colleges and universities in the country, Howard University. Paul asked attendees, "How did the Republican Party, the party of the Great Emancipator, lose the trust and faith of an entire race?"

About four years later, in February 2017, Republican Texas Senator Ted Cruz was interviewed by Fox News about Democratic antiracist opposition to Republican attorney general nominee Senator Jeff Sessions. Cruz said in response, "Listen, the Democrats are the party of the Ku Klux Klan."

Three years after that, during the Republican National Convention held in August 2020, a Black man named Clarence Henderson took the floor to state, "I'm a Republican. And I support Donald Trump. If that sounds strange, you don't know your history. It was the Republican Party that passed the Thirteenth Amendment, abolishing slavery."

During the three presidential elections surrounding these comments—2012, 2016, and 2020—Black voters were overwhelmingly in favor of the *Democratic* candidate, with an average of 93.3 percent support. What is going on here? On the one hand, these speakers present the Republican party as the party of Black people. A Republican president effectively ended slavery; a Republican Congress passed the landmark constitutional amendments guaranteeing a person's freedom from slavery, the right to citizenship, and the right to vote. According to them and other Republican pundits, it was the Democrats, on the other hand, whose slaveowner aristocracy started the Civil War. It was a group of Democrats who founded the KKK. So why are Black Americans voting Democratic at overwhelming rates?

The students in the auditorium at Howard for Rand Paul's speech knew why. When Paul asked them if they knew that Republicans had founded the NAACP, students in the audience groaned. They were groaning because they know what is missing from the appeals of Paul and Cruz and others who refer to the impressive accomplishments of the Republican Party in racial progress. What is missing is a full history, most importantly the last six or seven decades of it. For many of those students, it doesn't take an elite education to learn about the effects of Republican policies on people like them. They learned by living their entire lives as Black Americans.

But this isn't about demonizing a particular political party. To be sure, the Democratic Party does not have a stellar record of racial progress in the rare times they have held power since the 1960s. To explain the current Black support for the Democratic Party, one must understand history. But to understand why Republican candidates choose to ignore those recent decades, one must understand the value of injecting race and racial symbolism into political discourse.

## THE POWER OF EMOTION ON RACIAL ISSUES VIEWS

Conversations about race often invoke the history of the United States in allowing, even encouraging, the enslaving of millions of our fellow people. Today's racism is the inheritance of slavery, which once propelled our country to economic dominance (Lockhart 2019). That this dominance is simultaneously fundamental to the American identity and tainted with the abhorrent method in which it was obtained partially explains why the struggle for racial equality continues in the United States.

The previous paragraph likely produced a reaction in you, and the direction that reaction took depends on who you are. For five seconds, if you'll indulge me, just sit with that reaction. What was that reaction? When you're done recalling it, whether it was anger, frustration, sadness, annoyance, boredom, or something else, ask yourself, *Why do I think I reacted that way?* For example, if your reaction was, "Meh, I've heard all this before," what does that really mean? Does it mean that this really is boring stuff? Or does it indicate something more, perhaps a sense of frustration? When was the last time you had that feeling, and what does it usually mean? Does that feeling always come up when the topic is racism, or America, or is it something else?

Part of the reason we are stuck when we talk about race in this country is because the reactions escalate immediately—especially online, where people seem to be in a competition to use the most exaggerated language possible to express their point—and there doesn't seem to be much reflecting going on.

We are allowed to have our reactions and our own understanding of experiences: they are part of what makes us unique. Those reactions reflect our life experience and our beliefs. Immediate reactions reflect something within us that is real yet subjective. It is rare for someone to have a thoroughly logical, yet immediate, reaction. If we want to avoid overreacting, we examine our reactions. *What am I feeling?* leads to *Why am I feeling this way? When do feelings like this usually happen? What does this say about me?* And, *how comfortable am I with it?*

Therapists recommend assessing how emotions affect us because emotions can motivate our behavior. That is, a strong reaction indicates that I care about something. If I like the feeling, I am motivated to seek more of it. If I do not like the feeling, I am motivated to change it. Given that modern psychotherapy is designed to bring about behavioral change, emotion can contain valuable therapeutic information.

Unexamined emotions can be funneled into any number of things because we haven't taken the time to determine their origin.[1] One of the most famous studies in psychology is Dutton and Aron's (1974) "rickety bridge" experiment. In the study, they had male participants cross an unsafe bridge over a steep drop. Then they were surveyed by a female interviewer and asked to write a story based on an ambiguous drawing of a woman. The results for these participants were compared to a group who crossed a much more stable bridge. The comparison showed that the men who crossed the rickety bridge were both more likely to include sexual content in the stories they created and more likely to attempt to contact the female interviewer. The researchers concluded that the participants misattributed their emotional reaction: arousal from crossing the bridge was interpreted as sexual attraction toward the interviewer.

It's easy to misattribute emotion, or get carried away with it, whether it is mistaking being scared for being attracted to someone or it is mistaking discomfort with change for a personal affront. We must stop and examine the source of our reactions, rather than taking them for granted or as an indication of a final truth. When we do not, we can miss important information and become committed to our initial view, whether it was right or wrong.

Emotion is what makes discussions of race powerful. And once something is powerful, it becomes dangerous in the wrong hands. That's where politics comes in.

## THE SCORE

Perhaps I should start at the beginning, with Abraham Lincoln. I come neither to praise nor bury Lincoln. To wit, some of Lincoln's statements[2] have made him anathema to some racial progressives. Here it is instructive to look at him for what he was: an ingenious, pragmatic politician who intuited how and when to push for social change. To the extent that he made the Civil War a moral issue and succeeded, then sweet-talked to passage the Thirteenth Amendment outlawing chattel slavery, his presidency signifies an incredible step forward in racial progress. What makes history is not necessarily a president's personal proclivities toward Black Americans. It is the action taken in that regard. Thus, Lincoln retains a rightful place at or near the pinnacle of American presidents.

Lincoln was the first president to represent the relatively new Republican Party, formed from the ashes of the extinguished Whig Party. The Republican Party's identity was opposition to the slaveholding Southern oligarchy, hence the epithet contemporary rivals applied to Lincoln, "Black Republican."

When Lincoln was assassinated, the presidency was taken over by Andrew Johnson, whose Republican sympathies were limited by his profound sense of White identity: he indeed hated the aristocratic plantation owners, but in no way did he believe Black people deserved equal rights and Constitutional protections. When former Confederate leaders came begging to Johnson, abolitionists saw this as a chance to rebuild the South in a way that protected the newly freed Black Southerners (Stewart 2009).

In a reversal that may be familiar to many people of color,[3] Johnson instead applied clemency to these supposedly repentant Southerners. With the White, enslaving hegemony in the South reeling, Johnson let down his guard and all but invited them back into the union, including positions of power. This was the auspicious start to Southern Reconstruction, the attempt to rebuild the South using the North as a model of nineteenth-century egalitarianism and economy.

The North had entered a postwar boom of pride, population, and wealth, while the South was still physically, economically, and emotionally destroyed. There, the newly freed Black population became a convenient scapegoat for White Southerners' despair. This despair often was expressed through lynching, a barbaric practice that took many forms: chasing with bloodhounds, threats at gunpoint, and the vile "mob justice" of dragging, mutilating, hanging, and displaying the bodies—the "strange fruit[4]" populating Southern groves—of Black people murdered because they did not follow often-confusing orders of White men or admit to crimes they did not commit.

A reprieve came in the 1868 election to president of Republican U.S. Grant, Union hero of the Civil War, and almost mythic figure at the time. He intended to fulfill the promise of the Republican Party to protect the rights of Black Americans during Reconstruction, even if force was required to do it. In 1872, following passage of the Fifteenth Amendment enshrining Black voting rights, Black citizens voted overwhelmingly for Grant's reelection, and many ran for office as Republicans. With former Confederates sidelined, so began the rise of a Black Republican South.

Reports from the time, quoted at length in Eric Foner's (2014) master work on what came to be known as Reconstruction, show an engaged Black populace begging for a fair chance. What they asked for consistently was a chance to work the same land on which they had been enslaved, as their own land. Asking for this basic human, indisputably American, right was viewed as freeloading by the White Southern aristocracy. According to justifications at the time, the violence held at bay under the supposed protection of their plantation owners was unfettered by Emancipation. As Southerners exacted their revenge on the Black freedmen in their towns, lynchings increased (Pfeifer 2009).

The Republicans' forceful action for racial justice in the South disintegrated, along with Reconstruction, following the corruption of the 1876 election. The election was incredibly close, coming down to the electors of four states. Congress appointed a committee to determine the validity of conflicting slates of electors. The committee of fifteen had an edge of one, given to the majority party in Congress, the Republicans. The committee voted along party lines in each dispute and awarded the presidency to Republican Rutherford Hayes.

In what has come to be known by the deceptively innocuous name, "The Compromise of 1876," the Democrats only agreed to peacefully accept Hayes's election if he agreed to withdraw the federal troops protecting integrity of the polls and the rights of Southern Black citizens. A little more than a half century past the supposed Corrupt Bargain that cost Andrew Jackson his first shot at the presidency, a true Corrupt Bargain snuffed out the first major progress toward racial equality and cost Black citizens, effectively, most of the rights they had gained.

Like that, Reconstruction had ended, and a cruel "Redemption" had begun.


## THE HUMAN COST OF REDEMPTION

It is one of the most heart-wrenching stories in American history: the promise of freedom after hundreds of years of enslavement, the shining light at the end of the darkest tunnel, all snatched away. White Southerners unleashed a vindictive backlash fueled by rage that the "God-ordained" social order, even if for only a few years, had been turned on its head. All but abandoned by federal oversight, Southern Democrats used the law and political thievery to exact a calculated revenge.

The names of Black people were purged from voter rolls in multiple states. The disenfranchisement and dehumanization of Black citizens throughout the South was enshrined in what were known as Jim Crow laws, named after a common slave character in minstrel shows. These laws included various limits on acceptable behavior for Black citizens, such as when and where they could exist without being thrown in jail. When these laws weren't enough retribution, Whites could opt for vigilante "justice." It was common for White mobs to be disappointed when the police locked up the supposed offender before they had a chance to get to him. They often stormed the jailhouse and, in some cases, burned it to the ground to prevent even the sham trial awaiting the prisoner.

Part of this revenge re-created the functional reality of slavery under two different but complementary systems: sharecropping and peonage. Douglas Blackmon's (2008) Pulitzer-winning work, *Slavery by Another Name*, documents the iron grip of White landlords and the sadism of White sheriffs during this time. Sharecropping was the leasing of plantation land by White landowners to Black tenants who shared the crop produced on the land: rent and payment for other necessities were deducted from the income from the year's harvest. But determining the tenants' share and the value of the necessities, often mandated in the lease to be purchased at landlord-run shops at excessive prices, was the sole provenance of the landlord himself. Perversely, the ending of chattel slavery freed Southern landowners from the traditional pretense of patriarchal "mercy"[5] toward the Black people with whom they interacted, which rationalized the depraved exploitation of the system.

In *The Warmth of Other Suns*, Isabel Wilkerson (2010) explores the American Great Migration of the first half of the twentieth century, in which Black families—many of whom worked as sharecroppers or in agricultural jobs—left the oppression of the South to move to places like Syracuse, New

York, and Oakland, California, seeking opportunity and fair treatment. They did not always find both, which must have been a cruel lesson given the risks these pioneers took to get out of the South. Wilkerson tells the engrossing story of this seismic change, brought about by word of mouth and Black newsletters, through the lives of three Black Southerners: Ida Mae Gladney, George Swanson Starling, and Robert Pershing Foster.

What is clear from these tales is that emancipation did not guarantee freedom for Black Americans. Many of the migrants, like Ida Mae, were moving their families out of the restrictive jaws of sharecropping. They had the barest knowledge of what awaited them in cities like Chicago. What steeled them was the possibility of real freedom. Wilkerson tells us that perhaps the last straw for Ida Mae in her home in Chickasaw County, Mississippi, was being terrorized in the middle of the night by a group of White men looking for her husband's cousin.

The other side of the "new slavery" was peonage, or convict leasing. Southern sheriffs imprisoned Black citizens, often on trumped-up charges or minimal violations, then loaned them to local merchants as cheap labor. In one chilling thread, Blackmon traces the growth of the practice of working Black men to death at the Pratt mines in Alabama. Pratt supervisors withheld water, whipped their Black workers, and burdened them with literally backbreaking labor. Blackmon tells the story of one of these men, Green Cottenham, born free to parents who had been slaves, apprehended by authorities under false charges, and forced back into a different slavery at a place called Slope Number 12. Green was sentenced to this fate in 1908.

These developments were not ignored by Black Republicans. Timothy Thomas Fortune, who was a prominent journalist at the end of the nineteenth century, condemned the injustice of what the Republican Party had done to get Rutherford Hayes the presidency. Fortune (Meier 1956, 178) called the compromise that withdrew federal forces from the South "infamous barter and treachery." With the Republicans pulling back on protecting Black humanity and Southern Democrats aggressively retaking positions of power and violently intimidating Black citizens, the stage was set for the rise of a Solid Democratic South.

## THE FALL AND RISE OF THE BLACK VOTER

As the nineteenth century ended, Black citizens were asked to take a back seat to concerns such as the fallout of rapid industrialization and civil service corruption. Though incredible advances were taking place in Black intellectual history, such as the rise of W. E. B. Du Bois's incisive sociology as a counterpoint to Booker T. Washington's moderate doctrine of "cast down your bucket where you are," the political parties had moved on from a focus on Black civil rights, for the most part. In an exception rare for this race-agnostic era, Republican president Teddy Roosevelt invited Washington to dinner at the White House. The gesture drew insults and death threats for Roosevelt.

Roosevelt was not always willing to defend Black Americans. In 1906 a White woman's reported assault[6] and a bartender's shooting death in Brownsville, Texas, were pinned on the all-Black Buffalo Soldier regiment stationed in nearby Fort Brown. Though the soldiers' White officers argued that all had been on base at the time of the crimes, a riot broke out in Brownsville in which White town locals blamed the Black soldiers. Roosevelt dishonorably discharged the entire regiment. The incident soured many Black Republicans on the party of Roosevelt and his Republican successor, William Howard Taft (Meier 1956, 184–85).

By the 1920s, a decade of Republican dominance of federal government, the Republican party began to withdraw even further from pushing for the rights of its large, Black constituency. The decade had started with surprising promise for renewed focus on racial equality. In 1921, Republican president Warren Harding condemned lynching and forcefully argued for civil rights deep in Alabama "Klan Country" (Bailey 2016) and following the Tulsa massacre (Robenalt 2020) that left the town's Black commercial center burned to cinders, dozens dead, and about ten thousand Black people homeless.

Harding was dead less than two years after his Alabama speech, replaced by his vice president, "Silent Cal" Coolidge, who preferred to keep the government out of the way. When the Depression hit, the solution offered by Coolidge's Republican successor, Herbert Hoover, was so poorly considered and unequal to the task—let the charities handle it—that it seemed he was daring all Republicans, let alone Black Americans, to vote for someone else in the next election.

Heading into the 1932 election, Black Americans were beginning to assert their political power due to the Great Migration to the North, where they escaped Jim Crow, and membership in trade unions. Black workers had been denied membership in the most powerful union in the United States, the American Federation of Labor (AFL). They were beginning to be accepted[7] in the Congress of Industrial Organizations (CIO), though they had little say within the CIO at this early date.

It was the Democratic Party that was more sympathetic to organized labor, due to their extensive courting of White immigrant groups such as Irish, Germans, and Italians in large industrial cities. Within the Democratic party, the CIO, and thus Black citizens, could begin to have some political influence. This subtle shift is tracked in Eric Schickler's (2016) *Racial Realignment*, which documents the citizen-led transformation of the Democratic Party into one that could even fathom supporting civil rights by the time the events of the 1950s and 1960s made such a stance unavoidable.

Records show Black voters were still wary of the 1932 Democratic presidential nominee, Franklin D. Roosevelt, despite his famous speech about the "Forgotten Man" at the bottom of the economic structure. FDR's New Deal ushered in a wide variety of government programs designed to provide jobs. As the term went on, the CIO was positioned to push for Black hiring quotas in these new government positions. The Roosevelt administration, exemplified in the liberality of First Lady Eleanor Roosevelt, began to appeal to a Black constituency. As discussed in NPR's podcast on race, *Code Switch* (Demby and Marisol Meraji 2019), by 1936 Black Americans were ready to vote enthusiastically for another term for FDR. One headline, from *The New York New Amsterdam News*, announced it, "Big Negro Vote Backs FDR as New Deal Sweeps the Nation."

As historian Manning Marable (2007) describes, by the time the Cold War began, the loyalty of Black Americans to the party of Lincoln had been shaken substantially. A tentative faith in the Democratic party had been repaid in modest gains over the FDR and Truman administrations. FDR passed colorblind policies designed to lift all boats in the New Deal. His administration created a "Black Cabinet" to consult on public policy. His successor, Harry Truman, desegregated the armed forces to undo the damage of fellow Democrat Woodrow Wilson during World War I.

Black votes could not be taken for granted by either party. Whichever of the two would be able to embrace the issues that mattered to Black voters could aspire to the loyalty the Republican Party once enjoyed. Then came the 1950s, which put each party's commitment to Black Americans to the test.

### Identity Politics

Today, when the consistent record of Black voters supporting Democratic candidates comes up, two frequent replies come from the Republican side. One is that Black voters are mistaken: they are loyal to the Democratic party only because they are blinded to the good the Republican party can do for them. In the crude lingo of this perspective, they are still "on the plantation," with the implication that they should emancipate themselves and turn their backs on the Democrats. This line of thinking is most prominently delivered by conservative Black spokespersons, even some who probably should not be called upon to defend this viewpoint credibly or coherently. (This idea is explored in more detail in Chapter 8.)

The other response is that the Democrats are playing "identity politics" in which they ensure the Black vote by gearing their campaigns and issue stances toward minority groups. From this viewpoint, the votes of a certain group are expected based on membership in that group. An example is found is in the cringeworthy statement by President Joe Biden, when on the campaign trail in 2020, visiting popular radio show *The Breakfast Club*. When Biden claimed he needed to end the interview, host Charlamagne Tha God requested more time to question him. Biden responded, "If you have a problem figuring out whether you're for me or for Trump, then you ain't Black."

The idea that identity politics determines Democratic policy but not Republican policy is ridiculous on its face. Political scientist Ashley Jardina (2019) has documented, through a series of public opinion studies and social science experiments, the extent to which a sense of *White* identity unifies and drives strong attachment to the Republican Party, most notably in the person of Donald Trump. For example, Jardina showed that those with a strong sense of White identity were significantly more likely to support Trump, not only in 2016 but also starting in the primaries over other Republican candidates. Unsurprisingly, racial resentment, a common measure of modern racism, was a significant factor in whether people evaluated Trump more warmly. But even controlling for the effects of racial animus, White identity was a significant contributor to feelings of affection for Trump.

It is more accurate to state that both parties engage in a sort of identity politics. The Democrats, in treating the vast and diverse cultures categorized as Latino[8] as if they are a monolith, in expecting the votes of women despite having a selective definition of women's issues, and in using terminology regarding marginalized groups that can be simultaneously confusing and rapidly evolving. The Republicans do so in their fealty to the narrow biblical interpretation espoused by the Christian right and in their use of dog-whistle campaigns to motivate White voters.

A recent example is the conservatives' retort of, "All Lives Matter" to supporters of the antiracist Black Lives Matter movement. In the words of sociologist Joshua Paul (2019), this is an "anti-identity identity politics" that, oddly, attempts to remove race from the discussion of racism and racial politics. Despite claiming to be anti–identity politics, "All Lives Matter" is a position that defines itself, its identity, in contrast to BLM. It has no policy goals because "All Lives Matter"; outside the context of BLM, it holds little meaning. It's just another form of identity politics.

## THE CIVIL RIGHTS ERA

During the postwar 1950s, Black servicemen used to being treated like human beings in the armed services returned to a booming economy but the same social problems they left behind. Their families, many of whom had relocated north in the Great Migration of the preceding decades, did not find the acceptance and opportunities that seemed to be falling from trees for most White Americans at the time. This grassroots disillusion, combined with the organizational power of Black churches and the charismatic leadership of visionaries like the Reverend Dr. Martin Luther King Jr., established the foundation for a Black rights movement. All it needed was a spark.

The Supreme Court's 1954 *Brown v. Board of Education* ruling struck down "separate but equal" approaches that were commonplace in the Jim Crow era. *Brown* directly affected public schools, where it was determined segregation was unconstitutional. As could be expected, there was political resistance to the decision. Republican president Dwight Eisenhower was notably silent on the ruling.

Arkansas governor Orval Faubus forced Eisenhower's hand by allowing a mob to surround Central High School in Little Rock the day desegregation was to begin. Eisenhower sent in federal troops to enforce what was now the law of the land. With public sympathies in his favor, Eisenhower's attorney general, Herbert Brownell, proposed the Civil Rights Act of 1957. Eisenhower signed the act into law, which established a Civil Rights Division of the Justice Department and empowered federal prosecution of those interfering with a citizen's right to vote. The law was the first civil rights legislation of the twentieth century, though the negotiation process for passing it ensured it would be, by intention, relatively minor in impact.

The 1960 election gave Black Americans a choice between John F. Kennedy, an unproven but youthful Democrat, and Richard Nixon, a Republican who had served as vice president under the popular Eisenhower. Neither party could claim the consistent sympathies of Black voters. The election shaped up to be a close affair with the possibility of the Black vote being split.

Just days before the election, Martin Luther King was on his way to Reidsville, Georgia, to a maximum security prison for participating in a student-organized sit-in at Atlanta's Rich's department store. Worried about his fate, King's friends and wife, Coretta Scott King, were trying to reach the candidates to persuade them to use their power to get King released. Nixon, who had Black, pro baseball megastar Jackie Robinson among his close contacts on the issue, did not want to risk the support of White voters over taking additional action for King. Meanwhile, Kennedy eventually called Coretta to express his sympathy and concern for her husband (Levingston 2017). Word got out to the press, which increased the pressure for King's release. Perhaps more importantly for American politics, word spread through Black churches that Kennedy supported King.

The results of the 1960 election speak to the power of Kennedy's ninety-second phone call. In an election decided by close votes in multiple states like Illinois, Michigan, and South Carolina, Black voters made the difference in putting Kennedy in the White House. This set up Kennedy as symbolic of a new era of White partnership with Black efforts for civil rights. Kennedy's unfinished work also inspired his successor, Lyndon Johnson, to risk his and the Democratic Party's political future to spearhead the landmark Civil Rights Act of 1964 and the Voting Rights Act. By the late 1960s, it was clear which party was willing to do more to protect the civil rights of Black Americans.

That claim could no longer be made by the Party of Lincoln.

## THE DANGER OF POLITICAL TRIBALISM

Identity politics by themselves are not necessarily good or bad. It is how they are used that can create problems.

Was it bad for the mid-nineteenth-century Black citizens to overwhelmingly support the party more attentive to protecting their freedoms? Was it bad for mid-twentieth-century Black Americans to abandon the Republican Party in favor of the party whose president passed the Civil Rights Act and the Voting Rights Act, having direct, positive impact on their lives? Was it bad for early-twenty-first-century Mexican Americans and Salvadoran Americans to support the party whose leaders treated them and their relatives with dignity and humanity when discussing immigration policy? The answers show that "identity politics" have roots in human experiences.

Unfortunately, identity politics can be and have been used to divide. In her book, *Uncivil Agreement*, Liliana Mason (2018) explores the rapid partisan polarization over the last fifty years. One of the major trends she found is the entangling of what she calls "cross-cutting identities" we hold with political party. These identities include where we live, where we attend religious services (if at all), what we do in our spare time, and whom we do it with. It used to be that these identities exposed us to different types of people. We might be in a bowling league or attend synagogue or live in a neighborhood surrounded with people whose political views were not much like, or even opposite, ours. This exposed us to other views and humanized the "other side" of political issues. As documented by Bill Bishop in *The Big Sort*, this sort of heterogeneity of everyday environments—even our neighborhoods—has decreased in recent decades.

Homogenous sorting poses a major social problem. Social psychologists, prominently Muzafer Sherif (Sherif et al. 1974), have demonstrated how easy it is to demonize people outside our group. In his famous Robber's Cave study, a group of young boys was arbitrarily divided into groups and entered intergroup camp competitions. Though the experiment increased intragroup unity, it accelerated intergroup conflict. The best way to reverse the effect was to create a unifying goal toward which both groups could work together.

The tragedy of September 11, 2001, provided a too-real example of Americans coming together, like the boys in Sherif's study, for a common goal of survival against terroristic threat. Unfortunately, we know that was not the end. The effect wore off as people sorted back into political parties once the new reality settled in. Our coalescence in the face of the deadly coronavirus outbreak of 2020 was even shorter lived. We were back to our polarized camps just months later (Sides, Tausanovitch and Vavrick 2022). The situations are not equivalent, but these trends are one indicator of the shelf life of common goals to reverse polarization twenty years after 9/11.

We can see the problems created by sorting into politically polarized tribes of those who look and think alike. And researchers find that neither political party has a monopoly on tribalism (Clark, Liu, Winegard and Ditto 2019). They find that groups are "most biased about issues that are morally important and ambiguous." Given the moral weight applied to discussions of racism, as the concept expands and a consensus definition is harder to obtain, it is likely that political groups will become more tribal about their views on racial issues.

Yes, homogenous "tribes" are appealing to humans due to the evolutionary advantage of group loyalty. Just because it is natural doesn't mean it is helpful. Polarization not only affects policymakers and groups in a collective sense. It also impacts the people of color who are forced to deal with the negative repercussions when opposing a political party means opposing the people who support it.

These problems go beyond their toll on people of color. According to political scientists Morgan Marietta and David Barker (2019), a poison has seeped into our lives: misperceptions and blurred realities. Together, these constitute dueling fact perceptions (DFPs). DFPs mean that different people—in this case, different political parties—have different concepts of reality.

Marietta and Barker conducted a series of studies on how DFPs affect real life by creating a hypothetical character named Bob who disagrees with the participants on a fundamental aspect of reality. In one case, Bob believes racism doesn't exist anymore. Respondents who disagreed were 53 percent less likely to want to work with him. Does this mean those who believe in racism are intolerant and stubborn? Not necessarily. When the situation was reversed, and Bob claimed that racism still exists, respondents who disagreed were 37 percent less likely to want to work with Bob. The effect works both ways.

If we can't agree on basic facts, what is the starting point for a discussion? Let's say I'm a White woman who believes racism is wrong. If I see racism as mostly eliminated since the Civil Rights Era, with few exceptions due to bad apples, and the sources of information I trust do not challenge this belief, then I am unlikely to trust claims of racism, nor am I going to be persuaded with proof of institutional racism.

If I'm that person, and I can counter every piece of evidence of institutional racism with a DFP that either can't be proven or contradicts someone else's reality, of course I'm going to be offended and angry whenever racism is brought up in discussion. Therefore, and this is the real problem, *I can ignore the real damage* to people of color done by policies I support, *without thinking I am doing anything wrong*. I can believe I am against racism with almost no cognitive dissonance, and that leaves little room for reasonable discussion. Investment in one's own view without balanced or triangulated sources of information—in other words, without any rigorous testing of that view—blocks the conversations needed to solve real problems in this country, including racism.

## THE LEGACY OF THE SOUTHERN STRATEGY

The Southern Strategy is often cited as the turning point from the Republicans being the party of Lincoln and civil rights into being the party we know today. For most of the nineteenth and the first half of the twentieth century, the Democratic Party could rely on what was known as the "solid South," a bloc of states that voted Democratic partly because of the party's identification with White supremacy. The Southern Strategy was an attempt to use race to break the Democratic hold on the South. It is most identified with Republican Richard Nixon.

When Nixon ran for president in 1968, having seen the unexpected success of Alabama governor George Wallace's race baiting, he chose to refine Wallace's approach into something more palatable to Americans who did not want to feel they were supporting a racist. What he did was switch to a coded form of race baiting. Rather than complain about Black and White children learning side by side, he complained that school busing was a violation of states' rights. This negligee of obfuscation would provide enough plausible deniability to voters to feel comfortable supporting Nixon.

There is no doubt that the Southern Strategy was racism as a strategy to get a strong reaction, which motivates certain voters, and potentially wins an election. There is no doubt because Nixon had a strategist who admitted exactly that (Ehrlichman 1982). To pull back a bit, it is not necessary to find "n-word" tapes of Richard Nixon[9] to see the racist damage he caused. His goal was not to hurt or even insult Black people; it was to win an election. The method he chose was to appeal to the racial animus of Southern Democrats frustrated with their party's liberal turn on racial issues.

This is the problem when racial issues are stoked for political gain. The racial identity of human beings is tied up in political campaigns, campaigns intended to produce as strong a reaction as possible to motivate potential voters. Research (Nelson and Kinder 1996) shows that how an issue is described, or "framed," by politicians can influence how voters evaluate the measure. These frames often associate specific groups with the measure (e.g., busing = Black people), thus calling to attention feelings about those groups (e.g., Black people = scary/undeserving). So when Nixon brought up busing, he was bringing up an issue Wallace and others had already racialized (e.g., busing = Black people = feeling scared/resentful). He just reaped the benefits without mentioning race at all (e.g., scared/resentful = vote for Nixon).

However, as we saw in the rickety bridge study, when you get people worked up, it can have unintended effects. Politicians hope emotional appeals translate into action at the polls, but studies (Banks and Bell 2013; Brown 2016a) show the reactions evoked by the race-baiting politicians also turn into anger at minorities. We saw how that resulted, and continues to result, in raucous political rallies where Americans of color are often the targets of anger and violence. It's not just the moral stain of these appeals; it's also their real-life consequences that matter.

\*\*\*

Racism is an emotional thing, whether it is the strong reactions of White people being accused of racism or the Americans of color victimized by it. Likewise, slavery—in terms of how it is represented historically and how we discuss its effect on modern American society—is an emotional thing. The legacy forced on descendants of enslaved workers and the shame, avoidance, and defensiveness of the descendants of enslavers and those who look like them are real.

It is not enough to remind people who ended slavery. Based on the preceding, it should be clear that *throughout American history, racial discrimination has evolved side by side with politics content to ignore it or eager to use it to gain power.* Any appeal to Black and other Americans of color should propose solutions to the lopsided results they get from much of the American system, instead of invoking a supposed debt.

Meaningful conversations about race require an honest reckoning with American history. But in an age of dueling fact perceptions and spreading politicization, even how we teach and understand history has become another controversy fueled by differences in beliefs about race.

## NOTES

1. The determination of what an emotion is comprises a substantial area of research in psychology. The three foundational theories of emotion in psychology (James-Lange, Cannon-Bard, and Schachter-Singer) explain the different ways humans label emotional experiences, including influences on the subjective feeling. A fourth theory, Somatovisceral Afference Model of Emotion, combines elements of the prior theories to explain emotions that seem immediate and specific to a situation as well as those that are more ambiguous and require assessment. There is no final "law" that resolves the process of emotional arousal and assessment.

2. In 1862, Lincoln wrote to Horace Greeley, "If I could save the Union without freeing any slave I would do it, and if I could save it by freeing all the slaves I would do it." During the first version of the famous Lincoln-Douglass debates, held in 1858 over a senate race, Lincoln opened by stating, "I will say then that I am not, nor ever have been, in favor of bringing about in any way the social and political equality of the white and black races, [applause]. . . . And inasmuch as they cannot so live, while they do remain together there must be the position of superior and inferior, and I as much as any other man am in favor of having the superior position assigned to the white race." These quotes and some other remarks made by Lincoln leading into the decision to issue the Emancipation Proclamation have been posited as proof that Lincoln was racist.

3. Though David Brooks (2022) may not think so, people of color are indeed a "thing"; more exactly, they are people. I admit this is a catchall category that cannot possibly communicate the nuances and complex differences between Korean Americans and Indigenous Americans, for example. I use it, instead, to denote what used to be called "minorities." I prefer the term because *minority* has certain connotations, such as the discomfort experienced by people in spaces where they feel unwelcome or marginalized. Furthermore, the alternate term *non-White* centers Whiteness as a reference point. Contrary to what Mr. Brooks contends, on average, people of color experience America in different ways than White people, including experiences of American history (Chapter 3), disparities and discrimination (Chapters 4–5), and treatment by the two major political parties in this country (Chapters 7–9). The term can seem clumsy to some, but it is better than other options and has the major advantage of centralizing the humanity, i.e., *people* of color, of these groups. Therefore, that is the term I use throughout the book.

4. The 1939 Billie Holliday song "Strange Fruit" is a protest song about the lynching of Black Americans. It is based on a poem by writer Abel Meeropol. The song is credited by some as a harbinger of the Civil Rights Era in the mid-twentieth century.

5. On average, the treatment plantation owners applied to enslaved persons absolutely was not merciful in any way. However, there is great investment by some in keeping alive the fantasy of benevolent enslavers. During the leadup to the Civil War and in the decades following it, Southern politicians spoke loudly and often about how, in the South, "we know how to treat the Black man." As the temporal distance grew since Emancipation, Southern plantation families and their defenders switched to insisting that the enslaved people were treated "like part of the family." This flies

in the face of documentation of savage beatings based on amount or quality of work, repeated rape and abuse of Black enslaved women, division of families to generate income for the plantation owner, and other cruelties ranging from daily indignities to torture. This is over and above bringing the weight of deputized and official forces to keep these human beings enslaved. Calling any reprieve from this organized dehumanization "merciful" or appealing to exceptions in the face of extensive documentation is somewhere on the scale between disingenuous and delusional.

6. Accusations of assaulting a White woman were a common pretext for a particularly violent White mob response, including lynching, against Black Americans.

7. Black influence within the CIO is evaluated differently by different authors. David Roediger's (2005) award-winning *Working Toward Whiteness* takes a somewhat skeptical view of the embrace the CIO had of Black workers in the early twentieth century. Eric Schickler's *Racial Realignment* emphasizes the CIO's role as a "leading player" in broadening the scope of the New Deal to include civil rights (p. 52). However, this did not occur until the late 1930s.

8. Here and throughout the text I use the term *Latino*. The term *Hispanic* is often used, though there are issues with that term. The census created it to group people for counting, not to describe culture. In addition, the term itself prioritizes the Spanish origin of Mestizo peoples in what we know as Latin America; the people from these areas over the last five hundred years or so have Indigenous ancestors, which *Hispanic* does not acknowledge. It should be noted that modern Latinos have Spanish heritage because of conquest, colonization, and, in some cases, enslavement of people native to these lands. *Latinx* was created to avoid gendering the person or group being mentioned. Spanish and many other Romance languages gender nouns and modifiers and, given the paternalistic history of most nations, including those in what we know as Latin America, it is not surprising that *Latino* is the prevalent version of this term, rather than *Latina* (or the always-awkward *Latino/a*). I will defer on the use of *Latinx*, given its recent rise and the problems some have with its usage primarily by White or "elite" academics (Del Real 2020; McArdle 2021). To the extent that any of these terms are used in the United States, *Latino* seems the most appropriate. It is much more accurate, however, to identify these people using their country of origin such as *Guatemalan American* or *Mexican American*, as many American Latino citizens have done for decades (when not simply calling themselves "American").

9. Given releases of tapes containing Nixon's discussions with Ronald Reagan, it would not be shocking to unearth tapes of Nixon using the infamous racial slur. In those tapes, Reagan and Nixon joke about African diplomats, with Reagan calling them "monkeys." Later, Nixon is on tape defending Reagan's view (if not his language) and strategizing how to appeal to voters with Reagan's racist views.

## Chapter 3

# The Curious Power of
# Critical Race Theory

*The truth that survives is the lie that is pleasantest to believe.*

—H. L. Mencken, *The Free Lance,* October 23, 1915

In this chapter, I analyze the controversy over Critical Race Theory. The value of political symbols explains the backlash toward CRT and the apparent conflict between the Critical Race view of America and "traditional" American history. I analyze the psychology behind the typical, human reactions to this reckoning. Acknowledging these offers an opportunity to forge an honest American history.

\*\*\*

Suppose your friend has inherited a house. He invites you (with your great sense of style) over for a look; perhaps you can share your ideas on how to improve it. When you arrive, you are taken aback. Multiple walls are missing. There is a distressing hole in the roof over the living room that has been covered with tarp weighed down with bricks. Some windows are missing.

"Yes, it's a fine house. Passed down for generations now."

"But Joe," you say, "I am concerned. Look, I can walk right in without opening the door. The living room! What happens when it rains or snows or—"

"Listen," Joe cuts you off, "our family is very proud of this house. We've done everything we can to address the hole over the living room. Besides, I never go in there, so that won't be a problem." Now he's getting a little hot. "This house was built of the strongest materials. It will stand forever."

Dumbfounded, feeling that you have somehow offended your friend, you decide to leave the discussion for another day.

This is a tale of Critical Race Theory.


## PART I: THE THEORY

Critical Race Theory (CRT) holds tremendous power. You could learn as much from listening to the theory's opponents and supporters alike. One group is screaming from the rooftops about how dangerous it is, especially to children. They hold that CRT amounts to pernicious indoctrination. CRT opposers are so worried that they are recruiting people from out of state (Gross 2021; Hockstein 2021; Wong 2021) to weigh in on that most local of local issues, school board meetings. They are calling in to radio shows about it, watching TV specials about it, and they are angry (Cooper 2021; Ecarma 2021; Gertz 2021). The other group is trying to wave away its importance while simultaneously struggling to explain what it is. Many of the second group's reactions do not serve the theory; they are the Wizard of Oz demanding that no one look behind the curtain. Both reactions, the former in its organized desperation and the latter in its contradictory behavior, tell us that there is indeed something to Critical Race Theory.

Critical Race Theory was developed by several influential legal minds, including Kimberlé Crenshaw, Richard Delgado, Mari Matsuda, and the late Derrick Bell, as a method for analyzing the ways in which the law upholds and perpetuates racial inequality in the United States. As Crenshaw has said, CRT is less a theory than a "verb," in that it is intended to be a way of critiquing and making sense of the impact of the legal system on people of color.

What constitutes CRT varies slightly, depending on which theorist you read or speak with. However, there are several interrelated ideas that form the basis of CRT. The first is that racial inequality is hardwired into American society (Carbado and Roithmayr 2014). Therefore, racism is, as Derrick Bell put it, "ordinary." Additionally, racial progress is only truly allowed when the interests of people of color are aligned with the interests of White citizens. Bell (1995) called this "interest convergence."

CRT considers the role of racism when critiquing societal systems, such as examining how outdated laws written with racist intent have survived and continue to disadvantage Americans of color. CRT is constructivist, meaning that it acknowledges that laws and histories are never fully neutral because they depend on human beings, whose personal construction of reality is reflected in those systems. This also means that CRT recognizes and values experiential knowledge (Brown 2008), that is, the stories of the lives of people of color.

Proponents of CRT believe we should acknowledge that all policies and systems are inherently biased by the point of view of their creators. In

American society, those biases tend to perpetuate White supremacy. For example, CRT can be used to evaluate the assumptions underlying a supposedly race-neutral policy such as Stand Your Ground, the defense invoked in George Zimmerman's killing of Trayvon Martin.

The odds of a White-on-Black homicide being ruled as justified in Stand Your Ground cases was found to be 281 percent higher than a White-on-White homicide (Roman 2013). Applying CRT to Stand Your Ground would involve asking some questions. Why does a policy that does not specify skin color result in discriminatory treatment of Black people? Why are these laws proposed, and what supposed problem are they meant to address? What are the experiences of Black people when Stand Your Ground is used in their defense? When used against them?

Devon Carbado and Daria Roithmayr (2014) explain why colorblind laws disproportionately hurt Black citizens. They state American society communicates that colorblindness is good and attention to race is bad, but CRT takes the stance that attention to race can be good (e.g., affirmative action) or bad (e.g., discrimination). They build on previous work to introduce what they call a "Black suspicion paradigm."

The Black suspicion paradigm works like a flowchart. Mental shortcuts that take advantage of associations between mental concepts are called heuristics. The media and other elements of American culture give us associations (e.g., Black people and criminality) and images (e.g., the archetypal Black criminal). These lead to an availability heuristic in which people draw on the dominant association to recall Black people when crime is the topic; they also lead to a representativeness heuristic in which Black people are assumed to be criminals.

In the next step, these strong associations lead to a Black suspicion heuristic in which Black people in general are regarded with suspicion. The paradigm explains how associations and images can shape behavior such as racial profiling, sentencing disparities, and discriminatory policy. Whether the associations and images are outdated or are being reversed in some media is immaterial due to the powerful influence of these heuristics.

In the Stand Your Ground example, the Black suspicion paradigm explains the court decisions based on these laws. It also explains the skepticism with which many Black and other people of color view Stand Your Ground laws (Bates 2017; Bayram 2021; Henderson and Zerkin 2013; Kessler and Cotter 2020; Southern Poverty Law Center 2020), even though they are written in "colorblind" fashion that should theoretically protect their right to self-defense.

To understand what CRT is and why it has produced such strong reactions, let's step away from how CRT originated to examine why it grew in public awareness. For many, CRT became a thing when Nikole Hannah-Jones's magnum opus, the *1619 Project*, was released in August 2019. In it, Hannah-Jones examined popularized US history from the point of view of the descendants of enslaved people. One could not help but conclude after reading it, if they didn't already hold this belief, that racism and slavery have been a central part of the identity of the United States dating back to its inception. This was an example of CRT's function as a verb: a process of reexamining a traditional viewpoint through a lens that acknowledges the realities of racism and the experiences of the people involved. The result was a new version of history that did not whitewash the injustices built into the "new and more perfect union" and powerfully challenged widespread beliefs about this country.

The reaction to the *1619 Project* was most pointedly negative[1] among those who romanticize the nation's founding and identity as a bastion of freedom.

For those who see only the shining City on a Hill, this application of CRT to American history is a threat to the national identity. For those whose view of opportunity is obscured by redlined neighborhoods and dangerous stressors, whose success is belied by glass ceilings and family histories rife with experiences of injustice, Hannah-Jones's work is a revelation. For some Americans of color, it may be more than that. Seeing the suffering of their ancestors acknowledged can be a form of healing.

The backlash to the *1619 Project* presages the backlash to CRT. But while the former was focused on a specific work, the latter is based on something far less specific. In fact, it can be argued convincingly that it is *intentionally* a backlash to something less specific.

## PART II: THE BACKLASH

To hear him tell it, the backlash against Critical Race Theory began with a single man.

As told to Benjamin Wallace-Wells (2021) in an article for the *New Yorker*, Christopher Rufo believes he engineered that backlash after concluding that CRT was the "perfect villain." It's not hard to believe Rufo's claim: he has made frequent media appearances denouncing CRT, most notably on Fox News, since mid-2020. Rufo says he was looking for a term to describe the modern culture war conservatives were fighting. This new culture war ramped up in reaction to the cultural sensitivity trainings organizations offered in response to antiracist protests in the summer of 2020.

Rufo has assumed the role of right-wing expert on CRT in his appearances, linking CRT with critical legal studies, constructivism, Marxism, and eventually many cultural grievances that tend to be held by social conservatives. Rufo's tack is to argue pointedly against these philosophical elements of CRT.

Rufo then subtly expands "CRT" to include all attempts to acknowledge race as a social factor. Modern approaches to American history, for example, are not examined on their own merit; they are merely lumped under the CRT umbrella, an umbrella Rufo has already argued is "Marxist" and dangerous.

This leap is evident in efforts like those of Virginia Military Institute alumni to block reforms aimed at eradicating what a state-ordered investigation concluded was a racist and sexist culture at the school (Shapira 2022). Those alumni complain that CRT is embedded in any efforts to increase equity at VMI. At that point, Rufo's philosophical critiques no longer apply: CRT is behind anything and everything associated with race. But that does not seem to matter.

As writer Michael Harriot noted, teaching CRT to elementary school children makes as much sense as teaching them algebra or calculus (Harriot and Cooper 2021). To claim that this is what is happening is intellectually dishonest. In a chat sponsored by the *Washington Post*, one questioner asked journalist and author Karen Attiah, "Why not just shrug and accept the term has changed meaning?" Attiah responded that changing the name of CRT, a field "pioneered by Black scholars," would be unfair to their work.

That said, words change meaning over time. Meanings don't come from the dictionary; usage determines meaning and the dictionary records it. Think about how a word like "queer" has evolved in just the last fifty years in its predominant usage from "weird," to epithet, to reclaimed epithet, to form of self-identification. These meanings coexist to this day. If there is intellectual dishonesty in how CRT is being represented, there is some dishonesty in refusing to engage by insisting that CRT means something different than what critics are opposing.

To be clear, CRT opponents do not have the right to redefine it. What Rufo and his ilk did, and are doing, is dishonest. Furthermore, it is manipulative and intentionally divisive in an area already so personal to many Americans—the equivalent of throwing gasoline on a fire. There may not be much purpose in arguing about this point, though, because Critical Race theorists then face the uphill battle of *re*defining a theory that has already been "defined" in the public eye, albeit in deliberately inaccurate fashion. Fighting a linguistic battle distracts from what should a superordinate goal: exposing the flaws in the arguments of CRT foes. Such a strategy shows an understanding of the very human reactions of many of those who are prey to the backlash and addresses how antiracists can avoid falling into the traps set for them.

For example, Attiah explains how attacks on CRT serve as a "smokescreen" to challenge social justice and "content that affirms and uplifts non-white students." As Wendy Leo Moore and Joyce Bell (2019) put it in their research, CRT is a response to colorblind racism. In his paper on CRT, Edward Taylor (1998, 3) explains, "Color blindness makes no sense in a society in which people, on the basis of group membership alone, have historically been, and continue to be, treated differently." It is appropriate to revise the history we teach, even at the elementary school level, to reflect what this country is and how we got here.

That isn't critical race theory; it's honesty.

To continue to pretend that Dr. King and non-violence "solved" American racism or limit discussions of meaningful social events like the Trail of Tears is dishonest. This impacts the formation of the "cultural memory" of all students. In analysis of colorblind standards in social studies curricula, researchers (Heilig, Brown, and Brown 2012) found that information around race and racism often did not make the cut for "necessary" inclusion in classroom lessons. As the researchers ask in that paper, whose knowledge counts?

The opposition to CRT has not been forced to grapple with this fundamental question.

## Why the Backlash Works

The strategy of redefining CRT as a catchall antiracist villain is not a new one. Politicians know that having an enemy is a potent way to motivate voters. The Congressional turnover in 2010 was partially the result of an anti-socialism campaign maligning "Obamacare." The turnover in 2018 was partially motivated by a strong, negative reaction to progressive enemy Donald Trump. It is hard not to see the anti-CRT campaign as cynical and manipulative. But do opposers of antiracism in schools have a point?

People have deep attachments to the symbols in their lives. No one would argue that stomping on the Bible will literally injure an all-powerful God; a book is a manmade object with neither its own feelings nor an invisible connection to a deity's nervous system. Logical or not, most Christians would have a strong, automatic, negative reaction to this act. This, too, is the reason why cultural appropriation is problematic. Not because music or art or clothing doesn't "belong to everyone," but because these elements are valuable cultural symbols to which ethnic and racial groups have strong attachments.

Research on cultural identity and emotion has shown that culture serves people's fundamental needs (Bonn 2015). As a result, the symbols we identify with our culture generate strong attachments in us because they feed our human need for "safety, security, and predictability." Troisi and Wright (2017) reviewed prior research to offer a psychological explanation for the attachment to "comfort food." They found that comfort foods were related to the fundamental human need to belong: these foods served as symbolic connections to culture and valued relationships. Another group of researchers (Yap, Cheon, Hong and Christopoulus 2019) studied the process of cultural attachment, in which cultural symbols provide emotional security. They present research that underlines the value of emotion when learning about culture and, later, reencountering cultural symbols.

Who are the most likely to be attached to and protective of American symbols? Social Dominance Theory (SDT; Sidanius, Feshbach, Levin and Pratto 1997) is one indicator. SDT was developed to explain how group identities operate in a hierarchical society. According to SDT, the group at the top of the hierarchy (i.e., White Americans) is most strongly connected to national symbols and feels a sense of "ownership" over them. These connections have real-world effects, such as the finding by Carter and Perez (2016) that White people most attached to national symbols were most likely to be hostile toward immigrants of color, especially those from Latin America. Social Dominance Theory speaks directly to the mostly White backlash to CRT. The real and meaningful attachments many White people have to national symbols are threatened by accounts that affect, or even contradict, the meaning of these symbols.

The American norm of colorblindness is appealing to many, especially White citizens. That is because downplaying racial differences absolves White people of guilt related to discrimination and reinforces the American value of egalitarianism (Forman and Lewis 2006). Therefore, not only are White people more likely to be attached to popularized American history, but they also are more likely to oppose efforts to reassess it through more direct discussion of the role of race or racism.

The anti-CRT campaign is derailing the dialogue about racial issues in America during a time in which these issues are more nationally salient than they have been in decades. The moral weight many White Americans gave to the 2020 antiracist protesters, including a reevaluation of the role of White supremacy in this country, has been chipped away by the CRT opposition because they are threatened by challenges to their valued cultural symbols. Analysis of a large database of experimental research by social scientist John Jost and colleagues (Jost, Stern, Rule and Sterling 2017) found that fear and threat work to the advantage of conservative forces.

When policies are racialized by conservative politicians, White voters tend to move against them, as noted in research by Bennett and Walker (2018). CRT, already racial in nature, is intentionally being used to break multiracial coalitions—the CRT opposition has admitted as much. Rather than discuss the reasons people might have intense feelings about digging into White supremacy, including a reflex resistance to acknowledging the importance of race, a group of political pundits, PACs, and think tanks are content to exploit that vulnerability to motivate cash donations and votes.

Another reason people say they oppose CRT is that it "makes White children feel bad or guilty" (*The View* 2021). Yet an honest accounting of American history, as noted by Brittney Cooper (Harriot and Cooper 2021), would include a White legacy of antiracism, including the work of abolitionists such as William Lloyd Garrison and the ill-fated, righteous antislavery of John Brown. Dr. Cooper adds that erasing the bad deeds of prior generations and their reverberations actually does a disservice to today's White children. Discrimination and segregation are part of American history, but they did not need to occur: they are not part of human nature. By opening a discussion of these elements, which continue to wound the humanity of their fellow citizens, White children are offered a powerful way of counteracting any guilt by building new connections with those different from themselves.

It is imperative that those who want to see racial progress engage with as many people as possible. A moral mandate holds great power to motivate not only legislative improvements but also lasting social change. There is little to be gained from hunting for villains in the past or condemning today's White Americans. The past is past, just as we say in therapy. It is useful insofar as we learn from it.

White people in this country, just like all Americans, are responsible for its future. Diagnosing the present, just like in therapy, is meant to help us figure out our next step. Celebrating the guilt of White people, to the extent anyone is doing so, is like a client attending enough therapy to get diagnosed and then quitting so they can use the diagnosis to get sympathy. The diagnosis is not the work. But a diagnosis is informative, and White reactions to racism can give us information, too.

Shortly after Glenn Youngkin was elected governor of Virginia, supposedly due to his opposition to CRT, I conducted a preliminary experiment (Tilley 2022) to see whether using the words "critical race theory" mattered or not to White voters. The setup was that participants took several psychological measures. Then the participants[2] were divided into three, randomly assigned groups of equal size. All groups read an article about an upcoming school board election in their area. The article was the same except for one phrase. In the CRT group, the participant read about a candidate who states, "My opponent's opposition to critical race theory is a distraction." In the Neutral group, the participant read about the candidate's support for "an honest accounting of racism within American history classes." In the Humanistic group, the participant read about the candidate's support for CRT (which was not named) as translated into humanistic terms,[3] i.e., "racist systems dehumanize us all."

I wanted to see whether the actual term *CRT* mattered, or whether White voters were opposed to the concepts Rufo put under the umbrella regardless of the name. I also wanted to compare support for a humanistic approach to CRT to other versions. Overall, support for the candidate was significantly higher for participants with high racial empathy.[4] When I looked at the results by group, I found something interesting.

The participants with high racial colorblindness scores[5] rated the candidate significantly lower[6] in the Neutral and Humanistic conditions. There was no significant difference in the CRT condition, though. I interpret this result to mean a couple of things. One is that it seems it is the umbrella concepts, not just the name of CRT, that most White voters oppose. Even when describing the concepts in humanistic terms, colorblind racism pushes participants away from them. The other is that, when CRT was named, it hurt approval ratings from even those who acknowledge the realities of racism. The latter finding supports research showing the power of symbolic threats to build opposition to a policy.

## PART III: A RECKONING

It is said that the winners write the history books. This is undoubtedly so; the society that survives passes down its version of events, which is, in turn, passed down to succeeding generations as recorded history. History, in that sense, is a form of propaganda. It is up to the inheritors of history to decide whether to accept it as told, in which case it begins to die, or attempt to learn from it and about it, thereby strengthening both the history and the society it reflects. The only intellectually honest way to do so is to challenge it constructively, with the intent neither to crush it nor affirm it, so that the history that survives is fuller and more accurate.

That is the way history is supposed to work. It is what keeps Germany from erasing the rise of the Third Reich and the atrocities of the Holocaust from their national identity. But what happens when we are prevented from challenging and strengthening our history? To shirk that duty is to allow history to degenerate into mythology.

There are people who disagree with taking an antiracist approach to American history. They want their children to hear the same story of America that they were told, and their grandparents were told. By their logic, if it was good enough for them and their predecessors, it is good enough for their children.

The question posed by CRT analysis of US history is, which view is the truth? The experiences of the enslaved and today's Black Americans are true to them and very real. At the same time, the investment most White people, and some people of color as well, have in the popular telling of US history is quite real. It does no good to say, "Okay, we're going to tell the truth now," and wipe out centuries of tradition. There must be a reckoning, a conversation among differing worldviews, that leads to a better accounting of how this country was founded, why the laws are the way they are, and the relative impact of traditional American heroes such as the Founding Fathers.

If you are one of those people who believe traditional American history reflects only facts, I feel compelled to ask, does your point of view stand scrutiny? When I think of the loyalty many of us have to our worldviews, I think of religion and how deeply we hold our beliefs. In many religions, there is a tradition of constructive questioning. Not challenging out of cynicism, but challenging to strengthen your understanding.

Suppose you tell someone you believe in God, and they answer, "How can you believe in God when there is so much suffering in the world?" If you have not given your belief much thought, if you have not questioned why you believe what you do or wrestled with the dilemmas presented by the wantonness of life, you would have a hard time coming up with a satisfactory[7] answer. But by continually asking these questions—perhaps even praying or meditating about them or discussing them with others—you can approach a deeper understanding of your belief. By questioning your faith, you have made it stronger.

In the same way, we should engage in some introspection about why we hold the beliefs we do about race and the American system. Are there other viewpoints on how this country was founded, other views on the merits of Thomas Jefferson or other Founding Fathers? Am I sure that we have equality of opportunity in this country? If am I not persuaded by data that show discriminatory effects of the American system, why is that? What investment do I have in believing that our system is fair to everyone—or that it was intended to be fair in the first place? What would it mean to me, about me, if our system was not as fair as I had assumed?

On the other hand, if I believe in pervasive racial discrimination in this country, why do I hold this belief? What role does the "original sin" of slavery play in how I see my country? If someone tells me racism has decreased and now White people are being discriminated against, or that their White family was poor or immigrant and they hold no White privilege, what can I say to that? As we approach 175 years after the Civil War, why is the history of American chattel slavery relevant?

We should be able to answer those questions, too. Our views on American history must be able to stand critical thinking in continual, evolving pursuit of intellectual honesty. Otherwise, our conversation about race cannot proceed fruitfully.

This is not to say that those who push back against an honest accounting of history are just as accurate as those who demand the truth. Slavery was real. Its effects were real, and this country's people, especially Black Americans, still suffer for its reverberations. To deny this is to depart from reality. The part on both sides of this issue that is equally real is the emotional connection the people feel to their viewpoint. The humanity of all involved demonstrates that it is not a diluted half-measure that will solve the issue (e.g., "Slavery existed, it was bad, but it ended") but a truthful history. How we discuss that history must account for real, human reactions to learning about a legacy of pain and destruction.

None of this is easy. Nor is any of it, it should be noted, cynical or anti-American. On the contrary, it can be said that caring enough about our society to undergo this process is intensely patriotic. Thomas Jefferson once said that well-intentioned government should have nothing to fear from criticism. Jefferson, in an honest accounting of American history, is still a towering figure. His monstrous personal behavior and demurring on how to resolve slavery (which left him in abundant company at the time) do not negate his legacy as a singularly influential American. His approach to freedom is echoed by another American original, the author James Baldwin, who stated that his love for America is commensurate with his right to criticize it. There is little substantial reason on the right or left to fear the truth about America.

## THE PSYCHOLOGY OF DISTURBANCES AND INCONGRUENCES

Person-centered therapy, the psychotherapy developed based on valuing the unique humanity each of us possesses, teaches clients the importance of congruence. When we are congruent, we are able to live our best lives. The congruence we seek is between two versions of ourselves. One is the ideal self, which is who we want to be. This might include seeing ourselves as helpful, loveable, patient. The other is the image created by interacting with the world. This version of ourselves is based on the totality of our experience, not just our best behavior, and includes feedback we get from others. When our ideal self does not match our reality, we are said to be incongruent. In that state, it is hard to achieve our potential.

For example, if I believe it is integral to my identity that I am a kind and patient person, what is it like for me when someone personally insults me? It is disturbing because of the insult, sure, but there is an extra level of disturbance tied to my identity. I cannot allow myself to respond in a way that might be interpreted as rude. If I do, it is not just offense that I must deal with; it is the disturbance of behaving in a way that contradicts my self-image.

From a psychological perspective, judgments and feedback contradictory to our ideal selves can threaten our authenticity. If the idealized self is unattainable, we wind up encountering a world in which we are constantly experiencing incongruence. Psychological distress occurs when we ignore this valuable feedback. This protectiveness of an unrealistic self prevents us from maximizing our potential.

What if I believe I "don't have a racist bone in my body," but I am accused of being racist? The incongruence between my experience and my idealized self creates a disturbance. How do I deal with that disturbance? There are several ways. I can reevaluate who I believe I am, I can accept that I am not a perfect person (which involves letting go of the idealized "non-racist" self-view), or I can deny the value of the feedback I received. Whether the latter is problematic for me will depend on whether I continue to have these discordant experiences or whether I was right, i.e., the accuser was incorrect. But you can't skip to the end; you need to pause to look within before any progress can be made.

In the case of our country, the umbrella version of CRT that people like Christopher Rufo have worked so hard to make "toxic" (Iati 2021) boils down to challenges to the pat view of American history. What proponents of honesty about racism are saying is that the experience of people of color in this country is incongruent with the national identity as a colorblind land of equality and justice.

If we see this feedback as inconvenient, we might brush it off to protect this identity. We do so at our own peril. We become doomed to repeat the same disturbing experiences of incongruence until something changes.

The attachment many Americans have to the idealized self of the United States is deep-seated and vividly real. There is appeal in holding on to such an attachment; it feels good to think you are kind and patient, or without a drop of racism in you, or living in a land of freedom, equality, and justice for all. It is a great risk to let go of this idealized version by acknowledging and accepting its flaws. It is tempting to continue to reinvest in the idealized version. It is macaroni and cheese, Mom's meat loaf, carne asada tacos, a steaming bowl of pho—comfort food—for many Americans.

Those who wish to acknowledge systemic racism or flaws in American heroes are not doing so because they hate America. On the contrary, they want America to change so they can fully celebrate and enjoy the freedom, opportunity, and justice America promises. That version of patriotism is shared by Thomas Jefferson and James Baldwin. The value of this change, especially for those attached to the idealized self of America, is that it will draw us closer to a congruent place where reality aligns with ideals and the promise of this country will be fulfilled.

\*\*\*

If we are to learn as much as we can from history, if we are to maximize our unprecedented access to information, we must consider the past as accurately as we can. Our history is a house built by the stories of successive generations. Marginalizing some of these stories and the truth they tell, in the name of an idealized American self, leaves out load-bearing walls. The result is a weak house. We make our history more robust by integrating more information, more perspectives. By building those walls, we strengthen the house so it can better withstand hardship.

*The controversy about Critical Race Theory is really about who owns American history; less gatekeeping and more honesty humanizes and strengthens our shared story.* Today's White Americans, especially White schoolchildren, are not responsible for what happened in the past. What they, we all, are responsible for is the future. A racialized and hierarchical society is never going to be congruent with the glittering idea of America so many of us learned about and want to protect. Ignoring our flaws guarantees that our future will look like our present, which was formed by that same problematic past.

We can vote, petition, and push for an America that values each human being. It is a matter of historical fact that past generations failed to do so. If we want a better future, we can have it. We do not need to live in an unsound house. The work of repairing and rebuilding the house we inherited as American history can only come if we first are willing to challenge ourselves and our assumptions about this country.

## NOTES

1. The *1619 Project* came under predictable criticism from conservative elites, but it also was critiqued for its historical accuracy. One of the project's historian fact-checkers (Harris 2020) has written that her concerns with accuracy were ignored by the *New York Times Magazine*, which published the project. She establishes, though, that the bulk of external criticism of the project is not about accuracy, but rather about establishing a view of American history that minimizes the role of slavery. Another high-profile letter from historians (Bynum, McPherson, Oakes, Wilentz and Wood 2019) was sent to the *Times* requesting that the project be revised to correct the account of the American Revolution being motivated by the protection of slavery. They, too, note that the theme of slavery's centrality in American history is not at issue. The *Times* (Silverstein 2019) subsequently declined the request for revision because, "The work of various historians . . . supports the contention that . . . growing antislavery sentiment in Britain and increasing imperial regulation helped motivate the Revolution."

2. The total number of participants was 180 White volunteers, with sixty in each experimental group.

3. For more, see Treviño, Harris and Wallace 2008.

4. *Psychosocial Costs of Racism to Whites* (Spainerman and Heppner 2004) measures beliefs about the impact of racism on White people.

5. The Color-Blind Racial Attitudes Scale (Neville et al. 2000) measures adherence to colorblind racial (CBR) beliefs such as denial of racism, denial of White privilege, and blatant racial issues.

6. The ratings were on a 0–100 thermometer scale with 100 indicating full support of the candidate. The average for high colorblindness scorers in the Neutral group ($m=36.0$) was significantly lower than others ($m=63.5$, $p=.003$). The average for high colorblindness scorers in the Humanistic group ($m=34.3$) was significantly lower than others ($m=61.3$, $p=.007$).

7. A prepackaged, pat answer that ignores the complexity of the question does not indicate deep consideration, either. As my seventh-grade teacher, Sister Moira, would say in math class: Show your work.

# PART II

# Reality

## *What's Going On*

# Chapter 4

# Yes, the Struggle Is Real

## The Harvest of Racism

*Ah! You destroyer never destroyed, betrayer never betrayed! When you have finished destroying, you will be destroyed; when you have stopped betraying, you will be betrayed.*

—Isaiah 33:1

The analysis in this chapter and the following chapter builds the case that disparities experienced by Americans of color constitute a fundamentally unjust state of affairs, an important ingredient in building the moral conviction to fight racism. In this chapter, I present the realities of racism. I start with the psychology of the narrowest definition of *racism*, one restricted to interpersonal hate. Central to the continued relevance of race are the realities of experiencing racism. I provide one powerful example in the research on Black mothers. I close by exploring the realities of the misunderstood concept of microaggressions.

\*\*\*

White supremacy, Critical Race Theory, being woke, dog-whistling, systemic racism, misogynoir, unconscious bias . . . the drum beats on.

Perhaps all this is too esoteric. All this talk in America about racism as this invisible force that helps White people and harms Black people—could it just be theoretical? Is all this really happening? Is the Black struggle real?

The South lost, and Robert E. Lee isn't walking through that door. The plantations have been converted to museums. The firehoses in Alabama are back to just fighting fires. The lunch counters and drinking fountains and restrooms have been integrated. COINTELPRO has disintegrated. For eight years, Barack Obama, a Black man, was president.

Well, is it still real?

For the skeptics reading *Woke Racism* and cursing Robin DiAngelo, cheering on Ben Shapiro and Ye, this chapter shows the state of racism today. Not racism as a theoretical concept. Racism in the way it affects Black people, harms our brothers and sisters, keeps us from uniting.

Time has moved on, past John F. Kennedy's Camelot, when racism was most evident in individual vitriol: bombing Black churches, spitting at little Black girls, lynching Black boys, burning crosses. So, did Malcom X, the Student Nonviolent Coordinating Committee, Martin Luther King Jr., Fannie Lou Hamer, Stokely Carmichael, Angela Davis and Fred Hampton and the rapid cultural changes of the 1960s and 1970s get us across the finish line? Was Black Is Beautiful, disco, *The Cosby Show*, the Rainbow Coalition, White kids listening to hip-hop, Denzel and Hallie winning Oscar gold on the same night, enough? Was Barack Obama enough?

If that is the case, then racism is dead. But if racism is dead, let's first look at what is going on in this country, and then you tell me how to explain it without using that terrible word.


## RACISM AS HATE


Before getting into any discussion of how the totality of racism in American society harms Black people, let us begin with the narrowest definition of *racism*. The obvious, "old-fashioned" definition of *racism* on which there seems to be a measure of social agreement is believing someone is inferior based on race. Racism is implicated in the commission of most hate crimes, 57.6 percent according to the latest FBI (2021) data. The hate that comes from racist beliefs, whether we call it *bigotry* or some other term, has real-world consequences.

I start with racist hate because this is the racism that is easiest to see and scorn. When White people say, "I don't have a racist bone in my body," it is likely because they believe they don't *hate* any person of color. The malice and distancing implied by this limited definition of racism—one that recalls the KKK, lynching, and now tiki torches—is predicated on the centrality of hate in it.

Today, this hateful racism is forcefully denied. It is denied, often, with moral outrage. I learned as much when I studied colorblind racism and moral conviction. I surveyed a representative sample of 751 Americans[1] about their racial beliefs and how strongly they are held. I found that Republican racial conservatives, those who believed that racism was largely dead[2] and that Whites were being discriminated against as much as Black people, hold their beliefs with a sense of moral conviction.[3] This conviction was significantly related to a sense of White solidarity.[4] Not surprisingly, the group holding their racial views with the highest level of moral conviction[5] were Democrats who had strongly progressive views on race.

The book *Psychology of Hate* is an overview of research on how hate operates and why it often results in violence, particularly between groups or toward people of color. In the book, Ervin Staub (2005) writes about the social conditions necessary for hate. The first is difficult life conditions. This could include perceived difficulties, meaning that the economic anxiety so many theorize as behind the right-wing populist movement in the United States does not need to be reflective of reality. What creates a sense of resentment is the perception that other people are on their way up the social ladder (Bobo 1999) while I am stuck.

The second condition is connecting some other group to that resentment. If I am not happy with my life, I may choose to blame all my difficulties on my next-door neighbor. Once I blame him, and that impulse solidifies into a belief, we are likely to have negative interactions. That is because my belief is like a filter that alters my expectations and my interpretations of events, a self-fulfilling prophecy. But scapegoats don't need to be so idiosyncratic. They can be handed to me by my ideology.

Let's suppose I am a devoted Lakers fan and my neighbor is a Celtics fan. My neighbor on the other side is also a Lakers fan. It may be that I have had negative encounters with both, but the ones with my Celtics-loving neighbor stick out to me. Furthermore, I am likely to remember those negative encounters if I believe that Celtics fans in general are making our neighborhood or city, state, or country a worse place.

Being a Lakers fan didn't make me hate Celtics fans, just like simply being a White person doesn't mean that you hate Black people. However, if the influential people in my life are telling me the Celtics are not good for this country—if Magic Johnson is on Twitter telling me the Celtics are evil—it is possible I have absorbed some of these beliefs. What can magnify this effect is my level of devotion to this part of my identity. If I am the type to fly Lakers flags from my car and refer to the team as "we," I am even more likely to align myself with these beliefs. Then it is easy to blame my problems on Celtic fans, my group's chosen scapegoat, and in particular, the Celtic fan in my neighborhood.

According to psychologist Robert Sternberg (2005), scapegoating is group-oriented by nature. The cues come from the groups we value and are oriented toward an outgroup: a group we do not belong to or identify with. The scapegoat is showing itself to be worthy of hatred or it is threatening my group's interests. As I focus on the supposed flaws of this outgroup, I am shifting away from my individual identity as a flawed human being who makes mistakes toward my status as a member of my group. Thus, it is an affront to good Lakers fans, even the storied Lakers identity, that this Celtics-loving neighbor is not respecting me. I no longer view him as a flawed human being who makes mistakes; instead, I view him as just one more example of What's Wrong with Celtics Fans.

It is not hard to see how such thinking can lead to me not just avoiding my neighbor but hating him. Likewise, it is not hard to imagine an encounter with him, one that could have the same characteristics as an encounter with my other neighbor, getting violent.

This is more than a thought exercise. Consider the hate some Christians have for Muslims. Let's say I am one of those Christians, and the influential groups in my church disparage Muslims. Clearly not all Christians are attacking every suspected Muslim they encounter. What makes me absorb my church's logic so deeply that I am willing to perpetrate violence? It could be low self-esteem that tempts me to devalue others so I might feel better about myself. It could be my life feels out of my control, and the way to gain control is to accept that these issues are the fault of some specific group. It could be that my information is limited, I don't know much about Muslims, and the only things I hear about them are negative, so it is easy for me to feel threatened by them.

As noted, I might believe Muslims are such a threat because someone whom I believe represents me has told me so repeatedly. As Sternberg writes, "Often, people do not create stories, but rather cynical leaders create stories for them." Demagogues interested in profiting from intergroup animus can rally the ingroup by creating and attacking an outgroup. Appeals to the solidarity of a larger group against an offending, smaller group are hard for many to resist. The power of symbols, especially those tied to one's identity, increases the likelihood of absorbing this rationale and, as history has shown us repeatedly, violence.

The data are clear that hate groups grow and violence increases when politicians and other powerful actors scapegoat minority groups. A study (Piazza 2020) of the connection between politician speech and domestic terrorism found that politicians' hate speech was a positive and significant predictor of subsequent domestic terror attacks. The analysis indicated that the relation between the two was not endogenous, meaning that the speech was partially causative of the violence that followed. The author concludes, "Politicians' words have security consequences." Researchers (Bilewicz and Soral 2020) have found that the anonymity and democratization of the public sphere built into social media exacerbate the spread of dehumanizing views.

When Donald Trump referred to the deadly coronavirus as "Kung flu" and the "China virus," those words mattered. It wasn't just insensitive to use those words; it endangered Asian Americans. The Anti-Defamation League (ADL 2021) produces an annual study of online harassment. The ADL classifies as severe harassment physical threats, doxing, and sustained harassment. In 2020, the year of lockdowns amid an unsettling global pandemic, Asian Americans experienced a 72 percent increase in severe harassment. After Trump got COVID, there was a 25 percent rise in anti–Asian American negativity on Twitter. Overall, FBI data (Barr 2021) showed that hate crimes against Asian Americans rose 76 percent in 2020. The rash of anti-Asian violence witnessed in 2020 did not go away. As the pandemic continued into 2021, at least nine thousand hate incidents targeting Asian Americans were reported (Yellow Horse et al. 2021).

Did Trump cause all those hate crimes with his words? Certainly, his words preceded a rise in violence. And he had what Theodore Roosevelt called a bully pulpit[6] to spread that message. As research shows, politicians' hate speech means more than the words of your average citizen; such words often precede violence.

We all understand how troubling and baffling an unseen, evolving pandemic can be. It's a natural human response to search for an outlet for escalating anxiety. Channeling that excess energy into hate toward an outgroup did not keep a single person from dying of COVID-related complications. It didn't remove a single mask mandate or reopen one classroom. Rather, it spread new suffering and terrorized innocent people.

Maybe there would be less eye-rolling and hyperbolic outrage about changing terminology if people understood the impact words can have.

## THE BREAKS

Despite growing investment in fighting racism, especially since 2020, a substantial segment of Americans believes racism and its impact on people of color are limited or nonexistent phenomena. For example, polling (Griffin, Quasem, Sides and Tesler 2021) shows that about a fifth of Americans believe that Black people experience either little or no racism. Republicans are the most conservative on this question: as of January 2021, 71 percent of Republicans disagreed that there was a significant amount of discrimination in the United States. The study also found that 32 percent of all participants disagreed that residual effects of slavery and discrimination played a role in disproportionate poverty among Black Americans.

When people of color share experiences of discrimination and the effects of racism, a common response from racism deniers is that these aren't data. They're, supposedly, feelings. (And, as someone[7] is fond of saying, facts don't care about feelings.) Such a response makes the dispute personal.[8] First, these are reports of experiences that are real. Denying another person's experience dehumanizes and marginalizes that person, amplifying the impact of racism.

Second, as a psychologist, it is important to analyze the argument's discounting of feelings. Feelings do, in fact, matter. They are an indicator of a real problem. And numerous, rigorous, scientific studies have demonstrated the impact of experiences of discrimination and perceived racism on feelings and overall mental health. It is troubling to see measurable mental health patterns treated like passing whims.

So, how do experiences of discrimination or bigotry harm a human being?

If there were any question that post–Civil Rights Era racism exists and it affects people of color, decades of sociological and psychological scientific study have responded with vigor. As David Williams (2018) writes in his excellent, thorough review of the impact of stress on people of color, these studies have produced "broad agreement" that acute and chronic experiences of discrimination and bigotry significantly hurt mental health. Such impairments touch multiple areas of mental health, including self-esteem, increased incidences and severity of mood disorders such as depression and anxiety, and more severe psychiatric disorders. In fact, research shows that experiences of discrimination are related to an increased likelihood of Asian Americans and Latino Americans being diagnosed with almost any mental disorder. Indeed, a group of psychologists (Pieterse, Todd, Neville and Carter 2012) who reviewed the research on mental health in Black American adults concluded that experiences of racism should "be considered within the context of trauma."

Counseling psychologists Thema Bryant-Davis and Carlota Ocampo (2005) have analyzed the striking similarities between racism's effects and the patterns of post-trauma response to rape, domestic violence, and child abuse. They provide several specific behavioral examples. Child abuse victims and victims of racism alike can develop a set of "don't rules," such as *don't feel your feelings* and *don't trust yourself or others*. Rape victims and victims of racism both are prey to a puzzling social response that places the burden of proof on them and judges them for showing anger in response to their trauma. Bryant-Davis and Ocampo add that domestic violence and racism both gain their power from the victim's limited access to economic resources. The effects of racism on the mental health of people of color demonstrate that the differential outcomes and "mere words" of racist treatment are deeply wounding.

Apart from the numerous direct effects, feelings of "survivor guilt" often afflict those who witness the trauma of others. Survivor guilt is related to alienation from one's racial group and stressful questions about one's authenticity as a member. Though there are obvious limits to such comparisons, the parallels in several areas, especially the psychological risks such as post-traumatic stress, are substantially more than coincidence. Bryant-Davis and Ocampo recommend that therapists pursue applicable treatments from the trauma therapy field to help racism's victims.

People of color have been forthright in sharing their experiences of discrimination and racialized bigotry in decades of sociological research and a variety of forms of historical documentation. The experience of anti-Black racism—feeling hated, invisible, misunderstood, dehumanized—is famously a theme in the work of writers such as Toni Morrison, Langston Hughes, Audre Lorde, and James Baldwin. The late bell hooks (1995) laid bare the impact of racism by recounting her pain and anger through penetrating social analysis. George Yancy (2018) recounted his traumatic experience when readers responded to him with unnerving vitriol for writing about racism. Mary-Frances Winters (2020) has written about the far-reaching impact of racism and discrimination on Black people, not only at the national level, but also on her and her family.

A report by the Government Accountability Office (2021) found that, according to the latest data, 1.3 million students reported some form of hostile behavior directed at them over the course of one year. Bullying and hate crimes due specifically to race or skin color were "the most common, by far," involved in almost 80 percent of all hate crimes documented in the study. Bullying due to race includes student comments like, "Go back to your country," "I'm going to lynch you," and calling Black students "savages." This experience has led students in several schools to stage walkouts (De Luca 2021) in solidarity for bullied classmates of color, notably in the case of ten-year-old Isabella "Izzy" Tichenor (Tanner 2021). Izzy committed suicide after being bullied by classmates *and her teacher* for being Black and autistic.

## THE REALITIES OF "REVERSE" RACISM

White people make up 61.6 percent of the US population, according to the 2020 Census. The rate of White CEOs in the last twenty years (Zwiegenhaft 2020) shows that White people hold an overwhelming advantage at that position. Despite a 10.6 percent increase in the number of CEOs of color over that period, 85.8 percent of CEOs are White. Though college attendance has grown for people of color, White students with high school GPAs 3.5 and above are 11 percent more likely to attend four-year universities than their Black counterparts (M. Hanson 2022). The average unemployment rate since 1973 (Bureau of Labor Statistics 2021) shows that White people have had the lowest unemployment of any group, except for Asian Americans, from 2004 to 2019.

Still, a substantial portion of White Americans, 55 percent in one recent poll (Hill-Harris X 2019), believe White people are being discriminated against. Curiously, polling also shows that less than 20 percent of White respondents had experienced discrimination themselves (Gonyea 2017).

Based on the history of the United States, it would be reasonable to suggest that most White people have not experienced discrimination with any sort of weight behind it. If, in a college dorm, a Black student calls a White student a "cracker," that indeed could hurt. But there is no history of Black dominance over White people, no substantial threat of backfire for reporting the incident, no consistent pressure to performatively shrug off the pain, no society telling the White person, in so many words, "This epithet is a reminder that we do not value you."

Recently, conservatives and libertarians have decried what they see as an antiracist ascendance, especially on college campuses. Yet the facts about the numerous health disparities discussed above—the rotten fruits of racism—sharply contradict any notion that the racial order has been meaningfully upended. Until that point, should it ever occur, it is more realistic to look at society as it is.


## RACISM AND THE CASE OF BLACK MOTHERS

Discrimination can trigger what researchers (Fleming, Lamont and Welburn 2012) have called a "defilement of self": feeling victimized, scrutinized, disrespected, underappreciated, and misunderstood. The effects of discrimination are additive beyond socioeconomic status in accounting for all forms of mental health differences between White people and people of color. In other words, it is hard enough on one's mental health being poor or jobless, but being a poor or jobless person of color is worse. Many people of color, especially Black people, engage a "heightened vigilance" as an anticipatory form of coping with racism; this behavior is linked to sleep difficulties, increased risk of problems with cardiovascular functioning, higher odds of hypertension, and lower overall mental health.

The effects of racism spread beyond its immediate victims. Studies have shown that Black children experience racism vicariously through exposure to their parents' encounters with discrimination and bigotry. Nia Heard-Garris and colleagues (2018) conducted a systematic review of the impacts of vicarious racism on, primarily, Black children. They found links with problems in general child illness, mental health, substance abuse, self-esteem, frequency of sick-child visits to medical facilities, and even cognitive development.

"Well," goes the reply, "it's all in how you respond to it. Be stronger, just brush it off." This is a common line of reasoning among those resisting the evidence of racism in modern society: ascribing a level of control based on a false understanding of the situation. An extreme version of this thinking (and yawning dearth of historical perspective) is exemplified by rapper Kanye "Ye" West blaming enslaved people for not escaping as he said he would have. This takes responsibility off the unfair system and places it on those at its mercy.

In stark contrast to the supposed weakness of people of color stands a strange complementary idea: that American people of color, especially Black people, are adept at resisting oppression and have thrived in the face of adversity. These narratives burden people of color with almost unreachable expectations, which then are used to criticize them should they fall short. As Karen Pyke (2010, 563) wrote in her qualitative study of internalized racism among Asian Americans, the oppressed are cast as "impervious to pain, ever-resilient, and possessing a virtually superhuman ability to endure hardship. If the oppressed feel no pain, the oppressors can easily deny its infliction."

We know that human beings are not impervious to pain, nor are they able to endure hardship without hurting. Weathering is the process in which a lifetime of exposure to racist slights, marginalization, and the effects of discrimination gradually wear down the mental and physical resources of Black Americans (Giscombé and Lobel 2005). Weathering is one prominent explanation for the alarming prenatal and neonatal health disparities afflicting Black mothers. Black infants are twice as likely as Whites to die before reaching one year old, Black low birth weight and preterm death rates are significantly higher than White rates, and Black children have higher odds of cognitive deficits commonly tied to low birth weight.

Medical researchers do not blame biology. Physicians Dr. Richard David and Dr. James Collins (2007) conclude their analysis of racism's medical effects by stating, "It is highly unlikely for any given population to have concentrated multiple deleterious mutations in such a way that they are at higher risk for almost all of the common complex disorders *on a genetic basis* [emphasis added]." A series of studies support this conclusion: when Black Afro-Caribbean and African immigrant mothers move to the United States, they typically have higher birth weights and outcomes than American-born Black mothers. This is a damning bit of evidence that race is, as antiracists have insisted, a social construct and not a biological category.

Then perhaps these problems are due to the mothers' behavior. The research again contradicts this possibility: these effects remain after accounting for lifestyle elements such as smoking, alcohol use, and unhealthy eating. They are also not fully explained by socioeconomic conditions such as poverty, low education, and lesser access to quality health care. That means that "getting a better job" or other bootstrap solutions remain empty rhetoric here.

Before we jump to blame a faulty mindset in those American mothers—be it internalized racism or supposed cultural deficits—studies show that it is the *American racial environment* that is most likely to blame. A study covering almost a half million Black infants (Andrasfay and Goldman 2020) found that the advantage foreign-born Black mothers have over native Black mothers declines steeply in the next generation. So as the immigrant mothers give birth to American daughters, who give birth to their second-generation American daughters, and so on, whatever advantage the immigrant Black mothers had is lost.

Sadly, what they are losing is so much more than a categorical advantage. This is where another type of weathering comes in. Immigrants famously love the United States. It is not hard to find anecdotes of immigrants telling Americans how good we have it and that we shouldn't complain. In late 2021, pro basketball player and displaced Turk Enes Kanter said as much while criticizing LeBron James for his outspokenness on American racism. True, America is a wonderful country.

The initial wave of immigrants in a family are willing to work hard at (often multiple) low-paying jobs with the expectation of building a life for future generations (Rosenberg, Desai and Kan 2002). The American dream informs us that the next generation should be better off, and so forth. That is the story told about the Irish, Italians, and other now-White immigrant groups. But when the next generation and the one after see that the hard work is not paying off, this chips away at the shield of hope used to deflect their stress. This is a generational form of weathering in which each successive group of family descendants feels more fully the brunt of discrimination and other forms of racism. Such erosion of hope is a perverse artifact of acculturation for Black immigrants.

Pause a second and think about the ramifications of this research. It isn't biology. It isn't economics. It isn't personal behavior. It is the sorry treatment Black women are subjected to in this country—a "unique and more aggressive" version of racism, according to work by psychologist Maria Jones and her colleagues (Jones, Womack, Jérémie-Brink and Dickens 2021)—that impacts their mental health over a lifetime, as well as potentially impairing the mental health and cognitive development of their children. Not only that, but it also affects whether those children survive even to celebrate a first birthday. There may be no line of research more utterly devastating to claims that racism does not exist.

## IS RACISM DEFINED BY HATE?

The science of studying racism, and the accompanying dialogue when media outlets pay attention to the findings, tends to produce a good deal of terminology. Terms like *unconscious bias* and *privilege* (and, to an extent, *woke*[9]) spread in awareness from academic circles to common usage in news media and popular culture. Perhaps no term used to discuss racism is as misunderstood as *microaggression*.

In 2005, psychologist J. Manuel Casas (2005, 502) argued for an expanded conceptualization of racism that included "the everyday, mundane, negative opinions, attitudes, and ideologies and the seemingly subtle acts and conditions of discrimination against minorities." In a landmark 2007 paper on cross-cultural therapy, psychologist Derald Wing Sue and colleagues (2007) described racial microaggressions: brief, commonplace, sometimes unintentional indignities to which people of color are subjected. What Sue, Casas, and others are highlighting is another way that racism—whether born from hostility, beliefs in fundamental difference, carelessness, or dehumanization—seeps into the lives of people of color.[10]

Ijeoma Oluo includes a chapter in her inviting and informative book, *So You Want to Talk about Race*, listing a variety of microaggressions to which people of color are exposed. These include, "Where are you from?" and "You are so articulate." They might also include requests to touch a Black person's hair or telling a Korean American woman she looks "so exotic." To a person who has not been subjected to remarks like these regularly, these seem relatively innocuous. To a person of color, the behaviors are a barrier: you must not be from here, you are not like us, you are your skin and not another human, I expect very little from you. These are the hidden messages, as Dr. Sue calls them, that turn the mundane into the hurtful.

Research (Santiago-Rivera, Adames, Chavez-Dueñas and Benson-Flórez 2016) has found these indignities to be related to the higher levels of stress reported by people of color in America. Additionally, those most likely to perpetrate microaggressions are also more likely to deny the continued existence of racism and have some antipathy toward Black people (Kanter et al. 2017). This means that White people's doubts about racism's existence are not theoretical: they directly and negatively impact the health of the people of color around them.

A few years ago at the American Psychological Association's (APA) Division 45[11] biennial conference, I had the pleasure of attending a panel about the impact of racism on mental health. Speaking in that panel was researcher and psychology professor Dr. Tabbye Chavous. Dr. Chavous and other members of the panel detailed one of the reasons microaggressions are so hurtful.

As research has shown, exposure to racism tends to hurt self-esteem not only through internalized racism (Brondolo, Ng, Pierre and Lane 2016) but also through weathering over time. The panel noted that one of the devious features of microaggressions is the multiple levels of stress they cause. Because the situations are so vague, the victim not only has to deal with the pain of the perceived slight. They also must deal with confusion over the intent of the behavior, how to respond to it, and the aftermath of their response. It is easy to see how one supposedly small incident can reverberate throughout a person's day, and that is just one incident. Dealing with these manifold stressors takes a toll on the mental health of people of color.

It can be easy for White people, especially those who do not identify with a marginalized population, to claim that these are "just questions" or "innocent comments" when they aren't asked these puzzling things every day. White people aren't often forced to decide whether and how to defend their humanity daily. Those who believe these comments or questions can be just brushed off should consider the toll it takes to ignore what feels like a relentless series of indignities. Furthermore, it is not just the incidents themselves, but also the self-doubt, stress, and social awkwardness they trigger that must be shouldered and navigated by victims of microaggressions.

For those who believe the effects documented throughout this chapter are the result of unlikely, isolated interactions with "bad apple" racists, the research annihilates this contention. If hurt feelings were all that resulted from racist interactions, we would not see evidence of mental health disparities to match the economic and social disparities that disadvantage people of color in this country. Additionally, it gives lie to the aphorism, "it's only feelings," as if feelings don't matter or are easily changed. A century of psychological research demonstrates the opposite quite clearly. For the remaining skeptics, consider the last time telling someone to "cheer up" or "calm down" was effective.

Unfortunately, mental health needs for Black Americans are more likely go unmet than for other racial and ethnic groups. There are several reasons for this, perhaps chief among them the long history of White psychotherapists' poor response to the unique stressors encountered by people of color. Partially in response to news of this disturbing pattern, the APA finally released a set of guidelines in 2002 for multicultural training for therapists. The APA periodically revises these guidelines in pursuit of better treatment for people of color.

The other side of the equation is that there is also a long history of distrust in the mental health system common to Black Americans. Black Americans often report not feeling their needs met by a therapist pool that is primarily White. A survey of mental health views among Black Americans found that a major reason for not seeking therapy was a low perception of the effectiveness of such treatment. In the context of research on therapy process, such a belief can be damaging even when people do seek help: one of the widely cited "common factors" (Snyder and Taylor 2000) in successful treatment is hope that things will be better after therapy.

\*\*\*

It's been well over half a century since the landmark legislative achievements of the civil rights movement: the Civil Rights Act of 1964 and the Voting Rights Act of 1965. Those took place with the moral force of a nation behind them, amidst President Lyndon Johnson's Great Society program to decrease poverty and discrimination. For all the promising signs of progress, racism still hurts Americans of color in multiple areas.

We teach our children that education is part of the American dream. In one of the unqualified successes of the post–Civil Rights Era, high school graduation rates have increased to the point that over 90 percent of Black Americans between the ages of twenty-five and twenty-nine have their diploma. Post-secondary education was an ingredient in the rise of immigrant groups in the mid-twentieth century, when it became both more crucial and more accessible. That is, for some. The 101 "most selective" public institutions[12] in the United States are doing a worse job of accepting Black students than they were over twenty years ago. Choosing to attend a Historically Black College or University is no escape from racism: in 2022, at least three waves of bomb threats hit HBCUs, resulting in temporary closure of sixteen campuses (Lumpkin and Svrluga 2022).

At the most basic level, most of us can say, "At least I have my health." Here, sadly, Black Americans again experience disparities. As noted, a lifetime of racism has a deadly impact on Black infant survival rates. Black Americans have shorter life expectancies than other ethnic groups (Taylor 2019). The COVID pandemic stole the lives of loved ones and forced hard choices for almost all Americans; Black Americans suffered a disproportionate death rate (Hill and Artiga 2022). The health and economic effects of the pandemic forced many to dip into emergency savings that were far lower for Black families, widening the family wealth gap (Weller and Figueroa 2021).

Acknowledging the gains since Jim Crow does not mean we must ignore the existence of racism. Given the persistent disparities almost everywhere for people of color, the question that must be asked is, where is the moral conviction that energized a nation in the 1960s? Was it a lost moment in time, or the manifestation of a country's commitment to equality and justice?

If it is the latter, if we are to commit to the American dream, we must start by acknowledging that racism continues to exist and affect the lives of people of color for the worse. It is no less than a moral failure to continue to look the other way because progress has already been made, because there has already been a Black president, because White people have it hard too, because it somehow isn't the job of a country that pledges that there be liberty and justice for all, or any of the other pat reasons. *Racism is still real, and it is dangerous in many ways to Americans of color.* Simply put, believing racism is limited to hate, thereby avoiding any introspection about one's own racist tendencies by telling yourself "I don't hate anyone," is dishonest.

America deserves the allegiance of its citizens for what it is and what it can be. For many people of color, what it is falls short far too often. One potential reason why the American experience is lesser for people of color is that there is more hurting them than bigotry.

## NOTES

1. Participants were recruited from Amazon's Mechanical Turk. The sample was 59 percent male and 48.2 percent Republican. Participants were 66.8 percent White, 21.8 percent Black, 8.3 percent Latino, and the remainder Asian American or Pacific Islander. Income was representative of a middle-class group: 44.2 percent reported income below $50,000 and 77 percent below $75,000. Participants verified consent and then answered the surveys via a link to Google Forms.

2. This was measured by the Color Blind Racial Attitudes Scale (CoBRAS). For more on the scale, see Chapter 6.

3. Moral conviction was measured with the Moral Conviction Measure (Skitka and Morgan 2014; Brandt, Wisneski and Skitka 2015), a three-item measure of the extent to which an attitude about a specific object (here, racism) is held with moral conviction. There was no significant difference between Republicans and Democrats on moral conviction.

4. White solidarity was taken from the first two items of a measure of White Vulnerability created by Fowler, Medenica, and Cohen (2017).

5. When I split the data by the midpoint of the CoBRAS into "high" and "low" groups, then compared Moral Conviction Scores by political party, low-colorblindness Democrats had the highest moral conviction (13.25 out of 15) of the four groups and high-colorblindness Democrats had the lowest moral conviction (10.8). Each Democrat group was significantly different from all other groups at $p<.001$.

6. Great communicator though he was, Roosevelt could hardly have predicted the value of even radio, used brilliantly by his fifth cousin Franklin, let alone Twitter and other social media in political messaging.

7. Popular right-wing personality Ben Shapiro. I suppose his mantra is better than the viral Trump 2020 campaign slogan, "Fuck Your Feelings."

8. People of color can feel justified offense when someone disputes their real experience with racism. Prior experience may have shown them that people arguing against the existence of racism have an ulterior motive for doing so, especially if they

have shown themselves to be bigoted in other ways. Above all, arguing against a real experience with pain discounts the experience and is likely to make said pain worse. As much as the term *gaslighting* became vogue during the Trump presidency, these "that wasn't racism" arguments share much in common with that dynamic.

9. Woke took a slightly different path to mainstream White awareness than some of these other terms (Bayne 2022; Harriot 2021). As others have noted, woke was mid-twentieth-century African American Vernacular English often used in the context of a warning to peers, "Stay woke," be aware of your surroundings, and take care of yourself and your people. This came to be slang for those who are on guard against the ways racism threatens people of color, usually Black people. In its recent incarnation, *woke* has been applied to or claimed by White people who acknowledge their privilege and show sensitivity to the experiences of people of color. This usage has been parodied into an insult by racial conservatives toward supposedly oversensitive, liberal White people.

10. Sue and others do not limit the application of microaggressions to people of color. Sue's subsequent work (Sue 2010) clarifies that microaggressions can be perpetrated based not only on race, but on gender and sexual orientation.

11. APA Division 45 is the Society for the Psychological Study of Culture, Ethnicity, and Race.

12. Most selective was defined as state flagship colleges, colleges with high SAT scores, and colleges classified as such by the Carnegie Foundation Classification rubric (St. Amour 2020).

## Chapter 5

# Systemic Racism and the Post-Racial Lie

*What injures the hive injures the bee.*

—Marcus Aurelius, *Meditations*

In this chapter, I continue the case for racism as real and unjust, begun in the previous chapter. This chapter covers racism's systemic aspects, which are disparities that can be reproduced by the inertia of societal systems without ill intent from individuals. I begin, though, by presenting my theory for why it is hard for so many Americans to accept that racism has systemic aspects. I analyze research demonstrating how systemic racism operates within and affects American society. I close with a detailed example of the many ways systemic racial disparities—which I define as *systemic racism*—hurt Americans of color from youth onward.

\*\*\*

Let it never be said that a book about racism didn't contain at least some good news.

Over the last fifty-plus years since the end of the Civil Rights Era, White Americans seem to have been getting less racist. As reported by many surveys,[1] belief in Black inferiority, support for segregation and discrimination, distaste for interracial marriage, and denial of anti-Black discrimination have all decreased markedly since the 1960s. This may indicate that the sacrifices of the civil rights movement, including the ultimate sacrifice in too many instances, were worth something. They not only achieved landmark equality-focused legislation, but they actually changed hearts and minds.

This should be cause for rejoicing. But some view reports of decreasing racism with a jaundiced eye. After all, if racism is decreasing, then why are people of color still struggling at disproportionate rates to White people? Why, when people of color thrive, is this not rewarded fairly? Why do Americans of color fight harder to get less?

This is not an individual problem. It's hard to point to specific actors who make Latino and Black Americans more likely to be poor, more likely to be unemployed, less likely to graduate from high school, more likely to be incarcerated, more likely to deal with mental illness, or less likely to get a loan or own a home. *This is systemic racism*: the sum of numerous disadvantages that have a profound effect on the lives of Americans of color. Rather than going through the litany of ways race impacts Americans' lives, we talk about it as a system. This simplifies a complex reality, but it also complicates a story that racism is fought at the individual level. And that, supposedly, is a battle already won.

So, what good is a decrease in these racist beliefs if the lives of people of color are still vulnerable to persistent disparities? Are we a nation grappling with, as Eduardo Bonilla-Silva (2018) memorably put it, racism without racists? Why, so many years removed from the death of Jim Crow, are we still here discussing racism? How can it be that, in this post-Obama America, racism lives? The same people rejoicing without reservation that things have gotten better are also stuck puzzling out an answer to these questions.

This groping, this disappointment, this exasperation come from a place of pain. The pain was caused by a lie this nation swallowed during the Civil Rights Era. It was a lie that was tempting to believe for many reasons, foremost among them that it preyed on a popular vision of America as a shining City on a Hill where those yearning to breathe free could do so. But it was a lie nonetheless.

The lie Americans believed was that, if individual citizens stopped judging people based on their color—if White people stopped hating Black people— race would no longer matter. When race no longer matters, we have defeated racism. The lie is an assumption, perhaps born of premature hope, that vastly underestimated the challenge of ending racism. Having heard the demands of the civil rights movement and changed beliefs and even feelings about Black people, you almost can't blame White people for asking, shouldn't that be enough?

Based on current racial socioeconomic disparities, it is not. Thus, we are not yet a post-racial nation. Still, this question embodies the resistance to addressing disparities that harm many Americans. We start with this resistance because understanding it can give us insight into how to overcome it.

The previous chapter outlined the pain and suffering interpersonal encounters with racism and discrimination can cause. There is good cause to believe that interpersonal bigotry is not all that is afflicting Americans of color: racism is more than that. But, what, then? And what can one say in response to the White Americans pointing to the real trends presented above as indicative of racism's end? Before judging these people, let us stop to understand their pain. The pain is born of mourning, mourning for the death of that alluring Post-Racial Lie.

## UNITED IN GRIEF

One of the most popular conceptualizations of the bereavement process is the Kübler-Ross stages of grief. Elizabeth Kübler-Ross created stages to describe the experiences of those facing death: denial, anger, bargaining, depression, and acceptance. Though not necessarily a scientific[2] approach, the stages provide a picture of what it is like to process loss.

A more modern, empirically supported bereavement therapy (Rubin 1981; 1984; 1999) accounts for two separate tracks. One is the biological, behavioral, cognitive, emotional, and social impact of experiencing loss. These areas often interact with one another; thus, this track is known as the biopsychosocial track. An example is emotional stress, exacerbated by dwelling on unanswerable questions such as "Am I grieving appropriately?" disrupting sleep rhythms, which leads to avoiding social interactions.

The second track is the nature of the bond between the bereaved and the deceased. Therapists might ask the bereaved to explore this bond. What was the relationship like when they were alive? How has it changed, and how can it evolve? What does the bereaved find themselves yearning for in the wake of this loss?

The preceding assumes a person engaging with the loss and seeking treatment. Unfortunately, for a variety of reasons, people may react to death in ways that harm their functioning (Rubin, Witzum and Malkinson 2017) and prevent them from fully processing the loss. The risk of sinking into maladaptive patterns stands as notice that the grieving process should be handled thoughtfully.

The loss America experienced upon the debunking of that alluring Post-Racial Lie seems to fit both theories of bereavement. First, there has been persistent denial, by a significant segment of the White population, of the continued existence of racism (Sidanius, Singh, Hetts and Federico 2000). Considering comprehensive evidence to the contrary, this stands as a sad example of how the loss of this lie can create an emotional pull to an easy, but maladaptive, response.

Second, the Kübler-Ross bereavement stage of anger aptly encapsulates the frustration from some Americans that race and racism are still a topic. The anger that can come from confronting death often results from a sense that what is happening is unfair: the world is cruel; it isn't my (or my loved one's) time yet. The end of Jim Crow, increased racial sensitivity among White people, and the election of Barack Obama to the presidency are among many indicators of a just, colorblind society. So why aren't Americans of color placated and thankful? This is not fair, so the thinking goes.

The simplest indicator that Post-Racialism is a lie would be an actual rise in Jim Crow–style racism. It is unlikely that is the case, though there are some troubling indicators that racism is getting worse (e.g., Dubey 2020; Lotto 2016; Stein and Allcorn 2018). It is possible that some of the increased attention to racism is due to marginalized people creating a larger voice for themselves, whether through personal grit, societal progress, or the democratization of mass media. Though it could be things are again getting worse for people of color, it also could be that things have been bad on average. It's just that now that the five-alarm fire has been put out, other cries for help are being heard, and the fire's destruction can be understood.

This brings us to the third way the Post-Racial Lie has impacted White America: the relationship to the deceased. There is honesty in the desire for an end to talk of reparations, affirmative action, representativeness, terminology changes, and other redress. When people believe America gives everyone a fair shake, they are also likely to find Black people in violation of the tacit deal within the American dream: work hard and you will succeed. This much has been shown by research conceptualizing racial resentment as reflecting patriotic belief in an America that rewards hard work and epitomizes fairness.[3]

The connection between racial resentment and nationalistic patriotism matters because those who ardently adhere to a pristine, romanticized view of America are most motivated to believe the Post-Racial Lie. A change of heart during a period of roiling social change was not enough—in the great hour of need for citizens of color, America was not enough—and this stings those ready to celebrate victory. Either people of color are lying, or America failed. For the committed, confronting the realistic possibility of the latter cannot help but feel like a devastating loss.

The exposure of post-racial America as a lie occurred because the disproportionate victimization and suffering of Americans of color has been shown to go beyond interactions with bigots. The evidence is extensive; some of it is explored in the remainder of this chapter. That evidence demonstrates what systemic racism is: a fundamentally unjust state of affairs in which the odds of a person's success, mental health, indeed, lifespan are affected by their race.

## RACISM IS MORE I: IT DEPENDS

Whether you see racism as a category of individual, moral violations or something harder to delimit likely depends on your politics.

The Republican Party, evident from party leaders' statements on racial injustice (Courtney 2020; Klar 2020; Lemon 2020; Smith 2020) and findings on conservative racial views (Haltinner 2016; Mayorga-Gallo 2019), tends to conceptualize racism as limited to individual acts of hate against minorities. We might call this interpersonal racism. There are plentiful examples in modern conservative thought positioning colorblindness and denial of White privilege as—for lack of a better term—anti-racist (e.g., Friedersdorf 2020; Williams 2020).

The Democratic Party tends to consider a substantially larger set of issues as race-related. This includes racialized issues like affirmative action along with advocating for reforms in criminal justice (Baptiste 2019; Karma 2020), strengthening the social safety net (Porter 2020), expanding affordable health care (Bacon 2017), mandating fair housing policy (Rothstein 2017), and increased police accountability (Drakulich, Wozniak, Hagan and Johnson 2020; Swain 2018). Their proposed solutions often rely on liberal federal legislation in the tradition of the 1964 Civil Rights Act and the 1965 Voting Rights Act.

This difference in how party elites define and discuss racism shows up in data on the beliefs of voters. I measured voters' racial beliefs[4] using the Color Blind Racial Attitudes Scale (CoBRAS), which has a subscale for unawareness of institutional racism. The subscale includes items like, "Social policies, like affirmative action, discriminate unfairly against White people."

Using this subscale as a proxy for whether participants deny racism is a systemic issue, I compared the scores between Democrats and Republicans. Republicans had a significantly higher average score ($M$=30.5, $p$<.001) compared to Democrats ($M$=22.6). The 95 percent confidence interval, meaning we are 95 percent sure the real difference between the two scores in the population falls within a given range, was 6.9–8.9. This is a meaningful difference that amounts to about 16 to 21 percent of the total score on the scale: Republicans are less likely to see racism as systemic.

Despite disagreement on what racism constitutes, most people believe that racism involves dehumanization due to a racial difference. This is fertile ground to build a consensus on combating racism that carries moral weight.

## RACISM IS MORE II: CRIMINALIZATION

If it's clear that we are not in a post-racial era, then what to make of the existence of racism? Is racism still about individuals, or is it more than that?

On an afternoon in early 2020, a twenty-five-year-old man was jogging down a road in Glynn County, Georgia. This was not out of the ordinary; according to his father, he frequently exercised in the area. Back in high school, he was a pretty good linebacker on the football team.

Months earlier, a nearby neighborhood had reported several home break-ins. This has nothing to do with the jogger, yet it had everything to do with why he will never finish his plan to become an electrician. Why he will never lace up his sneakers again, laugh at a joke again, hug his family again.

A local man claimed he recognized the jogger as the man committing the local thefts. He grabbed a shotgun, his son grabbed a pistol, and they set off in their truck to confront the jogger.

They caught up to him. They tried to cut the jogger off with the truck, but he started running the other direction. A neighbor of the men in the truck attempted to box in the jogger with his car. A chase began.

Eventually the two drivers trapped the jogger with their vehicles; the son in the truck pulled a shotgun on him. The jogger tried to avoid the gunman. The son fired the gun, shooting the jogger. The jogger tried to wrestle the shotgun away from the son. Two shots later, one at point-blank range, and the jogger collapsed to the ground.

The jogger, as many people now know, was Ahmad Arbury, a Black man from Brunswick in the southeast part of Georgia, about forty miles north of the Florida-Georgia state line. The three men who chased him are White. Ahmad Arbury is dead now, and millions of people watched him die because his murder was recorded by a cell phone.

This was two White men, joined by a third, hunting and killing a Black man.

There are features of this murder that echo a history all too recent in this country. Entering the wrong neighborhood could get a Black person harassed, chased, beaten, tortured, killed. In 2020, much of the country wanted to believe those days were over, which explains the outrage over the video of Arbury's last living minute. Not that the events on the video themselves are not outrageous. There is an extra layer of outrage, there were White people marching in the streets, because it stands as evidence of the Post-Racial Lie.

If any event encapsulates what people mean when they say they racism is about hate, this is it. White men suspecting a Black man they don't know of a crime, then going outside the law to end that Black man's life. If they didn't have hate in their hearts, the thinking goes, they wouldn't have hunted him like an animal and killed him.

Is that it?

The father who thought Arbury was a criminal, the man whose son took Arbury's life, was a former police detective. Whether you think this detail has anything to do with the story likely has to do with whether you believe racism is mainly about individual hate or whether you believe it is more than that.

There is a long, tortured history between law officers and communities of color. In public opinion polling, Black people tend to report distrust in the police, though they often request more police involvement in their communities. Researchers (Prowse, Weaver and Mears 2019) virtually connected Black Americans in major cities to discuss police activity. In a variety of circumstances and different types of neighborhoods, the participants reported a paradox of policing in their communities: police were always around to harass but never around when needed. In one poll taken by the Democracy Fund's Voter Study Group (Griffin, Quasem, Sides and Tesler 2021), Black trust of the police stood at 5 points net favorability, meaning the number of Black respondents with a positive view of police exceeded the number with a negative view by only 5 percent. Ratings from Latino (27 percent) and Asian American/Pacific Islander (30 percent) participants were higher but still substantially lower than net favorability of the police among White participants (57 percent, an overall favorability of 78.5 percent).

The problems Black people tend to have with the police are not in their minds. Black men have about a 1 in 1000 risk of being killed by police in their lifetimes (Edwards, Lee and Esposito 2019). This number is twice the likelihood of all others and around triple the risk faced by White men. Black participants reported interactions with police that involved threats of force at a rate 2.65 times that reported by White participants.

Historian and professor Khalil Gibran Muhammad (2010) outlines the lengthy history of policing in the country, including the criminalization of Black men, using Philadelphia as a living example. In one grisly case, Muhammad writes that police disarmed Black Philadelphians during race riots in the summer of 1918, thereby aiding their attackers. The riots resulted in disproportionate arrests of Black men, most of whom had been attacked by rioters and were acting in self-defense.

Many publicly expressed skepticism that Arbury's killers would be convicted, much as they did during the trial of George Floyd's killer. This reaction, too, is not misplaced. Law professors Jeffrey Fagan and Alexis Campbell (2020) analyzed 3,933 police killings in their research. They found not only the same striking racial disparities in killings of Black citizens but also fundamental issues with how police are trained and regulated. These issues are rooted in judicial interpretations of the Fourth Amendment's protection against "unreasonable" search and seizure. These tend to give a wide berth to the "reasonableness" of police behavior, which in turn creates a high hurdle for prosecutors of police violence to clear. So not only does the system prioritize the police point of view, but it does so disproportionately at the expense of Black lives.

The criminalization of Black men, in particular, is one way in which a system can perpetuate racist discrimination. The open question of whether Ahmad Arbury was a sacrifice on the altar of racist hate or another Black man whose victimization was scaffolded by a racist system (or both) was not answered by his killers' trial. For that matter, the answer doesn't bring him back or change the hearts of three White men sitting in prison, nor does it fix the society that allowed him to be dehumanized. But if the answer is that racism is bigger than the hearts and minds of individuals, then the solution must be bigger as well.

## RACISM IS MORE III: THE GOAL

The result of the Post-Racial Lie is yet another America division, this time between those who believe racism is mostly limited to the actions of individuals and those who see it mostly as an unfair system. The crippling effects of interpersonal racism, both on the person hating and the victim of that hatred, have been discussed in the previous chapter. One group, believers that interpersonal racism is the problem, must be satisfied with the current norms discouraging this sort of bigotry. However, they are the same people likely to be disillusioned and hurt by the Post-Racial Lie.

The other group believes in a wider-ranging form of racism, which is rooted in an American paradox. Endorsement of Jim Crow racism has declined, yet racial discrimination and vast racial disparities in wealth and incarceration continue to exist (Bonilla-Silva 2001; 2014; 2015; Sears, Hetts, Sidanius and Bobo 2000). Kwame Ture (formerly Stokely Carmichael) and Charles Hamilton (1967) explained this by coining the term institutional racism, discrimination built into the operation of society. Institutional racism, often called systemic racism, does not rule out the possibility of interpersonal racism; rather, it explains why other sorts of discrimination have become a larger problem for modern Black Americans.

An interpersonal definition of *racism* has the appeal of having someone to blame for a situation. Blaming a system is a little harder to understand than blaming a person. For example, in the George Floyd case, many people jumped to blame Officer Derek Chauvin's personal racism for killing Floyd: he was a "bad apple" officer.

A racist system can reproduce racial disadvantages without foaming-at-the-mouth, racist boogeymen like Orval Faubus or George Wallace. An accidental, harmful by-product of focusing on a racist system is the removal of such boogeymen. Without visible villains, White people were free to question whether racism still existed. The implication of such a question is that Black people are wholly responsible[5] for their spot on the lowest rung of society. It is not hard to see that doubts about racism's existence can lower the motivation to support doing anything about it.

Those who blame Chauvin might may have been tempted to look through his social media feeds and prior behavior to see if there were other indicators he was a racist. But that would discount the impact of his training and experience as a police officer. As noted above, substantial research by Khalil Muhammad and work by Michelle Alexander (2012) demonstrate how American society, especially law enforcement, has come to see Black people as synonymous with criminality. This connection draws directly from a racist history in which Black Codes were developed to turn racism into law, which police patrols then enforced just as patrols once enforced the enslavement of Black citizens (Alexander 2012; Kendi 2016; Muhammad 2010; National Research Council 2014).

Richard Nixon's War on Drugs stands as an infamous application of policy designed on the racial politics of criminality. White voters who normally agreed with the moral imperative against racism could be peeled away from the Democratic party through Nixon's coded appeals to "law and order," which meant cracking down on anti-war protests and criminalizing poverty in ways that disproportionately incarcerated Black and Latino Americans (National Research Council 2014). The War was taken to historic heights when Ronald Reagan prioritized it, vastly increasing both the capacity and power of the carceral system, again to the disproportionate detriment of Americans of color. Such appeals have proven popular enough that recent Democrats like President Bill Clinton were able to use them to advance political goals, resulting in wins at the ballot box and harsher sentencing in the courts.

Not only does the criminal system have a racist history, but the present version still is infected by racist concepts. Research by anthropologist Cris Hughes and her colleagues (2016) has shown police officer trainees start out significantly more likely to have racist tendencies than non-trainees. This indicates that the profession is in a way self-selecting, that potential police officers start out with a degree of racial antipathy. The same research shows that gap with the public is larger once officers get their badge; one interpretation is that police training and culture contributes to further criminalization of people of color, primarily Black people.

That is what makes racism systemic. There are American systems built to disadvantage and exclude people of color. Those systems are not just tainted by this racist history. It is in their DNA, and it reproduces itself to this day. The socioeconomic elements discussed in this chapter share that DNA: they have origins in racist beliefs, and they continue to produce the originally intended disparities, even in the absence of interpersonal bigotry.

There is something else at work, too. It is harder for White people, especially those who see Black people as fundamentally different than them, to put themselves in the position of a Black victim than in the position of a White police officer. It is outside their realm of experience, yes, but so is being a police officer for most White people. Race is an artificial barrier that inhibits the ability to consider the impact of the situation, social roles, and other factors. Such tribal impulses blind many White people both to the potential for racist systems and the humanity they share with people of color.

If the goal was to eradicate the persistence of disparities that disadvantage people of color, Americans' attempt to solve racism—changing hearts and minds—didn't work. But it was rational to change the beliefs that justified the crumbling Jim Crow system, i.e., Black inferiority, to avoid re-creating it. The illumination by civil rights activists of what could be termed a series of moral violations in the mid-twentieth century via the strategy of non-violent resistance vividly contrasted White perpetrators with Black victims. This was a moral appeal for White Americans to reconsider the humanity of Black people.

The moral weight of this motivation had a psychological effect on those who left Jim Crow racist beliefs behind. On average, my research has found there isn't much difference between Democrats and Republicans when it comes to the level of moral conviction with which they hold their beliefs on racism. In a representative sample of 687 Democrats and Republicans, I found average moral conviction on racism and racial issues to be less than one point apart on a 15-point scale.

In Chapter 2, I noted what a problem it is that people can perpetuate racial disparities without believing they are doing anything wrong, because of the cover stories political parties use to gain power. In *The Coddling of the American Mind*, First Amendment lawyer Greg Lukianoff and sociologist Jonathan Haidt (2018) seem to dispute this interpretation. They (fairly, I believe) question the validity of demonizing someone for committing micro-aggressions or failing to challenge disparity-perpetuating systems.

They do so because they note that the people in question often do not have any ill *intent*, which is key in producing the moral revulsion toward racism and a major motivator in getting people to change their behavior. True enough. That doesn't mean it isn't still a problem for all those hurt in the meantime. Importantly, what about after these people learn the truth? After these folks see how their actions can hurt, if they don't change, they can no longer claim to be ignorant of the effects. Now they have moved from *unintentionally* hurting to *not caring* whether they hurt someone or not. That is a precarious place for these people to find moral justification.

This is precisely why those who see the injustice in racism must be able to engage with those who disagree with them. We must keep communications open, we must honor the humanity of everyone, even those we feel are working against the cause in which we believe, so that we can develop an understanding, not lecture.

It isn't a bad thing that times have changed so that fewer White people hold Jim-Crow era racist beliefs. Despite this change and the justified legacy of societal transformation from the Civil Rights Era, people of color still have it worse than White people, on average. So if it is not the morally justified abandonment of those racist beliefs that is the issue, what is it? It could be that the problem was bigger—or got bigger—than individual hearts and minds.

## RACISM IS MORE IV: THE ODDS

When I was in graduate school for counseling psychology, we read an essay by a feminist writer named Peggy McIntosh about an "invisible knapsack" that confers hidden benefits on White people. She called that knapsack *White privilege*.[6] Her thoughtful essay was instrumental in helping many of us in that classroom see the importance of understanding another's perspective when building a relationship. But in a country where most welfare recipients are White and rampant income inequality leaves a tenth of all White Americans below the poverty line, how does White privilege account for that?

Odds, or statistics, are an important way to represent reality. They are instrumental in social science's ability to reasonably predict reality. We rely on odds, which are explained by theories, because unlike "hard" sciences like physics, sociology and psychology don't have any laws. We can't have laws because human beings are each unique and reflect different combinations of genetics and environment in their personalities.

However, accumulated across an entire society, patterns begin to show up that can indicate likelihood of certain outcomes *on average*.

The idea of systemic racism is built on averages. If the odds are that one-third of all Black men are going to be in prison in their lives, that is a prediction based on statistical averages. To contradict that point by telling me that all the people you know who have been to prison have been White, that is an anecdote. Your acquaintances' experiences seem informative to you because you have a limited number of people in your life, as we all do.

Similarly, if you counter evidence of disparate outcomes of the criminal system with evidence of all the supposedly violent things Black men have done to deserve going behind bars, you are missing something else. Social scientists can use statistics to account for the effects of other variables (income, criminal charge, etc.) so that when we compare an average White outcome with an average Black outcome, we can do it while effectively hold-ing those other elements constant. Outliers and personal anecdotes are great illustrations but poor data.

The odds hold the key to understanding why "systemic racism" is racist. They also demonstrate how systemic racism gives White people with no dis-cernable advantage in life a measure of White privilege.

## THE COOPERS AND THE PORTERS

What follows is the story of two families, both of whom live on the north side of the same, large city in the same state here in America.[7] The neigh-borhoods where the Coopers and the Porters live are both considered lower-socioeconomic status. In those two families are the same number of young children: one girl and one boy each. Right now in the Porter house are Adrian, six years old, and Lucia, two. Over in the Cooper house live Joshua, six, and Lia,[8] four. The background of the Porter family is Scotch-Irish, French, and English. The Cooper family is Black.

It might seem absurd to say that Adrian or anyone in his family has "White privilege." After all, the Porters don't have connections, and they work low-paying jobs, just like Mr. and Mrs. Cooper do. Yet Adrian and Joshua, similar though they are in background, are different in one crucial way. The odds say these children, whose families both have such high hopes for them, are going to have very different lives.

### Education

Adrian and Joshua both are in first grade. You may know little children just like Adrian and Joshua. They both are considered precocious, curious, and able to verbalize their experiences. (What I mean is, they talk a lot. A lot.) They are the kind of kids to go bounding out of the car onto a playground to make new friends. Adrian and Joshua both go to public schools, but because they live in different neighborhoods of the north side, they go to different schools. The teachers at these schools are similar in training: they come from local colleges and credentialing programs. Even though many things are the same between Adrian and Joshua, their experience of grade school is likely to be very different.

Adrian's school, despite its location in a town with lots of children of color, is predominantly White. Joshua's public school, despite being located on the main road between the Porter house and the Cooper house, is mostly attended by Black and Mexican American children (Frankenberg 2019). Why are these schools so different?

Detailed by Richard Rothschild in *Color of Law*, the drive to desegregate public spaces during the civil rights movement was successful in some ways, but those successes were outweighed by laws preserving and perpetuating segregation. These laws include neighborhood covenants not to sell outside the White "race" and redlined areas in which real estate is devalued and intended for Black families. When the red lines were removed, no Black family was reimbursed for the devalued real estate and deterioration of their neighborhoods. Furthermore, inertia in Realtor practices and neighborhood reputations have acted together to maintain the effect of those lines.

*So what?* a skeptic might be thinking. *Realtor practices can be changed.* That may be. But consider another effect of redlining, one that harkens back to the reasoning justifying it in the first place, that people of color were less human than White people. Researchers have analyzed the environmental effects of redlining, which has been known to place communities of color close to environmental waste, downwind from industrial toxins, downstream from polluted water, and other health risks.

In 2022, environmental researchers from UC Berkeley and the University of Washington (Lane, Morello-Frosch, Marshall and Apte 2022) released a report on the environmental effects of redlining. The report was based on rigorous methodology that includes reliable data estimating nitrogen dioxide ($NO_2$) and airborne particulate levels in communities that had been redlined. According to the US Centers for Disease Control, $NO_2$ is irritable to the respiratory tract and lungs at low concentrations; by their estimates, only one or two high-concentration breaths can cause severe toxicity. The finding: redlining is "strongly associated with $NO_2$." The D-graded neighborhoods, the ones the federal Home Owners' Loan Corporation once rated as a hazardous investment risk to discourage White integration, have 56 percent higher pollution than A-graded neighborhoods. These neighborhoods, in most cases to this day, are home primarily to Americans of color.

In our city's north side, one public elementary school draws primarily from the closest neighborhood, which is predominantly White. The other school draws from the adjoining neighborhoods, which are more multicultural. The result is two schools on the same side of town with very different populations. I noticed this in my native San Diego, where in my teen years my parents could choose between two public high schools that were about equidistant from our home. One of these schools, Lincoln High, had a multiracial student body primarily composed of Black students. (Lincoln has changed in the last twenty years as the neighborhood has changed; now most students are Latino.) At my high school, which was mostly White with a large minority of Mexican American and Filipino American students and relatively few Black students, Lincoln had a reputation based on barely coded racial reasons: the school was "dangerous," the education was substandard, and, for good measure, the sports teams were always good but "undisciplined."

With Adrian and Joshua at separate schools that draw from families at similar income levels, the primary determinant of their experience is often the complexion of the students' skins. For something most Americans agree should not make a difference, studies show this has a devastating impact on the growth of these children. Even though Adrian and Joshua are both interested in reading, Joshua is less likely to be able to access a variety of books and see the different types of words and potentially growth-feeding, challenging material that Adrian can (Long 2016). Joshua's school has a very limited library without a trained library specialist and only one computer. Joshua is not an unfortunate outlier: poorer schools have less access to library and media resources, and minority schools are hardest hit by this trend.

A library is one crucial ingredient in student success and in building a lifelong value for learning. But funding shortfalls that are most likely to hurt schools like Joshua's have effects in other areas. Schools primarily attended by students of color with low numbers of White students produce documented performance gaps on standardized tests for Black versus White students (García 2020). Because Adrian and Joshua live in areas classified as high-poverty, it is unsurprising that the performance gap between Adrian's school and Joshua's school is even wider.

## Discipline

Recall that Joshua and Adrian are similarly talkative and, some would say, characters. Research shows that Joshua is more likely to be disciplined and, later, treated as older than he is and criminalized for behavior that might be ignored from Adrian (Riddle and Sinclair 2019). This extra discipline puts Joshua at higher risk for criminality later in his life. Dr. Nia Heard-Garris and colleagues' (2019) work, published by the American Medical Association, has shown that children personally involved with the juvenile justice system are at higher risk than their peers for poor mental health outcomes. Those children also exposed to parental incarceration were at higher risk for depression, anxiety, and post-traumatic stress disorder.

While Adrian, too, might be disciplined by his teachers, he is not at risk for the same outcomes as Joshua. And Adrian will not need to hear "The Talk" Black parents give to their sons about strictly monitoring his behavior to deescalate encounters with the police. The Talk was featured in Ta-Nehisi Coates's bracing literary conversation with his son, *Between the World and Me*, and also the focus of a recent book by Ama Karikari-Yawson (2020). Research has shown that frequency of encounters, their intrusiveness, and the young man's perception of injustice and disrespect are positively related with traumatic symptoms (Geller, Fagan, Tyler and Link 2014). The relation was significant even after accounting for the influence of a variety of factors, including criminal activity. And The Talk is not superstition or an overreaction: Black boys are six times as likely as White boys to be shot by police (Badolato et al. 2020).

Sometimes when children get into disciplinary trouble at school, a knee-jerk reaction is to blame the presence (or absence) of parents in the equation. But both of Joshua's parents live with him and are supportive of his education. That is not to say that mass incarceration of Black men cannot impact him (Alexander 2012). The odds here are also against Joshua, as one in three Black men will spend time in prison at some point in their lives. Research shows that having imprisoned family members is likely to hurt schoolwork and increases by 15 to 25 percent the odds of Joshua experiencing mental health issues (Williams 2018).

Adrian and Joshua both come from a tough place: a neighborhood with a high concentration of poverty. Their main advantage was coming from stable families. Fortunately for Adrian, he has a chance of rising to the middle class. In fact, recent work (Pager and Shepherd 2008) indicates that an environment like these boys have can lead to a future for Adrian that is about as good as what Joshua could expect growing up in a high-income, safe neighborhood. The authors state it plainly: "Even when Black and White boys grow up near each other, in houses with similar incomes, Black boys fare worse than White boys in 99 percent of America."

None of this is setting up Joshua for success. Systemic racism touches so many areas that, even if Joshua manages to avoid trouble during his education, he is likely to encounter it in other areas. A group of pediatricians (Trent, Dooley and Dougé 2019), including Dr. Maria Trent, director of the Adolescent Medicine Fellowship Program at Johns Hopkins, researched racism's impact on child and adolescent health. They conclude that racism "is a core social determinant of health that is a driver of health iniquities."

Any child can get sick. However, Black Americans are more likely to go uninsured, even after the gains made by the Affordable Care Act. This is partially because states in the South, where Black Americans are disproportionately represented, have resisted Medicaid expansion and instituted restrictions on the sort of safety-net social programs that provide a basic level of support for the needy. This means that a serious illness is more likely to bankrupt Black families than White ones.

## Career

Researchers have summarized decades of sociological, experimental, and legal findings in a review covering the effects of discrimination (Badger,

Miller, Pearce and Quealy 2018). The findings in employment go beyond the twofold Black-White disparity in unemployment rates to include the following staggering disparities. Out of two similar job candidates, the White one has a 50 to 240 percent higher likelihood of being called back. Black people spend more time looking for work on average and are 70 percent more likely to experience involuntary unemployment. Unfortunately for Joshua's educational aspirations, these disparities get *worse* as level of education increases.

Due to his family's lack of wealth, it is likely Joshua will need a loan during his life. White people have twelve times the wealth of Black people; Black people have 82 percent higher loan rejection rates and worse mortgage terms than White people. This is partially due to individual bias: when the final decision is taken out of the hands of loan officers via algorithms, Black people have higher acceptance rates. Still, they are more likely to need to resort to predatory or subprime lenders, even at the highest income levels.

When Black people search for housing, they are about 20 percent more likely to receive less information about available units, fewer opportunities to view units, less assistance with financing, and steering into less wealthy, segregated neighborhoods. Should he purchase a home, Joshua is likely to have his house undervalued by about $48,000 regardless of neighborhood (Perry, Rothwell and Harshbarger 2018), which affects his ability to pass wealth on to any children he might have.

Joshua could have almost every advantage imaginable—a fairy tale for a boy in his situation—and still wind up about as well off as he would have been had he simply stayed where he was and been White. That is devastating for any parent to hear. It also does significant damage to arguments claiming that White privilege does not exist. That concept is not about creating guilt or punishing White people: Adrian did nothing wrong. He is a curious, wonderful child in a tough situation. But Joshua is burdened with additional obstacles that can have trickle-down effects on any children he might have, thereby continuing the cycle.

Is it *possible* for Joshua to succeed? Of course. That is a different question than asking about his *odds* of success. If you think of life as a machine that requires the interaction of gears that represent who we are and gears that represent our environment, these boys have incredibly similar machines that can run well if given the chance. Racism gums up the gears of Joshua's machine. "White privilege" is the fact that Adrian's machine isn't gummed up.

\*\*\*

On a mid-2020 Thursday evening, a young Black woman named Kennedy Mitchum sent an email with a specific request: please correct what you say about racism so that it is "representative of what is actually happening in the world." The addressee was the *Merriam-Webster Dictionary*.

The next morning, she received a reply: the definition would be revised. Now, the second listing under *racism* reads, "The systemic oppression of a racial group to the social, economic, and political advantage of another." The first definition remains, "A belief that race is a fundamental determinant of human traits and capacities and that racial differences produce an inherent superiority of a particular race." Even in the dictionary, the two versions of racism exist side by side.

There is great joy, sunshine, creativity, resilience, and pride in the Black American experience, the Mexican American experience, the Vietnamese American experience, the Filipino American experience, the Indigenous American experience, and so many other uniquely American experiences for citizens of color. None of this discussion of racism should detract from that fact, nor should it detract from the tremendous progress and the impact persons of color have had in America.

However, in no way is it just that two people can be similar in every way except the color of their skin, yet that difference sets them down two unequal paths. One path is littered with additional obstacles that the other, tough as it may be, is free from.

As Kennedy Mitchum noted, if we only define *racism* interpersonally, it does not reflect the reality of people of color. These experiences contradict the notion that we live in a colorblind society. Whether one considers this concept technically racism is beside the point: multiple systems negatively and disproportionately affect the lives of people of color in America, which is a morally objectionable state of affairs. *A Post-Racial Lie covers American systems' reproduction of real disadvantages for people of color. Valuing one another's humanity demands that we reject this lie.*

The complexity of racism includes how we define it, and how adhering to a particular definition influences our behavior. We can learn how to address this complexity by studying the American people. The work of political and social scientists shows that certain racial beliefs can forsake, and sometimes impede, racial progress.

## NOTES

1. In addition to the primary source (Sears, Hetts, Sidanius and Bobo 2000), a variety of studies also cite similar numbers showing the decline of Jim Crow racist views as an indicator that racism has decreased, or at least evolved, in the post–Civil Rights Era.

2. Stroebe, Henk and Boerner (2017) have summarized concerns about Kübler-Ross's scientific methods as well as the applicability to the bereaved. The stages approach has been largely abandoned in psychiatric and counseling work but retains sociocultural influence.

3. The racial resentment research is quite comprehensive, but from the earliest conceptualization of the construct (Kinder & Sears, 1981), the element of distaste for apparent lack of patriotism among Black Americans has been present. (For a more detailed discussion of the connection, see Cramer 2020; Hutchings and Wong 2014; Kinder and Sanders 1996; Kinder and Sears 1981; and Sears and Henry 2005.)

4. These data were collected as part of the same study as the one cited in Chapter 4.

5. I want to be clear I am not absolving people of the consequences of their behavior. However, what is happening cannot be chalked up to mere personal choices or a phantom "failed culture" operating within the American culture. (This supposed failed Black culture also produces the same rates of drug use and religiosity as "White culture," to the extent that exists, so such an explanation lacks credibility.) Everyone should bear some responsibility for their choices, including Black people who commit crimes. That said, the larger sociological problem of criminality should be examined on more than an individual level. And what has been found indicates there are more than personal preferences and vague cultural mores at work.

6. It is well worthwhile for all readers, no matter the racial background, to seek out and read Dr. McIntosh's essay. The essay is free and available over the internet at https://psychology.umbc.edu/files/2016/10/White-Privilege_McIntosh-1989.pdf.

7. I am aware of a YouTube video with a similar conceit to the following section. The video (Act.tv 2019) introduces and explains systemic racism quite well. It cannot, due to limitations of the format, go into much detail about its complexities. To the extent that the following section is similar to the video, I let this section stand as a research-sourced explanation of systemic racism.

8. I focus here on the comparison between Joshua and Adrian because the Badger and colleagues research cited in this section notes that Black boys are particularly vulnerable to social, educational, and economic effects of discrimination. Space limitations prevent me from going into more detail about Lia, but her likely encumbrances differ from Joshua's. The way discrimination seems to affect Black girls, as proposed by Badger and colleagues, is in their health. Medical researchers cited above on infant mortality have studied allostatic load, which is accumulative risk across physiological systems due to various stressors. Black women are more likely to have a high load due to the unique combination of sexism and racism, and racialized sexism, they encounter. For example, Black women do not meet the "American standard" of beauty. Ample proof is in the Whiteness of "All-American" Abercrombie & Fitch ads of the 1990s or the cottage industry of Black hair-relaxing products. These stressors have been linked to higher Black infant mortality rate and low birth weights. Lia is also at risk of being prematurely sexualized, much in the same way Joshua is at risk for being prematurely and unfairly criminalized. Ironically, though Black women are historically oversexualized, their physical traits—one is reminded of the "Hottentot Venus"—are commoditized by White women, such as the Kardashian family, and for White women, as in the case of the early-2020s trend of "butt enhancement." If Lia

goes missing, as Black girls disproportionately do in this country, it is more likely she will be seen as a runaway and will not benefit from the outpouring of media attention that usually accompanies such cases. The Gabby Petito search in 2021 was a stark reminder of this disparity for some (e.g., Blow 2021; Jordan-Zachery 2021).

## Chapter 6

# What's the Matter with Modern Racism?

*The facts of life do not penetrate to the sphere in which our beliefs are cherished.*

—Marcel Proust, *In Search of Lost Time*

In this chapter, I present the case for an evolution of racism from the widely opposed Jim Crow version to a form of racism that enables the disparities presented in the preceding two chapters. I begin with a discussion of social norms and how they can explain this change over time. Studies also have shown there is a new form of racism, which I introduce starting with its most common measure, the racial resentment scale. I present research showing that political decisions about race often come down to emotion. This partially explains two other influential beliefs, status quo protection and colorblindness, that can undergird systemic racism.

\*\*\*

## WHAT IS NORMAL?

Psychologists, famously tasked with answering that question, understand the power of labeling something "normal" and something else "abnormal." *The Diagnostic and Statistical Manual* (*DSM*) reflects the latest scientific research, including what psychotherapists with significant theoretical expertise and experience determine to be a disorder. But each version of the *DSM* is like a dictionary: it does not dictate reality; it reflects it. Whether addiction to one's phone or social media fits the criteria for an addiction—and many clinicians believe it does (e.g., Lin et al. 2016; Panova and Carbonell 2018; Peckel 2017)—wouldn't have been a question twenty years ago. Hence, the *DSM* has evolved over the years. An important piece of whether behavior is considered disordered—abnormal—is whether the behavior is maladaptive: to what extent is it impairing the person's ability to function in society?

Even at the expert level, the determination of what is normal partially rests on society. We, collectively, determine what is normal because we set the standards for behavior in our society. These standards are called social norms. We need norms because they give us a sense of stability and comfort. We then understand how we are expected to behave, what we can expect from others, and what consequences are likely to occur.

You can break social norms; the consequences vary depending on how strong the norm is. When I taught undergraduate social psychology, I asked students to break a norm and write a report about the experience. I gave them five or so suggestions. I noticed a pattern in which norm students chose to violate. Most of the students over the years chose to sing out loud in a public place. Their experiences were largely joyful. Most of them received smiles from bystanders. Many even got others to join in on the signing.

I used to wonder why so many people chose to sing out loud. I have concluded that there are a couple of reasons. One is that these people might be self-selecting; that is, they already hum or sing softly in public anyway, so singing out loud is not a giant leap for them. The other is that this is a weak norm with little risk of negative enforcement. They may have thought, *How would I have responded if I saw someone doing this?* This is a natural human impulse that shows the power of the norm. You can anticipate a certain response based on your own, really a shared, sense of how the norm violation would be perceived.

A smaller group of students chose to violate the personal space norm. (This was pre-COVID.) The norm in the United States is that a certain amount of space should be left between people (Sorokowska, Sorokowski, Hilpert and Cantarero 2017): we don't share tables at fast-food places with people we don't know, we don't sit next to someone we don't know on the bus if there are plenty of open rows, and so on. These students received almost universally negative responses to their violations. The responses usually began with a turn of the head to quickly make eye contact establishing, *This isn't right.* Often, the responses escalated to some mumbling or repeated glances at the person. Rarely was the "violator" directly[1] addressed. The norm is something you should just *know*.

Before moving on, I want to mention one more group of students. In my first few years of teaching class, there were always a few who used to choose the option of going to the grocery store in pajamas. Over the years, I noticed that these students didn't get a lot out of the assignment, and eventually I replaced it. The papers these students wrote often expressed their disappointment at the reaction.

Why? Because the norm had changed. I see people in pajamas at Target, the 7-Eleven, the grocery store multiple times a week. Maybe you could get a norm-breaking reaction doing this at Nordstrom. Even then, I would guess it would be subdued compared to the reaction you would have gotten forty years ago.

Social norms are valuable barometers for where we are as a society. We are guided by the norm, but we also develop our own sense of which norms are more important than others, which need to be updated—think about the *Mad Men*–like behavior that used to be tolerated in offices—and what is likely to happen if we break the norm.

As such, societal norms surrounding race have changed. Beliefs like biological inferiority or "savagery" of Indigenous or Chinese people, for example, were once prevalent in American society and could be espoused openly. The sheer amount of change in social norms around race in the last seventy-plus years is a staggering indicator of progress. These norms changed due to the sacrifices of activists and educators. They flourished as access to higher education increased, television and the internet grew and diversified, and an interstate highway system was built that allowed for exploring new places and enabled concentrated populations of color more choice in where to live. Each step exposed White Americans to new people and cultural perspectives along the way.

Yet even as American society unquestionably became more accepting of people of color, even as there is less public abuse, even as more people of color are telling their stories through widely available art, even as fewer White people oppose interracial romance, even then, people of color continue to suffer more severely, and in more areas, than White people, all other things being equal. Social scientists have accounted for this evolution by investigating the possibility of a post–Jim Crow, "modern" form of racism: a set of beliefs and behaviors that that condone or perpetuate today's inequality and unjust treatment of people of color.

Why bother investigating a new form of racism? The norms changed, which discouraged Jim Crow racism, yet disadvantages to Americans of color persist. "Modern" racism is racism, plain and simple. There are reasons, though, that people resist broadening this concept. One noted in the previous chapter is the desire to celebrate measurable decreases in Jim Crow racism as a social, moral victory. In addition, when people view racism through the lens of the old norms, those behaviors easily meet moral opposition in context of today's norms. But we cannot easily use today's norms to evaluate yesterday's behaviors; the moral clarity needed in 1800 to support Black American service on juries, for example, is much greater[2] than what is required today. A similar mistake is being made by those who use yesterday's norms to evaluate today's behavior: social context and, more importantly, the racial progress since that time are being ignored.

Thus, to learn what would break the pattern, social scientists study the evolving set of beliefs that perpetuate injustice.

## RACIAL RESENTMENT

It is unlikely that the people endorsing Jim Crow–era beliefs like the biological inferiority of Black people are the main problem in an age that frowns upon, and even strictly punishes, expression of these views. The vastness of the extent of Black disadvantage in this country contradicts notions that hood-wearing Klansmen are the main culprit. Is it possible that another set of viewpoints might account for the inequality we see?

Some say, no, Black inequality is the fault of a culture that does not value hard work. That is where racial resentment comes in.

The idea that racism has evolved to something more than beliefs about biological inferiority has been investigated by David Sears and Donald Kinder (1971; Kinder and Sears 1981). It occurred to many, including these researchers, that racism could explain the resistance of White people to supporting policies that were designed to help minorities or were identified with minorities. In this line of thinking, racism had not been extinguished during the Civil Rights Era; rather, it had taken on a different form, as it had many times before (Bobo 2018). Belief in biological inferiority came to be known as old-fashioned racism, and post–Jim Crow racism took on a series of new names.

Before we go further, consider the automatic reaction many people have to a joke, meme, comment, image, or other trope: that's racist. When pressed, not everyone can answer *why*. The reason it is often hard for people to explain why something is racist is partially because it automatically violates their moral sensibility. A suite of studies by Jonathan Haidt and colleagues, described in his book *The Righteous Mind*, illustrates the automatic yet hard to logically justify reactions people have in response to moral violations. For example, the book includes a group of studies in which a story provokes a gut reaction of disgust despite including logical buttresses, such as in the hypothetical case of a man who has sex with a chicken carcass he buys at the supermarket. No one is harmed, yet most people judge the behavior as wrong.

This automatic sense of moral offense is helpful in alerting us to racism. However, it also can be confusing. Not everyone agrees on what qualifies as racist. When there is disagreement, it is helpful but not always accessible for people to be able to explain why something is racist. A clearer idea of what racism is, especially in the decades since the end of Jim Crow, would go a long way toward support for reversing its effects.

To test the concept of modern racism, Kinder and his colleague Lynn Sanders developed the racial resentment scale (Kinder and Sanders 1996). Racial resentment is rooted in work Donald Kinder and David Sears (1981) did in developing what they called symbolic racism. Symbolic racism is composed of two elements: sometimes subtle anti-Black affect and embracing of a "bootstrap" mentality, as in the idea that regardless of situation, people should be able to "pull themselves up by their bootstraps" by working hard.

The racial resentment scale was designed to obliquely get at racism rather than asking direct questions about interpersonal prejudice and biological inferiority. The questions were asked indirectly because of a concept called social desirability. Not many people in America, for example, are willing to say they have thought of eating dogs. Just reading that sentence likely caused many of you to recoil in disgust. But even if people did think about it, they would be unlikely to admit it because they likely want to avoid other people having the very reaction you just had (Krumpal 2013). Social desirability is a very important element in measuring taboo beliefs like racism. We can't ask, "Are you a racist?" and expect many honest responses.

Many studies using measures of modern racism use the results from the American National Election Survey (ANES), a collection of scientific opinion scales and demographic information drawn from an enormous sample during election years. Traditionally, the ANES has been administered in person, which means people are more on their guard than they would be in front of a computer screen. One study by European researchers partnering with American political scientists (Stark, van Maaren, Krosnik and Sood 2019) found that when ANES participants were subsequently given similar surveys months later using a computer, there was a small but significant increase in anti-Black views. That modern racism scales continue to get robust results despite this apparent effect is testament to their utility.

Researchers (Enders and Scott 2019) reviewing years of ANES interviews found racial resentment to be growing in its influence on political policy attitudes. Other work using the ANES (Wetts and Willer 2018) found racial resentment to predict opposition to welfare. They added that, "The documented link between Whites' racial resentment and opposition to welfare programs cannot be explained in terms of principled conservatism, with no role for racial prejudice" (817).

The racial resentment scale was used in a variety of ways to illustrate the strong and sustained backlash to President Obama. The scale has been shown to predict views on the economy under Obama (Tesler 2016b), support for Birtherism (Jardina and Traugott 2019), and voter defections from Obama in 2012 (Knuckey and Kim 2015). Notably, racial resentment was found to predict vote switching among Whites from Obama in 2012 to Trump in 2016 (Tesler 2016c). The use of the ANES and the General Social Survey, another large social study, allows authors to track average changes over time. Researchers tracking racial resentment (Tuch and Hughes 2011) effectively debunked the notion that President Obama's election signaled a post-racial America. They found that White Americans' racial views had not changed significantly since the 1980s.

Social scientists Alan Abramowitz and Jennifer McCoy (2019) conducted a series of studies finding that racial resentment explains Republican gains in recent elections. Researcher Steven Miller[3] (2018) found racial resentment, outweighing economic anxiety, to be the significant predictor of anti-immigrant opinion. He concluded that, "an ounce of racial resentment is worth a pound of economic anxiety."

## Is It Really Racism?

As the most prevalent measure of contemporary racism, the racial resentment scale has drawn criticism, claiming that it is not measuring what it purports to measure (e.g., Carmines, Sniderman and Easter 2011; Hurwitz and Peffley 2005; Schuman 2000; Sniderman, Crosby and Howell 2000). A good deal of this critique stems from assessments by political scientists Paul Sniderman and Philip Tetlock (1986), who see methodological issues with the racial resentment scale. A famous example of this critique came from researchers (Carney and Enos 2015) who switched out Black for Lithuanian in the racial resentment items and found "indistinguishable" differences in results, which indicated to them that racial resentment was measuring belief in a just world.

Belief in a just world is commonly associated with American conservatism: people who work hard are rewarded. The assumption embedded in that is, if you are not sharing in the spoils of capitalism, it is all your fault. This belief is unrealistic, but it is not racist. Those who push back against the use of the racial resentment scale, and the validity of a modern form of racism, contend that attempts to conceptualize a modern form of racism wind up including unrelated, conservative views.

For example, many tests of racial resentment use views on affirmative action as a barometer. The main critique, often called the principled conservatism view, is that people who oppose affirmative action can oppose it for purely ideological reasons assumed to be part of American conservativism, such as egalitarianism and opposition to active government. Thus, it is inaccurate and unfair to label these people as racists. Furthermore, this critique contends that Jim Crow racism is still influential and there is no need to "create" a new form of racism when the old one still exists.

The authors of the racial resentment scale and others have addressed many of these concerns. In one review, David Sears and colleagues (2000) note that the research used to support principled conservatism actually holds some evidence that modern conservative values and racism are "inextricably inter-twined." Their work (see also Gainous 2012) shows that increases in level of education strengthen the relation between ideology and racism; this means that having a better grasp on party policy helps people see the racial content of conservatism.

In other work, Sears and colleagues (2000) addressed the individualism part of the principled conservatism view. They show that in studies measuring individualism and racial resentment, nonracial individualism has little impact on views toward racial policies. If racial resentment were measuring just individualism, then it would not significantly predict racial policy views. However, *racialized* individualism—individualistic attributions for racial disadvantages—is the heart of racial resentment; this has a much stronger effect on racial policy beliefs.

Symbolic racism predicts White opposition to policies designed to help Black people, even when controlling for conservatism and limited-government attitudes (Rabinowitz, Sears, Sidanius and Krosnik 2009); the same model only weakly predicted race-ambiguous policy beliefs. Political scientists (Wallstein, Nteta, McCarthy and Tarsi 2017) found that racially resentful White participants, when exposed to subtle priming about Black people as opposed to White people, were more likely to oppose paying college athletes, even though this issue is unrelated to conservative principles.

Though the responses to principled conservatism have been quite compre-hensive, the debate about the racial resentment instrument has continued. The Fear, Institutionalized Racism, and Empathy (FIRE) measure (DeSante and Smith 2018) was created to address this critique. FIRE is based on analysis showing two dimensions of White racial attitudes: emotional (fear and lack of empathy) and status quo–protecting. After accounting for demograph-ics and economic perceptions, scores on FIRE predicted the probability of Democratic defections to Trump in 2016. Later research (Rhodes, La Raja, Nteta and Theodoris 2022) found higher scores on the FIRE scale, particu-larly denial of institutional racism, to be linked with denial that the events of January 6, 2021, were an insurrection, with 80 percent of high scorers calling it a "protest."

The remaining resistance to the legitimacy of racial resentment seems to have emboldened some to push back against the wealth of evidence showing that racism is influential in support for Donald Trump (Cherry 2019). What seems to be missing in this pushback is an accounting for why so many White people are not concerned about supporting policies that hurt so many of their fellow citizens. I understand having methodological concerns, but the discussion about symbolic racism should not be distracted from the point, which is how holding certain beliefs and supporting specific policies can have negative effects on the lives of people of color.

## RACE AND OUR BRAINS

The public work of mid-twentieth-century civil rights activists significantly contributed to changes in norms around race. A major aspect of their work was to create a moral contrast between peaceful justice-seekers and violent bigots. By doing so, they enabled Whites to see the stark realities that racist beliefs produced: enforcement of rules based on the beliefs resulted in bloodshed that tainted the American image.

True, the racism most people seem to oppose—outward antipathy toward people of color—still happens. Some White people still shout, tweet, and email racial epithets. Some White people still use negative racial stereotypes. Evidence that all this still happens doesn't disprove the existence of a modern form of racism, just like the simultaneous existence of apes and humans doesn't disprove biological evolution.

There are two main schools of academic thought on the existence of modern racism. One is that another form of racism has grown while Jim Crow–era racism has decreased. The other is that racism hasn't changed; researchers are mislabeling beliefs unrelated to race as racist. To be sure, there is a great deal of nuance and variance within those two positions, but those are the two main camps.

If it is no longer acceptable to express Jim Crow racist beliefs, less people will feel comfortable expressing them. But that doesn't make the feelings and reactions behind the expression go away. If those feelings can be expressed in ways that don't break the norm, there is little constraint on talking this new way. There's also little constraint on voting for those who do.

How an issue is described by politicians can influence how voters evaluate it; these descriptions, or frames, often associate specific groups with an issue, thus calling to attention feelings about those groups. Due to elite frames over the previous decades, such as Ronald Reagan's depictions of welfare recipients (Smith 1987), numerous policies have become linked to minority populations—usually, but not exclusively, Black Americans (Gilliam and Iyengar 2000; Valentino 1999). Thus, politicians strategically activate negative thoughts and feelings about people of color to motivate voters.

If a candidate for governor says she's going to slash the welfare rolls and turn down federal funds for the expansion of Medicaid, she is appealing to unconscious or taboo thoughts without violating the norm. In this example, the candidate is not only appealing to people who believe Black people are to blame for their plight. But she definitely is appealing to those who do. And the policy hurts people of color just the same. This is the same thinking behind the coded appeals of Richard Nixon's Southern Strategy discussed in Chapter 2.

Political scientists Milton Lodge and Charles Taber bring together bio-psychology and politics in their research. In their book *The Rationalizing Voter*, they draw on a series of experiments to show that much of our decision-making is directed by hidden, immediate reactions. It is only once the experiencing of a stimulus activates connections to other information in our minds, including feelings and prior experiences, that we arrive at the point where we begin "consciously" deliberating.

In one of these studies, Lodge and Taber (2013) used a priming task to show how related concepts speed up decisions and unrelated ones slow them down. Priming is presenting a stimulus before asking someone to complete a cognitive task. The stimulus is presented so briefly[4] that it cannot be processed consciously. However, our brains can access it, which can influence subsequent responses. When people are primed, it is expected that primes with established connections to memories, emotions, and other thoughts will have more influence on the subsequent task than a so-called neutral prime.

In the experiment, they used a set of issue primes: *affirmative action, tax the rich*, and *welfare*. The target words, which make up the conscious part of the task, were drawn from two categories. Some were Black stereotype words like *Afro, aggressive*, and *rap*; others were terms associated with political principles of individualism or egalitarianism like *self-reliance, earn*, and *opportunity*. After the issue prime, participants saw either one of the target words or a nonsense word and were asked whether they recognized the word.

Results show that all three issue primes sped up responses to political targets among those opposed to progressive taxation and welfare, which we would expect because they are conceptually linked. The three primes also sped up responses to stereotype targets among the same group. These findings not only indicate that affirmative action and race are linked. They also show that race cannot be separated from opposition to progressive taxation and welfare.

The influence of primes is partially due to how the brain is designed to work: information that is related is processed in a way to "connect" it. When this happens, our brain is practicing so that when the information comes up later, our attention is drawn to the other connected information in case it is needed. For example, smelling a particular candle might not just draw you back to winter at your grandparents' house, but it might also remind you to clean your garage because you used to spend time with your granddad in his garage. These connections are not something we consciously control, much like the sensory wonderland opened by the main character's crumbling of a madeleine cookie in tea at the start of Marcel Proust's *In Search of Lost Time*.

Political scientists also have been able to show how feelings powerfully influence political beliefs. In their book *The Affect Effect*, researchers W. Russell Newman, George Marcus, Ann Crigler, and Michael MacKuen provide evidence of the political impact of feelings. For example (MacKuen, Marcus, Neuman and Keele 2007), they were able to predict party defections—when people vote for the candidate outside their usual political affiliation—based on the level of anxiety voters experience. Furthermore, they found different effects for anxiety and anger, with anger having a conspicuous relation to prejudice.

Antoine Banks (2014), a political scientist who has done significant work on the relation between anger and prejudice, details the results of multiple, rigorous studies on the topic in his book *Anger and Racial Politics*. Banks shows several ways that anger is uniquely linked to policies designed to help Black people, such that support is lower when anger is induced. This effect does not hold for policies that are race-neutral, nor does it hold with anxiety in place of anger. His work aligns with the finding by Kinder and Sanders (1996) showing the stronger influence of anti-Black prejudice on White opinion of food stamps compared to other social welfare issues.

Black people are not alone in being objects of this strategy. Media portrayals of immigration have used negative images of Mexicans consistently, with evidence dating back decades (Fernandez and Pedroza 1982); an analysis of documents related to the 2008 and 2012 elections (Jo. Brown 2016) showed that immigration is increasingly becoming code for Latinos and a general "other-ness." Anthropologist Leo Chavez (2001) has studied the "alarmist imagery" of Mexican immigration found on US magazine covers. In 2010, research (Chavez, Whiteford and Hoewe 2010) on four major US newspapers' portrayals of immigration found that the foremost topic in the articles was crime.

People are unlikely to make many political decisions based on a thoughtful consideration of options, regardless of principle. They are more likely to make those decisions the way many of our decisions are made: quickly and biased by emotional reactions. That is not to say that all conservatives are racist, nor are all White people who oppose programs like affirmative action. However, it runs counter to how humans respond to political issues to assume that most White Americans can fight through negative associations, gut reactions, and other automatically activated biases, and still oppose policy to help people of color on fully race-agnostic grounds. It is likely, then, that many of the principled reasons provided for supporting or opposing a particular policy are actually rationalizations.

## STATUS QUO PROTECTION

Herbert Blumer's (1958) group position theory explains racial prejudice as resulting from competition based on where racial groups are in the social order. Building on this theory, Lawrence Bobo has a lengthy research program addressing the conflict between racial resentment and principled conservatism over why White people tend to oppose affirmative action. As Bobo (1999, 447) puts it, prejudice goes beyond stereotypes and hate to include "a commitment to relative status position of groups in a racialized social order." In group position theory, Whites oppose racial redress because Black people are a threat, real or imagined, to social resources to which they believe they have a right.

In an experiment controlling for demographics, conservativism, and racial attitudes, Bobo found that race itself—group position—matters in predicting views on racial policy. The results showed White participants most responsive to threat from the group seen as at the bottom of the social ladder, Black people. But Black participants were not equally threatened by the success or advancement of White people. The results further showed racial resentment and ideology, but not explicit measures of individualism and inegalitarianism, to be significant contributors to racial policy beliefs.

Overall, Bobo's findings indicate that beliefs about racial policy are related to the stakes you see involved in your group's place in the American social order. Group position is not to be confused with "tribalism," which posits that groups naturally competed throughout human history, obliquely justifying White racial animus. If views on racial policy were tribal, for example, Latino Americans would be just as likely as White Americans to oppose policy that is assumed to benefit Black Americans. But they are not.

Bobo and colleagues (Bobo, Klugel and Smith 1996) developed a term for the form of racism that condones the current American racial order: *laissez-faire racism.* They describe it as a combination of negative Black stereotypes, blaming Black people for socioeconomic disparities, and resistance to supporting policies that would ameliorate these disparities. Laissez-faire racism rests on White peoples' acceptance of anti-Black stereotypes that paint them as less intelligent, lazy, and desirous of government handouts.

Laissez-faire racism explains why many White Americans are unmoved in the face of rampant inequality in this country. This form of racism evolved to justify White privilege and explain Black disadvantages in the absence of a Jim Crow social structure that codified and enforced those differences. These differences are clearly unfair—one might say, morally unjustifiable. Laissez-faire racism reflects a willingness to "accept as much inequality as the market allows" justified by feelings of entitlement to resources and fear of losing them.

Though the status quo benefits White Americans, their awareness of this fact may create other psychological effects beyond wanting to protect it. White people's concern about how their behavior is perceived can lead to what Samuel Gaertner and Joel Dovidio (2004) call "aversive racism." Aversive racism is equal treatment of Black people in public but negativity about Black people in private. Normally, this would seem to be a mild form of racism. After all, if there is no open prejudice toward Black people, it cannot be as harmful. However, aversive racism shows that people discriminate selectively. When it is unclear whether the norm against racism applies, that is where bias shows.

Dovidio and Gaertner say many of the negative interactions between Black and White people can be explained by the contradiction between equality-affirming words and the resulting behavior. This contributes to a lack of trust from Black people toward the average White person, which creates a cycle of damaged relationships on average.

Amid nationwide protests in mid-2020, a movement began for corporations to demonstrate their sympathy for Black Americans. Businesses, universities, and other public groups pledged commitments to diversity, to investing in Black communities, to self-examine. This activity clearly reflected a norm change: after all, Black people have been experiencing discrimination and pain for a long while before 2020.

While the social justice–related behavior of corporations in 2020 and since may be no more than public relations posturing, at least they were doing something to recognize the pain racial discrimination was causing throughout the country. However, when it comes to *how* to implement those commitments, the social norm was weak.

As a result, you have breakfast food brand Aunt Jemima changing their name to Pearl Milling Company due to racist origins and imagery associated with the Aunt Jemima character. You have Amazon donating $10 million to social justice organizations with an accompanying employee donation-matching program. You also get JPMorgan Chase and Bank of America pledging loans and services to Black-owned businesses, investments that are likely to benefit mainly those banks. When investigative reporting followed up a year after these pledges, it was found that over 90 percent (Jan, McGregor and Hoyer 2021) of the money pledged went to the latter category. As of August 2021, less than 4 percent of the amount pledged a year prior[5] had been distributed, though some companies were not forthcoming about how much they had spent.

What stands out is the lack of commitment to criminal justice and reform of police training and procedures. These were two issues that were front-and-center in the 2020 protests, yet even applying a generous standard, this amounted to about 6 percent of the donations companies made. As noted above, donations were less than 10 percent of the money pledged in the first place. This generosity is still a good thing, but it is questionable how these actions met the calls for substantive, risky change.

The patterns unearthed in this investigation demonstrate both the power and the limits of social norms. Since the Jim Crow era, the social constraint against expressing racist thoughts or acting in a discriminatory way has been undergirded by a moral mandate. This has been valuable in reducing the pain experienced by many Americans in the following decades. If we think of this constraint as a cap on the pressure to express racist beliefs, aversive racism offers one release valve. This finding emphasizes the value of the moral mandate against racism: if it is weakened in some way, some of the pressure can be released in ways that can hurt people of color.

The pressure capped by our social norms against racism does not need to be released in hurtful ways. It can be relieved through more contact with people from different backgrounds and thoughtful engagement with one's beliefs about race. Decades of counseling psychology research have established that avoiding uncomfortable truths hurts ourselves and those around us, while honestly confronting and processing these truths can lead to healing. Aversive racists may be unconsciously hurtful, yet willing to apologize and look for common ground if their behavior is pointed out to them. It is hard to build those relationships, though, and make those breakthroughs when the conversation around race is at such a fevered pitch.

## THE POST-RACIAL LIE AND COLORBLINDNESS

These definitions of racism help us understand the psychological influences on opposing redress of racial grievance. As valuable as they have been, they seem to be ignoring the elephant in the room: the Post-Racial Lie. Taken at face value, American investment in colorblindness, exemplified by the refrain, "I don't see color," comes from a well-intentioned, though White-centering, place. It also prevents commitment to equity-pursuing policy that "sees" color by necessity.

Racial colorblindness is a belief system rooted in denial of the influence of race in society, of White privilege, and of institutional racism (Neville, Spainerman and Doan 2006). Sociologist Eduardo Bonilla-Silva (2018) has described colorblind racism (CBR) as the common tendency for White Americans especially to claim not to see race, that everyone is equal, or that discussing racial issues creates more racism. Adherence to colorblind policies tends to replicate current inequalities while shielding people from feeling any culpability in the results, effectively erasing the suffering of Black people (Forman and Lewis 2006). Bonilla-Silva (2018, 202) argues that colorblind racism is the "central racial ideology of the post-civil rights era."

It is not hard to draw this conclusion when 77 percent of Republicans polled say that seeing racism where it does not exist is a bigger problem than racism itself (Horowitz, Brown, and Cox 2019) and a majority of White, working-class Americans polled say that discrimination toward White people equals or exceeds discrimination toward Black people (Cox, Lienesch and Jones 2017). We have seen that the latter is not the case, nor is there a sufficient rationale for the former.

Psychologist Helen Neville and colleagues (2000) have developed a measure of CBR called the Color-Blind Racial Attitudes Scale (COBRAS). The CoBRAS is a twenty-item scale measuring colorblind attitudes toward racial issues. Participants are asked to respond to statements such as, "White people in the United States have certain advantages because of the color of their skin," and "Talking about racial issues causes unnecessary tension," on a six-point scale from strongly disagree to strongly agree.

Germine Awad and colleagues have used the CoBRAS to demonstrate that CBR predicts opposition to affirmative action and did so better than scores on the Modern Racism Scale (Awad, Cokley and Ravitch 2005; Hall 2015). Researchers have also found moderate correlations between two subscales of the CoBRAS (Blatant Racial Issues and Denial of Institutional Discrimination) and social dominance orientation (Worthington, Navarro, Loewy and Hart 2008). Social dominance orientation is a personality trait that denotes preference for a hierarchical society in which inequality favors one's ingroup.

Though the American Psychological Association has recommended cultural competence training as part of psychotherapy degree programs, some White therapists-in-training resist discussing the realities of race and racism. A few years ago, I was teaching a course designed to prepare students for their traineeship, which occurs at community mental health clinics. As I introduced a lecture on how culture impacts therapy, one student sighed and asked, "When are we going to be done talking about multiculturalism?" This is a minor resistance compared to what can happen in courses designed to encourage self-examination for racist beliefs and privilege. My colleagues have heard anti-multicultural tirades and heated arguments for the virtues of colorblindness. As a teacher's assistant, I saw students openly reject the deep empathy displayed by the White, male professor of a multiculturalism course when he shed tears as he discussed America's treatment of Indigenous peoples.

Reactions like these make the use of a scale like the CoBRAS with counseling students so relevant. Psychologist and researcher Derald Wing Sue (1998; 2011) and his collaborators have spent decades studying race and racism. They have found that these experiences are not exceptional: White therapists-in-training often struggle with acknowledging race or racism, which can prevent honest bonds with clients of color. Researchers (Gushue and Costantine 2007) have used the CoBRAS to show that CBR impedes the development of such bonds. Additional research indicates a link between CBR and low multicultural competence in psychotherapy trainees (Bray and Balkin 2013). Recall the documented shortfall of therapeutic services used by Black Americans: when White therapists struggle to understand their experience, clients have less hope things will get better and are less likely to stay in therapy.

When society has not moved beyond race—as established in the preceding two chapters—the colorblind desire to stop talking about race is like reading the last page of the book first. Post-racialism has led to a world where even discussing race can be seen by some as racist. It is not, and no one has offered coherent reasoning why it would be. Yet the Post-Racial Lie is powerful, and it has tricked too many people into seeking what appears to be an easy solution.

Clearly, these different psychological instruments are measuring something beyond simple conservatism. The results show that social scientists are studying something influential. In fact, these beliefs hold the key to understanding the mystery of the previous chapter. These beliefs, these emotional attachments, can explain how so many can tolerate a state of affairs that is fundamentally unjust to Americans of color. Calling it racism shouldn't be taken lightly. Whatever it is, to the extent that those beliefs prevent meaningful action on discrimination, it has the same effects as racism. And that is a problem.

\*\*\*

Symbolic racism. Laissez-faire racism. Aversive racism. Colorblind racism.

If you had never heard of any of these terms before, one would forgive you for being a bit disoriented. However, the modern discourse around race and racism is inherently disorienting. "Listen to Black people." "Okay," White people say, "but I want to be listened to, too." "We've heard from White people for long enough," say the antiracists. "But I'm not a racist," comes the reply. "Yes, you are. All White people are in some way." And then so many, too many, White people shut down.

Can you blame them?

Perhaps the most important advance in discourse about race over the last sixty years is the strong, near-universal social norm to oppose racism. When someone is called a racist, they are not likely to take it well, nor are they meant to. If the point of labeling something wrong in a moral sense—in labeling it racist—is to get that idea, behavior, image, or pattern changed, then let's look at our results. Black people are telling America in survey after survey that they experience discrimination and bigotry. The statistics bear this out. We have gotten much more sophisticated in sociology and political science about how we label and understand racism. But we have been in a holding pattern on major change for fifty years.

Why the disconnect? It's the same problem Kinder and Sanders were trying to confront in the 1980s. Today, what we have is a better way of pointing out the problem, but few mechanisms for getting the wrongdoer to change. It is imperative that researchers continue to refine and study how racism is defined, because how we define racism can influence how we address it, including the norms around it.

The beliefs of White Americans are important to understanding how racism operates, yet that should not obscure the responsibility of researchers to seek greater understanding of the many cultural and ethnic groups in the country. This includes how discrimination affects their lives, how they have been impacted by internalized racist ideas, their sense of group identity and how it affects feelings toward outgroups, and their beliefs about American society. A responsible approach to studying racism should cast a wide net in terms of participants, situations, settings, and methodology.

The definition of *racism* is not a philosophical exercise or argument. It is indisputable, as discussed in earlier chapters, that people of color—and specifically Black people—on average suffer more, encounter more barriers, and see worse outcomes in almost every meaningful area of American public life. As we have seen, that is not a problem with the biology or the culture of Black people. That is a problem with American society.

So, if racism is a larger systemic problem than an interpersonal one, why study individual attitudes? A racist system, as shown by Lawrence Bobo's research on lassiez-faire racism, is propped up by individuals who either deprioritize racial issues or ignore them while feeling justified for doing so. It isn't systemic views that perpetuate a racist system—after all, a system can't change its mind. It is the views of individuals that have power in a democracy to shape and redefine systems. Systemic racism would be harder to maintain if there were less disinterested and "colorblind" Americans and more Americans aware of how political choices based on misplaced resentments, manufactured fears, and faulty assumptions can impair both the lives of their fellow human beings and the progress of American society.

Sniderman and Tetlock themselves asked in their seminal challenge to symbolic racism, "Are conservative values promoting prejudice against Blacks?" Based on the effects of conservative policy, especially those that limit the power of the federal government to protect certain civil rights and feed growing economic inequality, the answer may be yes. This should be chilling to American conservatives who do not believe themselves to be racist. It may even be that there is no malice intended in their policy beliefs but the effects of some of the policies are malicious enough. The research is clear: *a certain set of beliefs, which we categorize as modern racism, leads to support for policies that disadvantage Americans of color.*

If labeling this national problem racism leads to a backlash, it is worth examining the character of that backlash rather than retreating from it. When the people with the lion's share of the burden get the lion's share of the attention, that is not called reverse racism. It is called honesty. Principle or philosophy does not explain the pesky reality of a problem that hurts everyone in our nation.

As movingly demonstrated by Heather McGhee in her work *The Sum of Us*, racism in America spiritually and materially harms everyone. Racist policies have a way of working against the White working class, too. White Americans, fairly or unfairly, must see their stakes in the fight against racism: they are the single largest group of Americans, and they are unlikely to take something being forced on them. None of us are. That resistance is one of several roadblocks to finding a just, higher ground on race.

## NOTES

1. There's also a social norm constraining the behavior of the responder. Directly correcting a stranger's behavior is outside the norm.

2. Speaking of clarity, allow me to be clear: if it is morally wrong now, it was morally wrong then. The difference, here, is in the sacrifices one must make to publicly oppose the wrong considering, in part, societal norms. For example, the sacrifices of the midcentury civil rights movement are unthinkable today for many White Americans. Most polls indicate a broad majority today would cheerfully support the work of Dr. King and the SNCC had they been given the chance, even though polls taken contemporaneous to the movement paint a much different picture (Boyon 2019; Cobb 2018; Enten 2022).

3. Not the former Trump advisor.

4. Thirty-nine milliseconds; this length of time occurs over twenty-five times within just one second.

5. Some changes require no money up front but do result in the company making less money down the line, such as banks adjusting the structure of credit assistance programs to benefit Black Americans more directly and significantly.

# PART III

# Politics

*Think*

# Chapter 7

# The Case of the 2016 Election

*No one could distinguish the sound of the joyful shouting from the sound
of those who were weeping; for the people raised a mighty clamor which
was heard far away.*

—Ezra 3:13

In this chapter, I examine the election of 2016 and subsequent public discourse about Trump voters through the lens of racial politics. I analyze the scientific research on the unique qualities of Trump voters from a humanistic perspective: what can we learn about these Americans that helps us get closer to a coalition against racism? Finally, I present original research showing how Donald Trump's racist commentary can worsen our national divide on race.

\*\*\*

In many recent books on race, there resides space for a discussion of 2016. Having read these books, I know I feel a shift in my emotions when I get to that chapter. It feels necessary yet still raw and unresolved. Even though we've had another presidential election since then, 2016 is when it seems like the racial discussion came to the forefront in a sustained way. There is a lot to say about 2016, but before I go any further, I should provide full disclosure.

I did not vote for Donald Trump. I know people who did. I still have these people in my life, some of them very close to me. I fully understand their reasoning, at least from what they have provided me, yet still I feel that if I were in the same position, I would not have made the same decision. That, right there, encapsulates the allure of dissecting 2016 for me: my *feelings* about my choice are quite strong.

However, I acknowledge that other people may have feelings just as strong. And that is how we found our nation in the wee hours of November 9, 2016. Many of us overjoyed at a surprise victory, and many of us completely shocked and crushed at a surprise defeat. Why was 2016 so pivotal for so many? Why are our feelings so caught up in this decision?


## 2008

In this case, it is helpful to go back into the past. Not too far back, just eight years earlier.

For many of the people who were shocked and crushed by 2016, 2008 was the opposite: the American dream writ large. Here was a son of a single mother, a mixed-race man who struggled with his identity and fitting in for much of his life, a non-traditional student who spent years after college working at the grass roots before going back to school for a law degree, the son of an African father elected president when we had never done so before. The year 2008 was supposed to usher in a new, post-racial era (Tesler 2016a), when the promise of Martin Luther King's oft-quoted "I Have a Dream" speech was finally realized.

It is worth unpacking why a post-racial America might be a good thing. Certainly, desire for it might be born of the aspiration for unity and a shared sense of American identity. A truly post-racial America would guarantee equal opportunities for everyone, minimal discrimination, and an end to the creeping suspicion that how one is being treated is based on certain assumptions about their race.

However, we cannot will such a world into existence. How does a change in president address the gaping disparities[1] in wealth, education, health, socioeconomic mobility, interaction with the criminal justice system, and other areas for Black Americans? Acting as if a single triumph, even the election of Barack Obama as president, transforms us into a post-racial country is like treating throat cancer with a lozenge. Perhaps most importantly, as noted by many Black voices, a post-racial or colorblind society must necessarily erase something, and that something, based on American history, is likely to be a Black identity and tradition.

Anyone with an immigrant Irish American granda or Italian American nonna could have heard how much prejudice there was against these "ethnics" when they arrived in America (Isenberg 2016; Potter 1978; Zinn 2003). They were dehumanized until they were here long enough to adopt the prevailing cultural viewpoint, including adopting the identity of the majority. Through this process, their humanity became valued. They could be seen as individuals with positive and negative traits, instead of being just another Irish drunk or backward Italian. When Italians and Irish and Germans "assimilated" and became regular Americans, what they were really doing was becoming White

(Roediger 2005; Steinberg 2001). It was by seeking group invisibility through the melting pot that they gained individual visibility.

Part of the post-racial story is that every other group has assimilated and succeeded, including those Latino Americans and Asian Americans in the process of doing so, except for Black people. The reason for all the disparities we see between Black Americans and White Americans must, therefore, be due to something Black people aren't doing that the European ethnic immigrants of the nineteenth century were willing to do. Namely, if only Black people would work harder, keep their families together, save their money, and follow the rules (Simmons and Bobo 2019) instead of waiting for the government to give them handouts or asking for special treatment in the marketplace, Black people could finally assimilate, and America could actualize its Utopian promise.

Studies show that the White people opposing social programs like affirmative action are likely to believe there is something wrong with Black people (Kinder and Sanders 1996); briefly, they don't like rewarding people who don't work as hard. If Black people are experiencing less wealth, shorter lifespans, and worse working conditions, then they are doing something wrong. There is something deeply human, though, in this reaction. How do these people know how hard anyone else works or what barriers to success those others face? They don't. They assume, as people often do.

Why do people assume? To make sense of how the world works so that we are not frozen when confronted with new information or new situations (Rosen 1988). And when we assume, we draw conclusions based on our own experience because that is what we know and that is what is most easily accessed by our minds (Nisbet and Ross 1980). In the therapeutic sense, assumptions can become problems simply because they are unlikely to be accurate (e.g., Beck, Rush, Shaw and Emery 1979). Assumptions are based on prior experience, flawed memories, biased interpretations of events, or misapplied logic. One of the major tenets of cognitive-behavioral therapy—the most prevalent approach to psychotherapy—is that assumptions influence behavior. If you want to change how things are going for you, you must be willing to examine the assumptions on which you base your actions.

Thus, we should be wary of the influence of assumptions on our views of others. If you're White and you assume all Black people face the same problems you did, you are tempted to assume they must overcome them "the way I did." If they don't, well, it must be a problem with the person.

A racial disconnect was operating in American society in 2008. Though hidden, scratch the surface and dangerous assumptions come to light (Kennedy 2011). When Obama was elected to the highest office in the land, there was rejoicing among those who sought post-racial nirvana. Not only did a Black man rise to this position, but he was also voted there through the trust shown in him by most American[2] voters. No more excuses. If the "Black guy with the funny name"[3] can reach the pinnacle, so should everyone else. This proved racism no longer holds people back.

Finally, there was no longer any need to talk about race, and we could all move on.

The honeymoon seemed to end before it started. A Fox News host (Sweney 2008) tried to tease a show segment on a quick Barack-to-Michelle dap by calling it a "terrorist fist jab."[4] As president, Obama appeared to side with Henry Louis Gates, a Black Harvard professor arrested for arguing with the police who tried to prevent him from entering his own home. Obama was castigated as "hating" White people (Calderone 2009), and his approval rating took a hit.[5]

Some researchers (e.g., Love and Tosolt 2010) have argued that reality, evidence of racism in Obama's America, created two competing thoughts in many. On the one hand, Obama's election conquered racism. On the other, reports from Americans of color established that racism remained alive. Rather than accept that the former was a fantasy, some chose to reject the latter. Part of the allure of the Post-Racial Lie is that we can finally stop talking about race. If we've made it to the Promised Land, why are we still talking about racism?

The frustration some people have with race even being raised as a topic is palpable. During the Colin Kaepernick controversy[6] in 2016, I was listening to sports talk radio when I heard an anti-Kaepernick caller state it about as plainly as I've ever heard: "Look, we elected Obama, didn't we? That proves that America is not racist."

Imagine the place you live has a rat problem. You have done everything you can think of to get rid of them, but you still have the rats. Finally, you find the person you think is the best exterminator. You did all of your homework on this process, Yelped until your eyes ached, and are convinced that this exterminator will finally get rid of your problem. The exterminator arrives and does their thing, and when it's over, you feel like you can breathe easily. You box up the rest of your rat traps. You stop cringing at tapping sounds. You stop obsessively sweeping the floors. You feel secure that you, your children, anyone you might have visiting can sit down or even nap on your couch and not have to worry about hearing, smelling, or seeing a rat.

A couple weeks later, a houseguest says, "You know, I had that exterminator by, and I'm not so sure he got rid of my rats the right way." Your confidence and security slowly ebb. Every now and then, you think you hear a *clickety-clackity-click* of rat feet scrambling on the other side of your drywall. Every speck on the floor is examined in case it might be rat droppings. Then someone asks you about the exterminator. How are you feeling?

Exhausted? Fooled? Lied to? Maybe a little angry?

## ENTER DONALD TRUMP

When President Obama announced that his priority legislation was going to be the Affordable Care Act, health-care reform that included a public option, the hidden issues with "post-racial" America surfaced. A group calling itself the Tea Party planned a series of rallies to fight against the tax increases included in the plan. They called the ACA socialist and evoked memories of Soviet state planning by renaming the reform "Obamacare."[7]

Despite confusion at what the Tea Party represented (Havercroft and Murphy 2018; Maxwell and Parent 2012; Sustar 2013; Williamson, Skocpol and Coggin 2011), it was very much about one thing: anger at President Obama. Worst of all, the imagery used in signs and on T-shirts hawked at these Tea Party events was old-fashioned racism.

The president was pictured as an African witch doctor, drawn as an ape, caricatured in Jim Crow style, and, chillingly, his iconic "Hope" poster was rebranded as "Rope" with his head in a noose. This was alongside signs and shirts telling him to go back to Kenya, one sign telling him to "hang in there" (beside a picture of a noose), and numerous versions calling him a Muslim,[8] which he is not. It was not uncommon to see confederate flags at these rallies, which are about as clear a sign against racial progress that there is.

Soon afterward, during a visit to *The View*, celebrity Donald Trump amplified the racist notion that President Obama—an American born in Hawaii—is not a citizen. "Why doesn't he show his birth certificate? There's something on that birth certificate that he doesn't like." Less than a week later, he was on *Fox & Friends*, and then the *Laura Ingraham Show*, repeating that President Obama didn't have the papers necessary to serve as president (Shear 2011). To end the controversy, President Obama was forced to show those papers. He released his long-form birth certificate in April 2011.

For those who follow history, this sounds familiar. During slavery, any White man could accost any Black person and demand their papers, whether those papers were documents explaining why an enslaved person was off the plantation (Stampp 1989) or they were actual Certificates of Freedom[9] if she or he were a free African American. In the year 2011, 150 years to the month after the start of the Civil War, a White man showed he could force the country's most powerful Black man to show his papers.

Therefore, when people like Donald Trump Jr. try to claim the revulsion so many folks on the left have for his father is indicative of some "Trump Derangement Syndrome," it is difficult to take them seriously. Why make up a disorder to explain something whose explanation is as clear as day? The people who dislike Trump, who couldn't think of much good to say about him from the jump, weren't doing so because "no one hated Trump until he went against the Democrats" (Zaru 2018). Or because he built a more successful economy than Obama; evidence is mixed at best that Trump significantly changed the trajectory of the pre-COVID economy (Casselman 2017; Long 2020). Or because he was a much-needed boogeyman for the left (Raimondo 2016); there hasn't been a shortage of those over the years. Even placing Trump's problematic history with Black Americans (Chang, Cornish, Kelly and Shapiro 2016; Itkowitz and Brice-Saddler 2019) aside, the birther issue was enough to label Trump a dangerous racist who could not be trusted.

And that was before he called Mexican immigrants rapists and drug-runners in his presidential candidacy announcement.

What Trump did in that 2015 announcement speech flies in the face of political strategy. Insulting Mexican immigrants, at least in theory, should make a presidential candidate unelectable. Sure, some people might still respond to that sort of ham-handed rhetoric, but in the twenty-first century it was expected that even in a Republican primary, enough voters would be ashamed of it (McCarthy 2015). Rather than marginalizing himself with these comments, Trump won the Republican primary.

Trump's public speeches as the Republican nominee featured consistent[10] anti-Muslim and anti-immigrant messages.[11] The rallies for these speeches featured aggressively sexist imagery and chants (Georgeac, Rattan and Effron 2018; Glick 2019) with sometimes violent clashes inside and outside the venues (DelReal and Sulluivan 2016; G. Saunders 2016). Occasionally, Trump would work up the crowd to turn on the few protesters who made it inside. During a North Carolina rally, a few anti-Trump protesters tried to heckle Trump. One of the protesters, a Black man named Rakeem Jones, was being escorted out of the building when an older White man in a cowboy hat sucker-punched him. In the ensuing scramble, the protesters were told, "Go home, niggers!" by a nearby rallygoer (Moyer, Starrs and Larimer 2016).

We know how the rest of the story went. Donald Trump did not pay for any of these actions. He was not made a pariah by Republican voters disgusted with his anti-immigrant comments. He was not the recipient of wholesale rejection by egalitarian American voters offended by his failure to control the frenzy his words seemed to create at his rallies, to show any sympathy toward refugees from war and famine, to apologize for supposed "locker-room talk" about how he can use starstruck women as sexual objects. On the contrary, he was elected president.

Imagine the place you live has a rat problem . . .

## BRING THE NOISE

In 2016, what to so many feels like a lifetime ago, Donald Trump was elected president in an "upset." So many writers, academics, polling experts, Democrats, Republicans, the apolitical, and the curious wondered in print and on social media how a candidate who openly insulted the growing Mexican American population, mocked the disabled, was caught on tape verbally debasing women, and popularized the racist notion that the country's first Black president was not an American—how did this person win? They began to ask, who voted for this man?

We were treated to articles and research on these Trump voters, some of it investigative but accusatory (McElwee 2016) and some of it sympathetic but patronizing (Abernathy 2017). Trump voters were alternately castigated for their racism (Bouie 2016), praised for disrupting a corrupt system (Bloom 2016), and almost always asked for a juicy quote. Like circus geeks, they were paraded in public for analysis and gawking: "Can you believe these people?"

A few years back, for a qualitative study I was conducting, I read every one of Trump's campaign speeches. Often these speeches were transcribed with crowd reactions, such as the boos whenever refugees from Syria were mentioned. I know exactly what Trump was telling his voters again and again because, for whatever his reputation as an improviser and an undisciplined speaker, he was remarkably consistent in his message.

As expected, I read a lot about how immigrants were coming to take the jobs of hardworking Americans. How refugee programs were letting in "radical Islamists" who were planning terrorist acts against the United States. How a woman named Katie Steinle was raped and killed by a still-at-large undocumented immigrant. How we needed to restore law and order to our streets to keep protesters for social justice in line.

What I did not expect, though, was the connection Trump was forging with these voters. He promised rally attendees that they were participating in a great movement, something special and exciting. They had the opportunity to shock the world and fix the way the American system operates. Most speeches closed with these calls to remember to vote, to be part of the movement, to take back their country.

There it was, there was the appeal. Beyond the racism and scare tactics there may be in Trump's method, he was not just offering people who were frustrated a buffet of scapegoats, he also was giving them something they could *do* about it. Immigrants, women who didn't know their place, Black people who were complaining about America, Muslims who refused to fit into "our Christian values,"[12] all of them were making America worse. It seemed to Trump like we had heard enough from all these groups. Supposedly, they had the media and power on their side. But if you got out and voted for Trump, you could tell those people to shut up—about sexism, racism, xenophobia, justice, and especially political correctness—and they would have to listen to you. Trump would speak for the silent, law-abiding, churchgoing, fundamentally good Americans and, in the process, make America great again.

## THE MIRAGE

There has been a lot of research on Trump voters, especially the "Obama-Trump" voters, those who reported voting for Obama in 2012 but Trump in 2016. The initial conclusion from some of the research was that these voters chose Trump due to their anxiety about the state of the economy (Sargent 2017; Saul 2016; Schiller 2016). One article (Porter 2016) concluded that Trump's votes were "where the jobs weren't." It made a lot of sense. The Rust Belt—the group of states along the Great Lakes where manufacturing was a key source of jobs in the decades following World War II—was where the changes from 2012 to 2016 were starkest, as Pennsylvania, Michigan, and Wisconsin went for Trump with Minnesota the lone, slight victory for Hillary Clinton. It might be that the economic policy of the Democrats threatened to leave this group behind again by prioritizing minority groups who primarily live in large, coastal cities.

Yet there were rumblings of another explanation. On November 12, 2016, *Saturday Night Live* aired a sketch guest-starring comedians Dave Chappelle and Chris Rock as part of a group of people watching the returns on election night 2016. Chappelle and Rock, the only Black people in the sketch, are portrayed as completely unsurprised by the turn of events. When Trump clinches the election and another partygoer gasps, "Oh my God, I think America is racist," Chappelle and Rock's characters react with mock surprise, with Chappelle's character adding, "I remember my great-grandfather told me something like that. But, you know, he was, like, a slave or something."

So, were Trump voters racists?

It is helpful here to take a step back from determining whether something like catering to people's basest instincts makes those who hear the call racists or not. Similarly, I'm not sure it is important to determine whether Trump himself is a racist. Witness the quixotic search for an "n-word tape" (Blake 2018) that proves Trump's racism by offering evidence he used what is traditionally seen as the most offensive racial slur in the English language. If it were found, what difference would it make? Would it make things better or worse for Black Americans?

From a pragmatic standpoint, if you want to start a dialogue with people and at least have them hear what you are saying, it is awfully tough to do so when you label them with one of the stickiest epithets in American society, "racist." Rather than litigating the racism of Trump voters by pinning it to a specific behavior or word, let's look at the evidence from political science and psychology. Much of that evidence is that the economic anxiety narrative was largely overblown not the least because the average Trump supporter was more economically secure and had a higher average income than the average Clinton voter (D. Saunders 2016). Numerous studies showed two much more influential variables than economics in determining who voted for Trump: racial resentment and status threat.

Racial resentment, as discussed in the previous chapter, is the idea that Black people have a lower socioeconomic status due to flaws in their culture. Those high on racial resentment take issue with redistributive economic programs and affirmative action because they see them as handouts to the undeserving, specifically Black people (Sears, Sidanius and Bobo 2000). Studies found that scoring higher on racial resentment translated to a significantly higher likelihood of supporting Trump in 2016. Similarly, the racial and ethnic isolation of some American towns has resulted in a substantial number of White voters vulnerable to the type of racially antagonistic appeals Trump presented (Rothwell and Diego-Rosell 2016). After all, it's easier to blame your problems on people you don't identify with or groups you don't see as part of your community (Cornielle, Yzerbyt, Rogier and Buidin 2001; Nisbet, Ostman and Shanahan 2008).

The other element was status threat. Status threat, or status anxiety, is based on the idea that society is arranged into a hierarchy with zero-sum rules. Seeing other groups begin to move up in the country creates a sense of threat to your status within the hierarchy, and the resulting anxiety can motivate political behavior. In 2016, those who believed the hierarchy was being upended, with White Christian males pushed to the bottom in favor of people of color and recent immigrants, were significantly more likely to vote for Trump. Several studies (e.g., Fowler, Medenica and Cohen 2017; Mutz 2018) showed the meaningful influence of status threat on political behavior, especially support for Trump, even when accounting for income levels and relative economic stability.

Make no mistake, status threat impairs racial justice. Status threat also works against a sense of common humanity, dividing people along a sense of territoriality that pits groups against one another. White Americans are not alone in being prey to this anxiety. For example, Latino Americans whose families have been established in this country for generations can also feel threatened by an influx of immigrants, not only from countries outside their heritage but also from their own "old country," especially if they sense new immigrants are not being asked to play by the rules or are getting special favors. It is not surprising these feelings are correlated with racial resentment.

In the short time since Trump's entry onto the scene, when he began "speaking the quiet part out loud" at rallies and in tweets, he has emboldened others to do the same. Numerous studies show the increase in hate crimes correlated with his candidacy (Williamson and Gelfand 2019) and election (Edwards and Rushin 2018; Hanci 2019). Reports even show that hate crimes rose 226 percent in counties following a 2016 Trump rally there (Feinberg, Branton and Martinez-Ebers 2019). This is a real problem. The people who commit hate crimes, as discussed in Chapter 4, do so for many reasons, one of which is a sense that they have been empowered by a leader whom they feel represents them.

Those prey to status threat and racial resentment may not see themselves as racist or xenophobic at all. Rather, they may see themselves as looking out for their family or victims of a broken government system. These are perceptions. Right or wrong, we have seen that, societally, the results of status threat and racial resentment are more division, less trust, and more exclusion. These decrease the prospects of coalescing around a common humanity.

The fears of Trump voters are misplaced, but they are fears, nonetheless. We have a better shot at conversation if we knowledge the humanity of our fellow Americans. There probably has been too much focus on the type to riot to disrupt the peaceful transfer of power because their guy lost. I have to remind myself to think about those who support Trump and wouldn't have gone to the Capitol on the sixth of January 2021. Where does their sympathy for the insurrection come from? If it were logical, it would not stand much scrutiny: most of the reasons amount to rationalization, something they would reject if they were coming from someone on the left trying to justify, say, the vandalization of a Portland courthouse. So, if we're talking about emotions rather than logic, why are these feelings so strong?

## THE MESSAGE

I was interested in studying whether these views on race, or a susceptibility to be motivated by them, was entangled with Trump or with being a Republican voter. Is Trump just playing on something that is already there, or is he actively making things worse? Perhaps more germane to our current situation, are Republicans willing to finally step away from some of the more outrageous statements Trump has made on race?

My study (2021) was composed of Republican participants divided into two equally sized groups. Both groups filled out some psychological measures, including the Color-Blind Racism Assessment Scale (CoBRAS). Participants were also asked to rate political figures like Donald Trump on a feeling thermometer from 0 to 100, with 100 indicating the most warmth or support.

The groups then had slightly different experiences. The condition for one group, called Racist, consisted of being shown a racist[13] Trump tweet. The other, called Dog Whistle, consisted of being shown a Trump tweet on race[14] that was subtler, but still stoking negativity about people of color. After seeing the tweet, the groups then resumed having the same experience: they were asked whether the tweet they saw was racist and completed a subscale of the CoBRAS called Blatant Racism. Using this subscale, I was able to ask participants to answer a few more questions about race that I could directly compare to their scores before seeing the tweet. In other words, did merely reading a Trump tweet on race actually encourage Republicans to express more racist beliefs?

The results clarified how Trump's statements on race influence Republican views. For those in the Racist condition, the one significant influence on whether they deemed the tweet racist was the participant's score on the CoBRAS. In other words, the more the participant denied White privilege and institutional racism, the less likely the participant was to label the tweet racist. The results got more interesting when I compared scores on the Blatant Racism subscale from before to after seeing the tweets. For those in the Racist condition, who saw a racist Trump tweet, their scores on the very same measure went up an average[15] of 13.5 percent. There was no significant difference on Blatant Racism scores from before to after reading the tweet in the Dog Whistle group.

The main influence on whether Republicans distanced themselves from supporters of these racially charged tweets was the extent to which they held colorblind racial attitudes. Those with high CBR were significantly more comfortable with supporters of the tweet. Previous studies (DeSante and Smith 2018; Schaffner, MacWilliams and Nteta 2018) have shown Republicans on average to have higher scores on the CoBRAS. In that context, these two findings are one potential reason we don't see Republicans rejecting the sort of racial rhetoric Trump used or walking away from a party that welcomes those with racist views.

A lot goes into political identity, and we know people are very attached to this label (e.g., Marietta and Barker 2019; Iyengar, Sood and Lelkes 2012). I don't believe all Republicans are racist, and it is unlikely all Trump voters are racist. The question that comes to my mind, though, is why are they comfortable associating with racists? Furthermore, are they aware that listening to some of what party leaders like Trump have to say on race pushes them, even subtly, toward expressing more skepticism that racism continues to exist in society? The results underline the fact that these sentiments are poisonous not only to the Black people they target but to the White people who hear them.

\*\*\*

Back to full disclosure, one of the people in my life who voted for Trump in 2016 is my father. I have looked up to my dad my whole life, and I see a wealth of good in who this man is. In the truest sense of Catholic laity, he is a man of God. He was a kind and giving dad. I remember my younger brother and I moaning in exaggerated agony when he would pull over to the side of the road to help people, and he did that a lot. I could not square this man with the image of the rabid, xenophobic, aggressive, sexist Trump voter.

For four years, when my mind would drift, often I contemplated what I could possibly say to dissuade him from voting for Trump again. Everything my dad stood for seemed to be violated by Trump's policies, Trump's "Pharisee on the street corner" version of Christianity, his tendency to aim down and insult those with less of anything than him, and his apparent narcissism. I wanted to tell my dad, think of your wife—my mother, a mixed-race woman with a Black father. Think of your grandchildren, who share a Mexican American heritage. Think of our family, Catholic to the core, raised to believe that you lift up those in pain and that the Kingdom of God belongs to the meek. For four years I built up in my head the argument I could make that would change my dad's vote.

The week before the 2020 election, I saw him and told him point-blank, as I was leaving his house, "We will need to talk again before Tuesday." He said, "Sure." Only I couldn't get a hold of him again before polls closed that November 3, despite showing up at his house twice. The best I could do was a voice mail and a text.

Had I blown it? Maybe. I took a step back and began to consider why this was so important to me, and why it might be so important to him. Even had I dragged him kicking and screaming away from voting for Trump—I told him at one point, "I don't care, write in Ronald Reagan if you have to"—what really would have changed? Would it erase the person he was and is to know he did vote for Trump, or that he plans on doing so again in 2024? I can say that it would not.

I do not want to appear Pollyannaish about the role of race in the 2016 election and beyond. That election continues to reverberate today, even after a bizarre 2020 presidential election, because of the reemergence of politics of identity—White, "native," male, and Christian positioned against darker skin, "foreign," female, and Muslim—as well as the power that comes with those identities. It appears as if many "closet racists" have felt encouraged by the former president's rhetoric (and seeming impunity) to begin acting out in public against Black people, whether they are visitors to the local pool or little girls trying to sell water on a hot day. At the same time, those individuals can live most of their lives without those prejudices surfacing and think of themselves as good, honest people.

A question I must ask is, if you paid attention and saw what that election did to our country, if you saw the pain that it caused Black people, recent immigrants, Muslims, and women (especially those exposed to sexual trauma), how can that be ignored? If you saw how seemingly easy it was for someone to scratch the surface of civility in this country and unleash anger and frustration, what does that say about the work that must be done to rebuild trust before we move forward? Because if you saw those things, you know we cannot have a national conversation on race the way things stand. We need to consider what we have learned to find an appropriate starting place, and that will take real work.

Neither the idealism of 2008 nor the roiling conflict of 2016 should define how we see racial identity in the United States. Trump didn't invent racism just like Obama didn't solve it. There is room to be disappointed in Obama without accusing Black culture of selfishness and laziness. There is also room to be disgusted with Trump without painting all his supporters as bigoted "deplorables." That room lies not in some logical or political compromise but our common humanity.

Racism is a moral wrong that hurts us all. The hurdle that must be over-come is helping people understand how decisions they make and beliefs they hold—both justified, in the minds of many—contribute to a morally disgraceful condition. That is a reality based on decades of research detailed in Chapters 4 and 5. Those who are clear-eyed about the impact of their political decisions are better equipped to change them. But how do we get to that point?

We have tried lecturing, the hard line, and escalating culture wars. The impulse to paper over racial conflict was met with harsh reality while the opposite impulse, to push back with an even stronger, racialized identity politics, has fallen prey to polarization. History and research show us that a more effective approach is to try to understand one another. Understanding and trust can lead us to a higher ground where we share humanity and a moral commitment to justice for all.

Yet the competing narratives within the political parties keep us divided. Many White people get defensive for what they think they're losing and for fear of being labeled racist. Americans of color can get exhausted from try-ing to express their humanity, or simply exist without harassment. The final lesson of 2016 is that *the racialization and polarization of American politics have wounded our prospects of coalescing against racism.* The only way to go forward is to go back, forsake the current talking points and counterpoints, and reset the discussion.

We all have fears, just like we all have dreams, and politics has a way of magnifying and manipulating them both. If we want things to change, we can start by viewing the person on the other side as a fellow human being. Be open to listening and communicate this clearly at the start. Even today, we can choose to how to disentangle the knot of racial polarization by trying to understand each other's feelings before rushing to express our own.

## NOTES

1. As noted in Chapters 4 and 5, Black Americans are on the losing end of a variety of disparities. They are less likely to be able to hold generational wealth (Weller and Roberts 2021), less likely to finish high school or attend and graduate college (Cook 2015), have a shorter lifespan (Harper, MacLehose and Kaufman 2014) and greater likelihood of mental illness including stress, have less socioeconomic mobility (Badger, Cain Miller, Pearce and Quealy 2018), and are more likely to interact with police, be arrested, and when convicted receive longer sentences (Alexander 2012) compared to White Americans.

2. But not most White voters (Pew 2009).

3. President Obama's words, not mine.

4. The host, E. D. Hill, later apologized. She still lost her show. The term was later satirized in a *New Yorker* cover captioned, "The Politics of Fear."

5. Subsequently, Obama hosted a "Beer Summit" at the White House with Gates and the responding officers. It was likely due to the blowback he received for his comments supporting Gates that this event was one of the few open attempts at interracial dialogue Obama made during his presidency.

6. During the 2016 NFL preseason, San Francisco 49ers quarterback Colin Kaepernick began sitting during the national anthem, stating that he would not stand for a flag that represents oppression. After this became public knowledge, he received significant blowback. He was then approached by a football player who had served in the military. This player suggested finding a different way to protest without "disrespecting" the troops who are commonly associated with the anthem. Kaepernick's compromise was to kneel instead. This demonstration began to catch on with a small number of athletes and became an eventual rallying cry for social conservatives: here were entitled athletes injecting social justice into "non-partisan" sports. The controversy, and the practice of kneeling, grew and likely peaked in 2020 after the death of George Floyd.

7. Obama, always one to push back carefully, said, "he had no problem" with the moniker because, "I do care" (Madison 2011).

8. The othering of President Obama by calling him Muslim is a separate discussion altogether. One can easily argue that calling him Muslim is a dual slur against Obama for not being American enough and against Muslims by using the religion as shorthand for sneaky, foreign infiltration of American institutions. Muslims have

traditionally struggled with marginalization and othering in American society, though this got significantly worse after the events of September 11, 2001.

9. "Free at Last?," an exhibit set up by the University of Pittsburgh library, allows viewers of the webpage to learn about and actually view freedom papers from the nineteenth century. View at http://exhibit.library.pitt.edu/freeatlast/papers_listing .html.

10. Having read all the speeches myself (Tilley 2020), I can verify that these messages were consistent to the tune of Trump mentioning Islam negatively in 62.9 percent of his speeches for 1.44 mentions per speech and anti-immigrant rhetoric in 77.4 percent of his speeches, averaging 5.06 mentions per speech.

11. Research also shows Trump's rise coincided with a rise in hate groups (Stryuk 2017).

12. Trump used these words in a little over a third (35.5 percent) of his speeches, averaging a mention once every other speech (0.58).

13. The "racist" condition tweet was sent during antiracist protests in Minnesota, some of which resulted in rioting. The text: "These THUGS are dishonoring the memory of George Floyd, and I won't let that happen. Just spoke to Governor Tim Walz and told him that the Military is with him all the way. Any difficulty and we will assume control but, when the looting starts, the shooting starts. Thank you!"

14. The "dog whistle" condition tweet was sent during the runup to the 2020 election. The text: "The 'suburban housewife' will be voting for me. They want safety & are thrilled that I ended the long running program where low income housing would invade their neighborhood. Biden would reinstall it, in a bigger form, with Corey Booker [sic] in charge! @foxandfriends @MariaBartiromo"

15. The average score for these participants was 10.85, versus 9.56 before reading the tweet.

*Chapter 8*

# The Persistent Whiteness
# of Republicanism

*I have the greatest affection for [Black people], but I know they're not going to make it for 500 years. They aren't. You know it, too. The Mexicans are a different cup of tea. They have a heritage. At the present time they steal, they're dishonest, but they do have some concept of family life. They don't live like a bunch of dogs, which the Negroes do live like.*

—President Richard Nixon, 1971

*I am of the view that Black Americans will move inexorably and naturally toward conservatism when we stop discouraging them. . . . Conservatives must open the door and lay out the welcome mat if there is going to be a chance of attracting Black Americans. There need be no ideological concessions, just a major attitudinal change.*

—Justice Clarence Thomas, 1987

*Why are we having all these people from shithole countries coming here?*

—President Donald Trump, 2018

In this chapter, I present the Republican Party's idea of racism and how it attempts to address it. I present two prominent conservative voices on racism and discuss its appeal. I discuss research on recent changes in Republican Party demographics, though the party remains overwhelmingly White. I present reasons why this might be. Republicans differ from Democrats in how they define racism, and that influences their largely colorblind racial policy. Finally, I analyze the Republican idea of racism from the perspective of a moral mandate to value humanity.

***

Having read in Chapter 2 about some of the responses Republicans receive when trying to appeal to voters of color, you know the GOP is swimming upstream in trying to move beyond its large, White base. Why might Black people, and people of color in general, be skeptical of the Republican Party? There are a few major reasons that stand out.

One is GOP politicians' strategy of appealing to racially resentful White voters. Even if the GOP didn't live up to any of their promises to cut welfare (which would disproportionately hurt Americans of color) or corporate taxes (which would disproportionately help White Americans), the party as a whole and many of its supporters at least condone this strategy. This strategy has borne fruit in the growing gap between Republicans' and Democrats' belief that anti-White racism has eclipsed anti-Black racism (Samuels and Lewis 2022). The second reason is that conservatives show low levels of favorability toward Black people (Chambers, Schlenker and Collisson 2012). This is a central problem in the Republican Party's ability to promote Black conservative voices in good faith.

Third, and most importantly, a neo-Nazi[1] presence is growing in the party, which brings us to Tucker Carlson.

Tucker Carlson is a prominent Fox News personality who, as of 2021, hosts the number one–rated prime-time program on cable news. Carlson has been credited with leading Fox News to the top of the ratings rankings and strengthening Fox's hold on the cable news genre (Katz 2022). By most respects, Carlson is the most important voice in conservative media since the salad days of Rush Limbaugh during the Clinton presidency.

It is not surprising, given his show's demographics, that Carlson addresses racism from the point of view of White Americans. Carlson goes beyond providing this outlet, though, to combat notions that racism exists at all. He called White supremacy and White nationalism "hoaxes" (Beauchamp 2019; Rodriguez 2019; Stelter 2019). He also has questioned whether the left has a definition for these terms, asking, "Can someone tell us in very clear language what a White supremacist is?" on the show following President Biden's inauguration (Porter 2021).

Carlson's employment of grievance politics reentered the news in the aftermath of the mass shooting in May 2022 at a Buffalo market, in which thirteen Black Americans were shot, ten fatally (Hayes, Johnson and Thornton 2022). The shooter chose the location because it was known to be a Black neighborhood, and he had written a lengthy, online manifesto espousing something known as the Great Replacement (Sullivan 2022). The theory was also credited for the New Zealand mosque shooting of 2019, in which the shooter posted a manifesto praising Donald Trump as a "symbol of renewed White identity."

The Great Replacement is a White supremacist conspiracy theory that accuses Democrats of accelerating demographic change in America to "replace" White voters with immigrants of color, who are presumed to have higher birth rates. The philosophy dates to the French nationalism of the early twentieth century (Anti-Defamation League 2022) and has been resuscitated by writer Renaud Camus (Feola 2021) in recent decades. Government and law professor Michael Feola (2022) analyzed themes in the Great Replacement and found that the threat implied in the conspiracy is of such a radical and existential nature that it practically compels correspondingly radical action exemplified by the Buffalo shooter.

Tucker Carlson has openly mused about the Great Replacement (Media Matters 2021; Michel 2021). He is not alone: Fox News hosts and personalities have discussed the supposed "plot" to replace White voters for years (Farhi 2022). But Carlson's reach, and the attention he has given the theory, have come under scrutiny. The *New York Times'* (Yourish et al. 2022) analysis of 1,150 episodes found four hundred discussed the Great Replacement and tacitly endorsed it. Carlson explained on September 22, 2021, "This is called the Great Replacement: the replacement of legacy Americans with more obedient people from faraway countries."

The Great Replacement shares much in common with studies on status threat, which was mentioned in Chapter 7 as a factor in Trump's 2016 victory. Status threat is tied to group identity: a change in demographic conditions can produce anxiety about a potential loss in status for one's group. Status threat has been linked to a variety of outcomes, most notably the activation of White identity (Jardina 2019; Major et al. 2018; Sides, Tesler and Vavrek 2017) and voting behavior in the 2016 election (Fowler et al. 2017; Mutz 2018; Reny et al. 2019). White Americans high in status threat are also more likely to sense anti-White animus in the current trend of racial progress (Craig and Richeson 2018; Jardina 2019; Norton and Summers 2011; Wilkins and Kaiser 2014).

A series of studies on status threat (Craig and Richeson 2014a, 2014b, 2018; Major et al. 2018; Outten et al. 2012; Wetts and Willer 2018) showed some participants information about demographics shifting toward a "majority-minority" population. These studies found these participants showed increased status threat and White identity, expression of more negative racial attitudes, increased support for race-related conservative positions (e.g., welfare "backlash"), and endorsement of special company policies geared toward Whites.

Research indicates that status threat is built from outgroup-directed animus, White identity, and a sense of protectiveness over economic, existential, and social "turf" related to that identity. Some of these ingredients figure into contemporary versions of racism. To learn more about this potential link, I studied correlations between status threat and colorblind racism with 618 participants.[2] I measured status threat in two ways. One, based on Diana Mutz's (2018) work, was Social Dominance Orientation. SDO, as introduced in Chapter 6, is a preference for a social order with one's own group preferably at the top. For example, SDO in multiple cultures has been found to decrease identification with oppressed minority groups (Pratto et al. 2000).

The other measure was using the White Vulnerability Scale developed by Fowler, Medenica, and Cohen (2017) to assess White Americans' sense of "losing ground" to immigrant groups. I found both measures of status threat to be significantly and moderately correlated[3] with denial of racism and belief in "reverse racism." What this means is that Carlson is not just "asking questions" or exposing viewers to alternate views on immigration: he may be activating, even stoking, racism denial and resentment of these immigrants.

Tucker Carlson is not just another crank on the internet. He has a giant audience and clips of his show are all over the Fox News YouTube page. However Carlson might define himself, he is a mouthpiece for modern American conservatism, which is aligned with the Republican Party. He has talked about this, and other White grievance-feeding topics, for years with impunity. That this racist[4] idea has purchase in the Republican Party must give American voters of color pause.

## IT'S YOUR THING

The results of the 2020 election contained a curious bit of data: President Donald Trump, man of many documented foibles discussing people of color, man half the country thought was racist (Lemon 2020), made *gains* among Black and Latino voters. From an identity politics perspective, this should not have happened. The Democratic candidate, now President Joe Biden, went to great lengths to signal his allegiance to Black Americans via his candidacy-saving endorsement from South Carolina representative Jim Clyburn, his promise to put a Black woman on the Supreme Court, his open antagonism toward Trump's racial insensitivity, and his choice of a Black and Indian American woman as vice president.

But demography is not destiny. Polling data (NPR Staff 2021) show that 12 percent of Black men voted for Trump, about twice as many as Black women. Trump improved his Black voter support by 2 percent compared to Mitt Romney, who ran against President Obama in 2012 (Roper Center 2013). The data indicate a continuation of Republican popularity trending upward among Black men (Ostfeld and Garcia 2020).

Trump also improved his standing with Latinos across the country by about 8 percent compared to 2016, both in expected areas such as Florida and in unexpected ones like Wisconsin and New Jersey (Swan 2021). Further research on 2020 Latino voters (Russonello and Mazzei 2021) indicates that the issues that mattered most to them were Trump's handling of the economy and the Republican Party's embrace of a religious identity politics. Natalie Jackson of the Public Religion Research Institute told the *Los Angeles Times* (Lauter 2021), "Hispanic Protestants look more like White Protestants than Hispanic Catholics." The *Times'* analysis includes a note that Latin American countries have seen a similar pattern, with Protestants there moving in a conservative direction.

The Democratic focus on fighting racism may have turned off some voters of color. The message, "We support you and we strongly oppose racism," was thin on the details at many points in the campaign. For example, one 2020 campaign ad (MSNBC 2020) focused on Black dignity and "hold[ing] police officers accountable" but lacked substance on the concurrent economic freefall that wound up hitting Black Americans harder than others.

Similarly, the seeming assumption among the Democrats that Latino voters would support them because of Trump's harsh anti-immigration rhetoric ignored the complexity of Latino voters and their interests. Famously, the group called Hispanics or Latinos is composed of Americans in various stages of generational acculturation, whose ancestors lived in a wide variety of countries, each with different cultures. Some of these groups, like Floridian Cuban Americans, are relatively conservative (e.g., Krogstad 2020) on the social issues that have consumed Democratic messaging over the last decade. As the Democratic Party has increased its focus on racial justice (Caputo and Rodriguez 2021; Cillizza 2021), some Latinos find themselves more connected to the "immigrant narrative" of assimilation (Schoen and Young 2021) and worried about the economy (Winston 2021).

Psychology illustrates that average group differences, while informative, tend to be less than the variance within that group. To use the example of Mexican Americans, strength of racial identity is influenced by family background and the local context. The first generation to move to the United States may be marked as "foreign" but strongly identify themselves with their new country. Some descendants may embrace cultural elements of the old country as part of their identity, including learning Spanish. Other generations may seek to further blend in to American (White) society. Parts of the transition are not left to choice, though: the color of the immigrant's skin, their accent, their name, where they live, and other factors may continue to identify them with the old country and potentially expose them to discrimination. For many, the logical path away from discrimination is assimilation.

The assimilation narrative has been studied in the context of Latino Trump supporters. Political scientist Rudy Alamillo (2019) studied voting behavior, racism, and racial identity among Latinos in the 2012 and 2016 elections. He found that the higher the level of denial of racism (as measured by two items from the CoBRAS), the more likely the participant was to vote for Trump. Racism denial was a more powerful predictor even than Republican identity. As discussed in the previous chapter, racism denial is important for predicting White voters' behavior as well. But it was more powerful for Latino voters in 2016 in contrast to 2012: moving from the lowest to the highest point on the racism denial items increased likelihood of Trump voting by a factor of five. Alamillo also found that the more White people in these Latinos' neighborhoods, the higher the likelihood of voting for Trump. Alamillo explained the two findings by noting that denying racism is a way to minimize stereotyped Latino "un-Americanness."

Racial identity affects Black conservatives differently. Leah Wright Rigeur's (2016) examination of decades of Black Republican activism shows Black Republicans' twin isolation from fellow Black Americans and from fellow Republicans. According to recent research by author and political scientist Andra Gillespie (2022), compared to Black liberals, Black conservatives are more optimistic about Black progress in the post–Jim Crow Era, more likely to desire to keep an open dialogue with White people, and more likely to emphasize self-reliance. Gillespie cites the work of Tasha Philpot, whose content analysis[5] and survey research indicated that White conservatives tend to emphasize morality and government while Black conservative thought tends to emphasize social welfare and religion.

Black Republican politicians have had recent success, including Mia Love in Utah and Tim Scott in South Carolina, and Dr. Ben Carson's popularity among conservatives. This appears to contradict studies showing conservatism is related to racial resentment (e.g., DeSante 2013; Gainous 2012; Sears, Hetts, Sidanius and Bobo 2000). Research by Hakeem Jefferson and Michael Tesler (2021) found that racial resentment does not foreclose supporting Black Republican candidates for political office. In fact, White conservatives are likely to support Black Republican candidates *because* of their Blackness. Black Republican candidates "provide cover" for a party whose policies and rhetoric often run counter to Black Americans' interests.

LeFleur Stephens-Dougan (2020) has analyzed political language, especially the appeals used to attract racially resentful White Americans. Her research indicates that politicians practice what she calls racial distancing. They signal that they will not disrupt the racial status quo; this may include invoking Black stereotypes or criticizing so-called Black culture. Because Black candidates are assumed to be looking out for Black voters first, they are under pressure to engage in racial distancing. This frees them to be more blatant in their use of stereotypes or critique, such as when Ben Carson referred to the Affordable Care Act as "slavery." Explicit racial appeals continue to have purchase, especially when coming from Black politicians.

Thus, the main benefits to Republicans highlighting their Black and Latino politicians are a) they can say things White Republicans cannot, b) these racial appeals appear to psychologically absolve White voters of guilt in holding such stereotypes, and c) diverse representation is a way to appeal to often-skeptical Americans of color. The latter of these benefits appeared to pay some dividends over the last six years, though it should not be underestimated that there is no law that the Republican Party's policies, such as tax cuts or business-friendly policies, can only appeal to White Americans.

Other trends should not be discounted. The immigrant assimilation narrative, mentioned above, appeals to certain Latinos, especially those in majority-White neighborhoods. There is a lengthy history of Cuban Americans and some South American immigrants opposing anything with the faintest whiff of socialism, which the Republican Party has worked to tar the Democratic Party with since at least the heyday of the New Deal almost a century ago. Recent macho Republican posturing, especially by Donald Trump, also appears to have made inroads in appealing to Black and Latino men (Logan 2020; Medina 2021; Muravchick and Shields 2020).

Though Democratic Party representatives claim Republican policies will hurt Black and Latino Americans overall, this message is not always clear, nor is it consistently clear how a firm antiracist stance translates to "bread and butter" gains for people who are disproportionately at the lower end of socioeconomic status. The Republican gains among American voters of color have been news since 2016. Yet for all the fuss, the fact remains that about four out of every five Republican voters are White.

## VOICE OF CONSERVATIVE MILLENNIALS

One of the most persistent Republican voices on racism is Ben Shapiro. Shapiro is the founder of conservative news site The Daily Wire. He has been publishing columns since he was seventeen years old. He had a stint as editor-at-large of right-wing Breitbart News. He hosts a podcast as a "voice for conservative millennials."

Shapiro has gained some fame over recent years for his willingness to engage in debate with almost anyone about political issues. This is an admirable trait. My YouTube feed, which is hardly an arch-conservative rabbit hole, will occasionally suggest videos of Shapiro "EVISCERATING" (always in caps), "OBLITERATING," or "leaving SPEECHLESS" liberal college students who attend his lectures.

One could argue that the most important purpose Shapiro serves to the conservative movement is to supply listeners and readers with a wealth of data and rationale to combat liberal talking points. Shapiro's ability to expose the flimsiness of some liberals' beliefs, especially those on a complex subject like systemic racism, should be a sign that the left wing has failed the job. After all, if progressives were clearer about why systemic racism exists, why it is wrong, and where to look for further information, there would be a lot less OBLITERATING going on.

For example, in one video from Shapiro's YouTube page (Shapiro 2021b), which does not show how the other panelists responded, Shapiro says he will accept evidence of systemic racism as soon as someone justifies to him the numerous ways in which the disproportionately negative outcomes experienced by Black Americans cannot be chalked up to culture.

An honest response would require unpacking each of his cited statistics on their own merit, i.e., what "racist origin story" might exist for each of these disparities, did that story get changed via legal or social means, following the change what evidence is there that the original racism seeps into modern experiences, have any real attempts been made to reverse the disparities, how have they succeeded or failed? This takes time, which debates are famously short on. Even if Shapiro gave college students an hour, most would not be able to supply those answers. The information is out there. It is in this book. It is in the books and research I cite. Recalling all of that at a moment's notice, as Shapiro does with his statistics, takes a mastery of a good deal of information that most cannot condense into a pithy retort.

So let us consider his contention that Black culture is the cause of educational, income, and incarceration disparities. Shapiro is notoriously critical of what he considers Black culture. He has repeatedly criticized rap and hip-hop music (Shapiro 2009). Rap and hip-hop culture embody what so many of the conservative critiques of Blackness in America are about. The messages hip-hop can communicate, "Black America's CNN," as Chuck D of Public Enemy famously put it, document not just excess and misogyny, but the full range of the human emotional spectrum as experienced in Black communities. Just think of rapper Tupac Shakur, who threatened violent vengeance and objectified women, yet also sang to us—the way he remembered Marvin Gaye used to sing to him—about the struggles of single motherhood and the pain of marginalization and rejection, over the same soul and funk hooks that soundtracked the Black is Beautiful movement.

Too often, hip-hop is often caricatured as lowbrow, problematic, and a bad influence. It is this caricature that Shapiro attacks, rather than treating it like any other art form. I personally don't like most country music, but I see why people like it. Rather than saying country is reflective of problems with rural White America (which I don't believe), I can simply say "it's not for me."

This difference is precisely why Shapiro leaves himself open to accusations of cultural racism, which is blaming people of color for their societal standing without considering alternate explanations.

"If only Black people worked harder" is not a new line of thought, nor is it one free of racial bias. Are the "deaths of despair" blighting the Rust Belt, Appalachia, and spreading throughout the country indicative of flaws in White culture? Perhaps. Or, perhaps, there are other factors that can be considered.

In a video "DEBUNKING" a viral explanation of systemic racism, Shapiro (Daily Wire 2021) says that educational inequities could be solved through the voucher system. We know that such is not always the case with voucher systems and that they tend to facilitate White flight (Abernathy 2005). Democrats historically support maintaining enrollment at local public schools because it keeps schools integrated.

Shapiro moves on to another complaint about systemic racism: it either means that racial disparities alone are proof of a racist system or that all systems are racist. Regarding the latter, he said that if it were so, everyone would oppose them. As he breezed forward, I paused the video. Since when do we have universal opposition to racist organizations? What Shapiro does without saying it, is switch between definitions of racism. Limited, interpersonal racism with a broad moral mandate against it is the sort of racism that it is hard to imagine an entire system imposing since the death of Jim Crow. Should organizations act in racist ways, as many continue to do in hiring and pay practices, I see no reason to assume they face a consensus opposition. In fact, prominent public figures who have acted in old-fashioned racist ways[6] have been defended repeatedly by high-profile voices on the right.

Shapiro says that systemic racism seeks to explain disparities through history while ignoring personal behavior. What, then, of the heart-wrenching results of studies on Black motherhood and child mortality rates discussed in Chapter 4? Recall that personal behavior was a major factor in the analysis, and holding behavior constant there still was an unfortunate, and sometimes lethal, disparity. The personal behavior argument vastly oversimplifies systemic racism, including decades of research in sociology, a field in which there is broad agreement that systemic racism is real.

Similarly, pretending that history ends at a specific date is a tactic that allows Shapiro to claim that rates of decline in some of these outcomes for Black families are not reflective of the inertia built into history. Simple question: what is easier, a sharp left turn or a slight left turn? The video Shapiro is critiquing plainly says that Black families lost significant wealth due to redlining, then he pretends that should not be a factor[7] in present-day economics.

He attempts to debunk studies showing the continued effects of redlining by citing another study saying that such studies don't account for credit risk. However, credit risk is a subjective matter that is determined by people, who are known to make mistakes and have biases. Finally, he attempts another fast-speaking summary of why statistics on current wealth loss due to redlining are questionable by citing the natural tendency to rate areas as high- or low-risk. History tells us plainly that high-risk and low-risk areas were designated as such specifically due to racial biases.

Shapiro also overstates the corrective ability of affirmative action to increase Black access to higher education, labeling it discriminatory. This is not surprising, given that it is a larger point within conservatism. Decades of social science research show that White people, and conservatives in general, are likely to be opposed to affirmative action policies to help people of color (e.g., Peffley and Hurwitz 1998; Sears and Henry 2003; Sears et al. 2000; Sidanius, Pratto and Bobo 1996; Sniderman, Brody and Tetlock 1991; Sniderman and Piazza 1993).

Research on how affirmative action is described (Haley and Sidanius 2006) divided survey participants into six groups, based on exposure to one of six different ways of describing affirmative action. White people were more opposed than others to affirmative action, no matter how it was described, which supported prior research. This may be because of preexisting assumptions the participants held, as Haley and Sidanius concluded, or it could be due to the high likelihood of White people holding system-justifying beliefs, as subsequent research (Phelan and Rudman 2011) indicated when studying negative attitudes about affirmative action.

What the research shows is that concerns about affirmative action are not related to its fairness but, rather, its ability to disrupt a system in which White people believe they have a reserved right to certain services, including higher education. Though some may resist this conclusion on the basis that conservatives do not support government intervention in the free market, further research has contradicted that conclusion. Over three studies, researchers (Rabinowitz, Sears, Sidanius and Krosnik 2009) showed that "White opposition to racial policies incorporates an explicitly racial component (823)," not a rejection of government help to specific groups.

Politics, no matter how often Shapiro talks about "facts," are related to feelings. That is how it is (e.g., Brader 2006; Ditto and Liu 2016; Lodge and Taber 2013; Neuman, Marcus, Crigler and MacKuen 2007; Pérez 2016), and that is how it will continue to be. There are people who will love Donald Trump no matter what he does, and there are people who will hate him no matter what he does. That is not a reason to completely reject what Shapiro says, but it is a strong caveat to his insistence that facts (really, inconsistently sourced statistics) are primary in politics, or even society.

Because politics, and much of our decision-making, incorporates various levels of emotion, it is not uncommon for us to hold political beliefs that cannot stand logical scrutiny. This is because we do not critically evaluate the reasoning behind every belief that we hold. Doing so is even less likely in the modern era of political polarization, wherein most people are unlikely to hear serious challenges to their viewpoints (Marietta and Barker 2019; Mason 2018). Though Shapiro and other conservatives sell their views as "facts" and "truth," they are just as likely to be based on feelings and biases as any other belief.

## TWO DEFINITIONS OF RACISM

To understand why racial groups—including White people—are not more evenly divided between parties, we must look at the policies and voter appeals of the Republican Party, including how the Republican Party conceptualizes racism. The major advantages racial conservatives have in discussions about the modern forms of racism, especially systemic racism, are inertia and simplicity. The racial project of the post–Jim Crow era achieved a norm establishing the immorality of racism and, thus, racist behavior. There is clear moral weight in presenting racism as limited to "bad apples," as conservatives like Jordan Peterson have said.

The case that racism is something more removes the agency for racism from morally objectionable bigots to systems (potentially designed by bigots) that have immoral results. Therefore, traditional Democratic solutions to racism address its systemic aspects. These include programs like affirmative action and expanding the social safety net. A Democratic motto for this approach might be, "It takes a village."

Republicans have offered solutions to racism that are much closer to the racial project of the post–Jim Crow era. Racism is something "in your heart"; it is an individual moral violation. Tellingly, the main governmental action Republicans recommend is to improve the economy, an artifact of post–Jim Crow–era faith in the end of discriminatory laws and the instatement of a much-ballyhooed "equal opportunity." If there are no longer legal barriers, the only responsible governmental action is to go back to the postwar focus on increasing the income potential of Americans (Levy 2021). The Republican motto for this approach might be, "A rising tide lifts all boats."

The faith Republican leaders and conservatives have in the death of a system of legalized discrimination has led to a politics of colorblindness. As discussed earlier, the Post Racial Lie appeals to all people because it represents victory over centuries of American racial struggle. Still, it remains a lie because people of color continue to be discriminated against and they suffer disproportionately negative outcomes on most conceivable measures of life quality, as examined in the second section of this book.

It is worth asking, do colorblind policies really help everyone?

One example is economic conservatism. When taxes were lowered in the Tax Cuts and Jobs Act of 2017, did that colorblind action benefit everyone equally? While the results are incomplete, the history of similar tax cuts indicates what will happen. As Ronald Reagan discovered decades ago, tax cuts do not pay for themselves through increased investment. When that happens, government expenditures are cut, which often results in reductions in programs like welfare and Medicaid. These programs are disproportionately used by Black Americans. That is not an accident.

Medicaid and, especially, welfare are often cut because doing so does not raise much of an uproar. These services are unpopular due to a decades-long smear campaign against welfare begun in the 1970s that tied Black Americans to "handouts." The strategy, perpetrated largely by Republican politicians, played on voters' racial resentments (Brown 2016b; Levin 2013; Slocum 2001; Smith 1987; Wells and Roda 2016).

Early indicators are that the tax cut did not do much to raise the average person's wages (Tax Policy Center 2021) and that it most helped Americans already at the top of the economic scale (Bischoff 2020; Gale and Haldeman 2021), a group that is disproportionately White. Furthermore, the tax cuts did not go to worker salaries or even through meaningful bonuses (Congressional Research Service 2019), which averaged out to 2 to 3 percent of the corporate tax cuts. It is not a stretch to imagine that income inequality will continue to grow, disproportionately hurting people of color.

Some colorblind policies can help, such as investing more in early childhood education. Americans of color, as noted in the second section of the book, have lower average income, often necessitating multiple jobs and earners per household. Childcare, thus, becomes a major priority. Universal pre-K can fill that gap for a year, saving those households money or freeing up daytime work hours, though that has been a policy advocated more publicly by the Democratic Party. There was bipartisan agreement on increasing the child tax credit, which could have benefited low-income workers of color, though that credit was allowed to expire by a deadlocked Congress in 2021.

Opportunity zones, proposed by a group of Congressmen including Republican senator Tim Scott, represent another colorblind approach. Opportunity zones incentivize rolling capital gains into investments in low-income communities. This is a conservative solution, using high income gains to support historically under-resourced communities. Scott (2021) stated that the Opportunity Zone program resulted in a $29 billion investment in "low-income, high poverty, racially diverse areas."

The Republican Party has less embraced colorblind solutions than advocated moving beyond race, offering conservative distaste for government regulation as an all-encompassing solution. Part of the reason for this is that racial colorblindness justifies the party's mostly hands-off approach to race.

Among the problems with colorblindness is that it offers, as sociologist James Jones (2018) puts it, an illusion of morality without any substance. The result is that racist structures stay intact, racial inequities continue, and colorblind actors can claim an empty moral high ground by offering "race-neutral" solutions. Jones notes that acts of redress for these inequities are moral when they go to the heart of the problem; what often happens instead is that inertia moderates demand for change and tends toward symbolic solutions that preserve the problematic structure (Baron and Bielby 1980).

Imagine a reckless driver jumps the curb by your house and runs over your young daughter, severely injuring her. Doctors tell you it cannot be guaranteed that she will be able to walk again. Say that driver offers you a bunch of money to avoid court, allowing the driver to go back to his life. Does that money right the wrong? If that example seems extreme, consider the situation of the Sackler family, who have been implicated in causing and feeding an epidemic of opioid addiction and death in multiple regions in the United States. Is the money the Sacklers usually pay to avoid further responsibility a fair settlement? Few believe it is. Even after the Sacklers paid billions in settlement money, a two-hour hearing forced them to listen the pained and dissatisfied family of victims of the epidemic.

A rhetoric of colorblindness, which many popular conservatives like Jordan Peterson and Ben Shapiro espouse, partially shields many Americans from engaging in an honest discussion about race and its place in American society. As many have said, what other major problem has been solved by deciding not to talk about it? I figured that, in 2020, plenty of people were already uncomfortable talking about race, period. The evasion that James Jones writes about was something I wanted evidence of during the racial reckoning.

In the summer of 2020, I conducted an online survey with 687 participants divided into two groups. Both groups answered the CoBRAS to measure racial colorblindness and the White Vulnerability scale, which is three items measuring feelings of threat from changing demographics in the United States. Following the measures, both groups read similar AP articles about the upcoming 2020 election. The article the first (control) group read stated that the economy was going to be the main factor in the election and greatly influence the approach of the next president in the next year. The second ("race") group read the same article, except I inserted "racial issues" instead of "the economy."

After reading the article, the participants were asked to share their initial reaction to it in a sentence or less. Then I asked them to rate their anger on a scale of 1–10. I wanted multiple ways of capturing responses to the prominence of race versus something face-neutral such as the economy. Following the study, I coded the spontaneous responses based on the emotion being shared. The codes included frustrated, sad, angry, happy, confused, anxious/worried, hurt, and neutral.

Compared to Black participants ($M$=5.02) in the race condition, White participants had higher levels of anger on a scale of 1–10 in reaction to the article ($M$=7.2, $p$<.001). Trump voters in the race condition ($M$=7.19) also scored significantly higher than all others ($M$=5.31, $p$<.001). White participants also had higher rates of spontaneously angry or frustrated responses to the article (20.7 percent) compared to participants of color (12 percent). These were slightly more negative than spontaneous responses of White participants in the control condition (17.1 percent). One response coded as angry from a White participant in the race condition read, "It makes me angry to see the media report only one side of this issue." Another coded as frustrated read, "It makes me feel like this is just focusing on one case to fit a narrative as liberalism is taking over the country."

I also ran linear regressions on reported anger levels to help explain my findings. To keep the surveys short, I did not collect a great deal of demographic information or additional psychological characteristics of participants. Even so, regression was able to explain an informative amount of variance.[8] The race regression ($R^2$=.28) had three significant contributors: politics, colorblindness, and White vulnerability. Overall, even mentioning race tends to anger White people more than others.

What do Republican racial policies have to do with colorblindness? The Republican Party, and the Democratic Party in many ways, has pursued colorblind racial policy precisely because of mass appeal of the strategy. Who doesn't want to live in a world of equality where we echo Dr. King's goal to "not be judged by the color of [our] skin but by the content of [our] character"?

But as shown above and in the previous chapters, Republicans do care about race; Republican voters tend to care to the extent that racial policy *upholds* the racial status quo, with White people in an advantageous position. Colorblind racial policy, because it tends to maintain the status quo, thus has a double benefit to Republicans: it has face value as a "non-racist" way to discuss race, yet it usually results in protecting the advantages enjoyed by, mostly, White Americans. However, as discussed in Chapters 5 and 6, the research shows that ignoring disparities due to race and denying contemporary relevance of racism—attributes of racial colorblindness—hurt Americans of color in a variety of ways.

Another reason Republicans pursue a strategy of colorblindness is to avoid the negative response observed in the study I conducted. Guilt about White privilege or complicity in systemic racism is a symptom of a problem. It is neither a good thing nor a bad thing; it is a reaction. Systemic racism, which the research plainly shows is real, is not a person with an agenda to hurt the feelings of White people. The easiest way to respond to White guilt is to consider what positivity can come from it. As noted in the chapter on Critical Race Theory, guilt is not static. Like any other reaction, it comes with choices on how to deal with it.

If my eight-year-old son does something I find disrespectful, sometimes I am frustrated enough that I loudly reprimand him. I love my son and I believe he is a wonderful, unique child. I have a standard for his behavior; I want him to learn the right way to do things. When I raise my voice, I am not modeling for him the correct way to respond to someone, so I feel guilty.

I can wallow in that guilt and get angry. I can project it back onto my son by blaming his behavior for my outburst. Or I can consider why it is there and try to do better next time. I have a choice.

From a counseling perspective, discussion should not end when White people feel guilty after learning about systemic racism. In my example, I was responsible for my reaction, but not the events to which I reacted. White people, including children, who learn about how supporting the racial status quo hurts their fellow people have nothing to do with building or even maintaining a racist system. They didn't know that voting for certain politicians ensures that nothing meaningful will change about the system—or will push it backward. But now they do, and they are empowered to do something about it. What they do represents a choice over which they will have full control, unlike the past events that contributed to the system.

The guilt, anger, and frustration that comes with White people learning about the operation of systemic racism can be part of a process. Typically, Whiteness is not thrust into a White person's daily experience the way racial identity can be conspicuous for people of color. When the humanity of the White people who learn about complicity in a racist system is valued, we can discuss the experience of a real cognitive dissonance between my self-image as a good person and the knowledge that my choices may hurt my fellow human beings. To be productive, it may be that a conversation about race will need to account for this discomfort and embrace discussion of it rather than maligning it.

\*\*\*

How well does the Republican view of racism fit a moral mandate to value humanity? There are two parts, how racism is defined and how it is addressed.

Republicans can argue that there is great moral weight in their interpersonal definition of racism: in it, there are clear perpetrators whose actions cross the line from what is right to something fundamentally wrong. The only weakness is that this definition is contradicted by a growing body of research showing that Americans of color are disproportionately harmed by more than encounters with bigoted individuals. As society begins to embrace a wider definition of racism, the clear moral authority of a limited definition is likely to erode, leaving Republicans looking like they (potentially, immorally) are ignoring the suffering of fellow Americans.

Republicans have a more complicated case for moral authority of how they propose to address racism. Research shows that colorblind policies such as the tax cuts Republican congresses have passed often do not help poor Americans of color, and over the last forty years have accelerated inequality. There are colorblind policies that have been shown to perform better, but they are not a Republican priority.

The limits of the interpersonal definition of racism are starkest here: addressing racism becomes about eliminating bad apples. One way to do this would be through education, but the most popular voices in the Republican Party vociferously object to this. Many White Americans have been convinced, as noted in Chapter 3, that bringing racism into schools' history curricula is a threat to their children or American society.

There is nothing right or wrong with a conservative approach to life or politics. Liberals would be incorrect in assuming the country automatically would get better if conservatives would "get out of the way." Conservatives are liberals' fellow human beings, with strongly held beliefs they wish to protect.

According to the work of social psychologist Jonathan Haidt (2012), conservatives have a more diverse "moral matrix" than liberals. He theorizes that liberals focus on care and fairness while conservatives additionally value loyalty, authority, and sanctity. Haidt's contention is that the reason liberals and conservatives are unable to find common ground on so many issues, especially moral ones, is because liberals do not understand[9] the additional moral foundations valued by conservatives.

As a result, while liberals value social justice in the name of fairness and care for fellow humans, conservatives may take issue with that focus for a variety of morally justified reasons. They may see antiracism as challenging the authority inherent in existing social order. They may assess the actions of social justice protesters and advocates as disloyal to the United States. They also may take issue with progressive solutions to systemic racism like affirmative action on the grounds that they limit the liberty of employers and job-seeking White people, or that they are a violation of their interpretation of fairness as proportionality.

One element we all may need to consider is that the inequality in this country is what is hurting it. Conservatives and Republicans are fond of stating that we should move beyond race. One way to do this is to address income inequality. Heather McGhee (2021) explored convincingly how racism, including systemic racism, has hurt and will continue to hurt poor White people. Her example of how a pool being closed to prevent its integration reverberated through the decades and affected an entire community illustrates how local the politics of systemic racism can be. The unfortunate side effect of the political manifestation of conservativism is that, for a variety of reasons, it tends to uphold an unjust system. Not merely a system unjust to Black people or Latinos, or Indigenous peoples, or Vietnamese Americans. All Americans.

Overall, the Republican case for a humanistic, moral mandate against racism is a mixed bag. It is understandable that people of color, especially Black Americans, are hesitant to belong to a party that minimizes the importance of race in the persistent inequities they experience, on average. Some of the solutions Republican politicians offer have potential, but strenuous action against racism is not popular with the party's rank-and-file.

*The Republican Party is mostly White because it is willing to appeal to White voters with policies and language that hurt many Americans of color.* Whether it is winking at White supremacists, cutting programs that disproportionately help Americans of color, looking the other way while their most recent president spouted a variety of racial insults, discounting experiences of discrimination, or a distaste for discussing race, the Republican Party has created a minefield out of fertile ground to grow beyond their White base. Yet the Democratic party also has fumbled opportunities to build an antiracist consensus.

## NOTES

1. They refer to themselves as "alt-right," but many of these people talk about impending race wars and White "extinction," espouse White ethnic nationalism and antisemitism, and share views that would not be unwelcome at a Ku Klux Klan meeting. To my eye, Nazis don't get to rebrand themselves as something else.

2. The participants reported 44 percent Republican and 40 percent Democrats. The data were collected on MTurk.

3. Correlations: CoBRAS and White Vulnerability ($r$=0.64, $p$<.001); CoBRAS and SDO ($r$=0.52, $p$<.001).

4. Carlson is fond of playing dumb or pretending no one will answer his "simple" questions, so I will bite: why is this theory racist? First, it assumes that immigrants, largely those with brown skin, have no other reasons for coming to America than to

overthrow White people. Second, the theory assumes that immigration is automatically harmful to the American way, which implies that the American way is the way "you"—the older, almost entirely White audience—believes America should be. Third, it quite literally is a White supremacist tenet to assume that people of color are more "obedient" or "docile." There is a lengthy history of using these terms to demean and demarcate people of color in the United States, most notably Indigenous Americans and enslaved Black people. Perhaps most importantly, Carlson's and the theory's proponents' rhetoric provokes a fearful and angry reaction to the unnamed forces of demographic change—easily projected onto fellow Americans of color—which feeds racist and deadly actions like those the Buffalo shooter took.

5. Philpot conducted a content analysis of "Black and mainstream newspapers over the second half of the 20th century" (Gillespie 2022, 1). Content analysis applies structured methodology to identify and categorize themes of communication over time or across communicators within a defined range.

6. Roseanne Barr, for instance, was defended by no less than popular conservative personality Alex Jones, rocker Ted Nugent, World Series–winning pitcher Curt Schilling, and the chair of Students for Trump (Cummings 2018).

7. Additionally, during the time Black economic outcomes continued to fall, America entered a post-industrial age that displaced many of the Black workers who moved north for steady, blue-collar jobs during the Great Migration. As the economy moved away from a focus on industry and a livable wage and politicians altered tax codes to "relieve" the wealthy, inequality exacerbated. As could be assumed, Black families were hit hardest because they were already in the most vulnerable position, having little inherited wealth—a disadvantage that is a direct result of prior racism. For more detail on the economic shifts in the late twentieth century, see Levy (2021).

8. Variance estimates the amount of differences among the scores that can be explained using the variables included. In that way it is a measure of accuracy of an explanatory model.

9. "Moral Tribes" by Joshua Greene offers a thorough rebuttal to the conclusion Haidt draws from his research.

# Chapter 9

# The Democratic Party

## Anti-Racism and Its Discontents

*It is not just Negroes, but really it is all of us, who must overcome the crippling legacy of bigotry and injustice. And we shall overcome.*

—President Lyndon B. Johnson, March 15, 1965

*One thing I'm convinced of is that working-class White people and working-class Black people and Brown people have more in common with each other than they do with those who, in fact, downsize corporations—what they call right-size, or what some might call downsize—and out-source jobs.*

—Reverend Jesse Jackson, 1997

*White supremacy is a poison.*

—President Joe Biden, May 17, 2022

Having addressed the Republican Party's approach to racism, I turn to the Democratic Party. To what extent do Democratic approaches to race show the belief that Black lives matter? Embedded, but rarely directly stated, in progressive antiracism is an assumption that Americans feel empathy for one another. Analysis of prominent critiques of modern progressivism often misunderstand this approach as intending to create White guilt. I then analyze the missteps of so-called cancel culture considering the goal of shared humanity. I close with an analysis of the Democratic idea of racism from the perspective of a moral mandate to value humanity.

***

The first time much of the country heard the phrase Black Lives Matter was some time during the second term of President Barack Obama. Those attuned to Twitter may have seen Alicia Garza's statement, "Black people. I love you. I love us. Our lives matter," or the hashtag #blacklivesmatter from Patrisse Cullors, in response to George Zimmerman's acquittal in the murder of Trayvon Martin (Black Lives Matter 2021). Others may have seen it at gatherings in 2014 mourning the death in police custody of Eric Garner in New York or the shooting of Michael Brown in Ferguson, Missouri (Howard University 2022). During the second half of 2014, protests in connection with the slogan "Black Lives Matter" occurred in Minnesota, New York, and Washington, DC. By January 2015, *Essence* magazine had placed those three words on its cover (Goodridge 2016).

Black Lives Matter, as a concept and a social movement, was followed by backlash in the slogan "All Lives Matter." The meaning of this slogan has been debated (Baker 2020; Capatides 2020; Victor 2016), though its opposition to Black Lives Matter remains clear. Indeed, the support of an "all lives matter" approach may indicate something more than a preference for equal billing. Experiments by sociologist Keon West and colleagues (West, Greenland and van Laar 2021) found that participants' implicit racism predicted their level of support for "All Lives Matter." Support for the slogan also was related to a "narrow definition" of discrimination, which was one of the hallmarks of a right-wing approach to racism discussed in the previous chapter.

The widespread protests in the summer of 2020 were prominently linked to Black Lives Matter, resurrecting support for the movement. Washington, DC, added "Black Lives Matter Plaza" on Sixteenth Street with the words spanning two city blocks. BLM yard signs, business notices, and bumper stickers seemed ubiquitous. In June, Black Lives Matter peaked at 67 percent support (Horowitz 2021), an unfathomable level just years before.

As 2020 wore on, support for BLM again declined (Bellamy 2021). It may be that the protests provoked fatigue in some moderates and previously sympathetic White Americans. It cannot be ignored, though, that right-wing commentators (Gonzalez 2021; V. Hanson 2022; Quinton 2021; Ramirez 2020) played a role in linking the movement to hate, rioting, and "reverse racism." In 2022, Republican Florida governor Ron DeSantis signed what he called the "Stop Woke Act" (Brugal 2022) to fight the sort of "indoctrination" assumed to be the mission of BLM and the larger antiracist movement.

The growth and decline cycles of the movement are reflective of a larger pattern in American society, which can be described as a pendulum. Glibly put, every action provokes an opposite reaction. The reality is more complex, given that the forces of reaction often align with vested social power: a protest for change necessarily challenges entrenched systems and their inertia.

We saw this in the 1960s, when fatigue over fires and protests in Watts and widespread anti-war demonstrations fueled reactionary support of George Wallace and ushered Richard Nixon into the White House. The "post-racial" afterglow of Barack Obama's presidency was interrupted by the rise of Donald Trump. Even the Reconstruction of the post–Civil War South, earned in bloody combat and pursued in the name of reunifying America, was followed by a merciless Redemption. This is the pattern of racial justice in the United States.

So, do Black lives matter or not?

For what it is worth—and, considering the flagging popularity of the movement in the fall of 2020, it was worth something—the Democratic platform (Democratic National Committee 2020) announced clearly in its Preamble, "We believe Black lives matter." If that is so, then what is the Democratic Party's solution to modern racism?

## A PROGRESSIVE VISION OF RACISM

In the last half-decade, one of the most vocal proponents of progressive anti-racism has been Dr. Ibram X. Kendi.

Dr. Kendi founded the Center of Antiracist Research at Boston University. Kendi has also become a lightning rod for his strong antiracist statements, many of which can be found in his book *How to Be an Antiracist*. The book outlines his philosophy that racism is a system that is propped up by a majority of Americans, most of them White, who believe that by being "not racist" they are fighting racism. Meanwhile, the system never meaningfully changes, and it continues to reproduce harmful disparities for people of color in a wide range of areas.

Dr. Kendi's point about the operation of racist systems should not be controversial. After all, decades of research in sociology as well as economics, social psychology, and political science support the contention that racism is embedded in the functioning of various American systems. As detailed in Chapter 5, while the original racists who built the systems are long gone, and the worst of the outrages perpetrated by the system have been addressed by changes in policy, the disparities persist. Dr. Kendi himself masterfully traced the evolution of racist systems and thought by citing centuries of examples and data in his prior book, *Stamped from the Beginning.*

There are some weaknesses in the conclusions Dr. Kendi draws from this information, true. But it does not feel like the backlash aimed at him over the last year is rooted in logical and principled objections. In writing from the center-left and from the right (e.g., Chait 2020; Douthat 2021; Rufo 2021; The Economist 2021) during that time, the objection appears to be more about what Kendi symbolizes. Dr. Kendi is the antiracism movement in its ascendance during mid-2020 and, if the critics are to be believed, its excesses since. As such, critiques of his work often evince frustration with progressive approaches to racism writ large. Some of these critiques, though, merit discussion.

Among the critics of Kendi's approach who took the time to spell out real objections is journalist Eric Levitz (2021a). One issue Levitz presents is Kendi's focus on communities, especially the "White community." By Kendi's telling, White people should be aware of their shared Whiteness because that helps hold each White person accountable for solving the social problems begun by prior White actors and they themselves perpetuate by lack of action as voters and social beings. This is the keystone of Dr. Kendi's antiracism: it cannot simply be people of color working for change; White people as the majority in the country and potential stakeholders in racial equality must be motivated to act.

This is sound reasoning. However, it requires a stronger sense of White identity, that is, White people must be aware of their Whiteness to acknowledge their inherited share in the pain caused to Americans of color. This poses some problems, as outlined by Ashley Jardina in *White Identity Politics*. She found increased White consciousness to be related to actions protecting Whiteness. Given White Americans' numerical plurality and outsize role controlling powerful corporations and government, stronger White identification could create problems for Americans of color.

For example, when the economy was down, threats to Whiteness did not motivate an examination of inequality. Instead, threats motivated scapegoating Latinos, which contributed greatly to support for Donald Trump in 2016. As Jardina (2019, 268) puts it, "The politics of White identity is marked by an insidious illusion, one in which Whites claim their group experiences discrimination in an effort to reinforce and maintain a system of racial inequality."

Kendi's definition of racism is much more expansive than the Republican version, and probably more expansive than the mainstream Democratic one. As noted in the second section of this book, there are decades of social science to support the notion that racism is something more than the actions of individuals, if we consider as racist all things that disproportionately hurt people of color by virtue of being people of color. This is the foundation of the Democratic Party's recent antiracist efforts. Kendi's definition, if I am reading it correctly, is that everything that results in racial inequity is racist. The subtle difference has been a point of contention in presenting his case (Klein 2021; Snyder 2021).

Kendi's reasoning for this definition, it should be noted, is not often addressed in critiques of his work. When I heard him speak at San Diego State (right before the pandemic shut down such gatherings), he explained that part of the rationale for his expansive definition of racism is to generate support for actions that will reduce racial disparities. This does align with a moral mandate against racism because it centers the humanity of the suffering. However, the shock of Kendi's approach, in which racism seems to be everywhere, is often too much for even some on the left (e.g., Chait 2020; Levitz 2021a).

As such, it may be so that Kendi's antiracism is ahead of its time, politically speaking. It also may be so that it accurately reflects reality for Americans of color.

## Morality, the Scope of Racism, and Personal Responsibility

The mainstream Democratic case against racism, based on the recent support for Black Lives Matter, party policy priorities, and the party platform in 2020, is somewhere to the right of Kendi, but well to the left of the Republicans' "bad apples" version. Regardless of the differences, if we cannot abide the conceptual shift from the interpersonal to the systemic, we are stuck. A limited definition of racism has great moral weight—it literally impugns the morality of every single actor who behaves in a racist manner—but it does not account for the expansive disparities experienced by Americans of color, many of which cannot be traced back to immoral individuals.

On the other hand, if we accept that racism can be perpetuated without intention, then there is a risk of diminishing the advantage of moral weight. Why should I change my behavior if it isn't intentionally hurting anyone? How is it morally wrong? The rub, of course, is that there are plenty of "unintentional" behaviors that do hurt people of color, such as implicit biases that advantage "White" names in the hiring process and voting for politicians advocating policies that happen to hurt people of color most. A strong argument can be made that, once a person becomes aware of the consequences of their actions, they should take those into account before repeating that behavior. What is unintentional has become intentional.

Let's consider that process with a low-stakes example. Let's suppose my wife and I have pet names for one another. We've used these since our time dating, and calling my wife by this name reminds me of an innocent and exciting time in our lives. If my wife tells me that she has decided that she doesn't like when I use this pet name—maybe she is tired of it, or she never liked it—what do I do?

Well, I can choose to keep using the name. It's a habit that reminds me of happy days, and I didn't mean any harm in the first place. Or I can consider that my choices, which I thought only involved me, were affecting her. Furthermore, though I would be losing something by giving up the name, I am *taking more* from her if I don't change, which is not fair. In light of this new information, if I don't change, I am intentionally ignoring how my words hurt my wife while claiming I didn't mean to. A more direct interpretation is that to continue my behavior after learning its effects is wrong.

Of course, for me to attend to any of this assumes I have empathy for my wife. (I do!) But this is not the case when people exclude those they see as members of an outgroup from being part of their "moral community." The concept of a moral community, explored by Jonathan Haidt in *The Righteous Mind*, is connected to moral capital, the resources that enable groups to suppress selfish impulses for the greater good of the community. The moral community is the group whom we believe shares our values and to whom our morality applies.

The repercussions of a moral community are starkest when considering well-defined outgroups such as distant nations with traditions that diverge greatly. From the perspective of many Christian conservatives in the United States, the traditions of devoted Muslims in Asia and Africa conflict with those valued in America. The panic associated with "Sharia law" that gripped a portion of the conservative American populace in the early 2010s (Lemons and Chambers-Leston 2014; Serwer 2011) is partially a function of the belief that law based on an outgroup morality would threaten the integrity of the United States' moral community.

Similarly, moral exclusion theory (Opotow 1990; 1995) posits that justice only applies to those within our moral community. Those who are excluded are "beyond our moral concerns" (Opotow, Gerson and Woodside 2005, 305), thus our motive to include, and empathize with, them is minimal. Researchers of moral exclusion theory have found robust international support for its influence (e.g., Hadarics 2020; Passini and Villano 2018). Psychology researcher Jesse Brinson (2011) has applied moral exclusion theory to racism, concluding that some Americans ignore the harm policies can do to people of color because those Americans see people of color as outside the boundaries of true justice.

History and research (e.g., Brinson 2011; Opotow et al. 2005; Pilecki 2017) show us that it is only by building bridges between groups that we can feel concern for one another's well-being. Such a process creates moral inclusion. For the process to succeed, it must be sustained and meaningful. It cannot rest on the tokenism of trumpeting exceptions, nor can it echo the fleeting, widespread support for BLM in 2020. Sustainable moral inclusion requires sacrifices from some, but it leads to outcomes that maximize the potential of this country.

To expand a moral community means extending humanity to those who disagree. That, as history has shown, is one way to higher ground. Modern Democratic politicians demonstrate a belief that Black lives matter. Their statements on social justice show humanity and moral inclusion. Their support of social safety net programs, such as the Affordable Care Act and Medicaid, that help disproportionately disadvantaged Black Americans are tangible attempts to value Black lives. Through the progressive wing has been more willing to promise reforms to the carceral and legal systems, both of which produce racially disparate outcomes, this zeal for justice has come under fire.

## THE SAME OLD SONG

The epithet probably most used to attack the left's social justice efforts is "woke." As noted earlier, "woke" started as Black slang that eventually made its way into the mainstream and was twisted into something else. Though many White people today would consider it caricature to proclaim themselves "woke," voices on the political right have been mocking the term since at least 2018 (Douthat 2018) and have expanded its umbrella, much like they did CRT, to include any earnest-seeming social justice effort (Doescher 2021; Reuters 2022; Robinson 2022; Sabes 2022).

One of the sharpest and most extended critiques of supposed "wokeness" has come from within the Democratic Party, in John McWhorter's (2021) book *Woke Racism*. McWhorter is a linguist and writer who frequently publishes his opinions in the *New York Times*. He also is a Black man, a self-identified cranky liberal, who serves as a voice for racial conservatism.[1]

I got a curious feeling reading McWhorter's complaints about leftist approaches to racism, which boils down to his problem with a group he calls "the Elect." McWhorter says the Elect decide how we talk about race in America. The Elect are the adherents of what McWhorter calls third-wave antiracism, which is focused on systemic racism and White complicity. McWhorter scores some solid points against the antiracist left, especially in the rush of some online vigilantes to cost people jobs, provoke resignations, and share sensitive information about those who transgress the "confusing and contradictory" tenets of modern antiracism. The curious feeling as I read McWhorter's "can you believe this crazy shit"–style anecdotes was emptiness: his critique was not so much an articulation of a moderate view on racism as it was a return of fire against the excesses of antiracism.

In McWhorter's (2022a, 2022b) recent writing on systemic racism, he questions the impulse behind liberals spreading the message that racism is at fault for the sort of racial disparities documented in Chapter 5. This is a central complaint about "wokeness." As he (McWhorter 2022b) puts it, "Why are we supposed to care whether they—meaning non-Black people—know it isn't our fault?" The reason, though, is covered in Chapter 6, in dozens of books, and hundreds of political science, psychological, and sociological experimental studies.[2]

Talking about racism, stigmatizing systemic racism, matters because the people who deny racism exists—who haven't gotten the "message" about racism—tend to be the same who vote reliably conservative. And the representatives elected by these voters are the same people who tend to stand in the way of repairing racial disparities, if not actively creating discrimination through gerrymandering and other shenanigans. This is not about a handful of openly racist jackasses getting elected to Congress. It starts at the local level, and it's on display in the results of every single election. We talk about today's racism to spread awareness and, ideally, give people more to think about when in the voting booth.

McWhorter (2021), though, contends that the conversation about race is a false goal. He believes it is a trick meant to enforce leftist "religion" of antiracism without engaging in an actual exchange of ideas. It is, of course, possible that many on the left do not want to hear what conservatives, especially White conservatives, have to say about racism. He is correct to warn that antiracist zeal could restrict honesty from the right during such a dialogue.

What is missing, though, is the historical context. There are reasons there hasn't been a conversation about race, and they have little to do with the current "woke" movement. They are rooted in the political expediency of appealing to White grievance. There was no conclusion to the conversation on race in the 1960s because Richard Nixon and George Wallace both found ways to benefit from derailing it. The backlash to today's racial reckoning is stronger than McWhorter gives credence.

Still, racial liberals and antiracists should want to listen to what those with opposing views have to say. That is an honest conversation about race. Too often what deniers of modern or systemic racism have to say is obscured by louder, more extreme voices on the right who are satisfied with the racial status quo and do not see the need for any conversation. It may be that racial liberals, due to their deep moral objections to racism and those who support it, have a hard time hearing what conservatives have to say. There is much to be gained from engaging conservatives on race, starting with that fundamental aspect of conversation: acknowledgment of the humanity of the other person and the validity of that person's opinions.

## THE HEART OF LIBERAL ANTIRACISM

I work on my university's Inclusion and Equity Council (IEC). I suppose I am not much different from the millions of Americans who decided to do something for racial justice in 2020 and since. True, a work committee can only change so much about the world. It is another drop in the bucket, ranking somewhere below community organizing and above changing your Twitter handle.

The IEC has members who come from a wide variety of backgrounds, and that includes a substantial number of White people. This is good, not just because I'm happy to see White people care. It's good because people of color shouldn't be asked to singlehandedly solve racial problems that affect everyone. It's also good because working toward a common goal should bring people of different backgrounds together.

When I think about committees like mine cropping up across this country, I am reminded how empathy, such an important factor in healing the racial divide, can take different forms. Empathy does not need to mean crying because you feel someone else's pain. Empathy does not need to be righteous anger at injustice done to a fellow human being. It can be what you do, how you spend your time, why you are in the room.

Back in Chapter 1, I wrote about Jonathan Haidt's (2001, 2012) Moral Foundations Theory. Haidt believes liberals base their morality on care and fairness, while conservatives tend to have what he sees as a more multifaceted morality, also founded on loyalty, authority, and purity. The singlemindedness of the people snidely maligned as "social justice warriors" reflects a morally justified dedication to fairness. They care about their fellow Americans. One may quibble with the methods they choose, but it is hard to question their resolve.

A group of researchers (Hasson et al. 2018) examined whether liberals differ from conservatives in their motivation to feel empathy for others. Considering the antiracist uprising in 2020 and since, it is not surprising this question was asked. But in the context of political psychology, there is a long tradition of research showing political ideologies are related to personality profiles, on average (e.g., Adorno, Frenkel-Brunswik, Levinson and Sanford 1950; Linder and Nosek 2009; Saucier and Cawman 2004; Settle, Dawes, Christakis and Fowler 2010).

The results show that liberals overall were more motivated than conservatives to experience empathy (Hasson et al. 2018). The authors propose that the identity of a liberal or progressive is tied to empathy; liberals value social goals, which empathy promotes by cuing liberals to the welfare of others. They conclude that liberals experienced empathy more deeply and connected it to a greater willingness to help others. These differences were related to liberal values. This does not mean that conservatives are not empathetic, just that the liberal focus on transcending the self in the name of the group motivates expressions of empathy even when it takes a lot of effort or there is low external incentive to help.

How do liberals develop this sense of empathy, particularly White liberals' empathy toward people of color? Educational researcher Chris Linder (2015) interviewed a group of college-aged White feminists who considered themselves antiracist to learn about their process of developing that identity. Based on the interviews, Linder identified a common process of working through guilt, fear, anger, and defensiveness about their White identity. What stands out is that a major part of transitioning from experiencing empathy to taking action was these women recognizing their White privilege. Rather than being weighed down by guilt, as some on the right assume is the case, they were motivated to use that privilege for good.

An interesting feature of the process Linder identified was that it is cyclical. These women moved from confidence and activity back to guilt, shame, and fear of seeming racist. Building an antiracist identity, for them, was not a virtue-signaling choice for their personal benefit; it was a struggle. Linder concluded that White antiracists should share their personal struggles to normalize them. This has the effect of reducing the feelings of isolation and "doing it wrong," echoing the imposter syndrome so many experience in their twenties.

These findings illustrate that racism does not just hurt people of color; it hurts White people too. James Baldwin famously wrote about the insecurity of Whiteness, the need to "create the Negro" for White people to build a sense of self. Racist systems benefit White Americans through increased access to social resources, educational opportunities, and a sense that one's worldview is supported by the majority culture in the country. But there are costs hidden in this bargain: anger and fear of people of color, sadness and helplessness about the existence of racism, guilt and shame, and a profound ambivalence.

Lisa Spainerman and Mary Heppner (2004) developed the Psychosocial Costs of Racism to Whites (PCRW) scale to measure the impact of societal racism on White people. Spainerman and Heppner have found that racism distorts White people's view of self, others, and reality as well as limiting their relationships to others by proscribing acceptable behavior. This includes discouragement from engaging meaningfully with people of color and disconnection from other Whites, such as pressure to stay silent in the face of racism. Their scale has three factors: White empathy, White guilt, and White fear of others.

Spainerman and colleagues (2006) tested the PRCW scale to see what these factors indicate about common ways in which White people interact with racism. Their work resulted in five clusters: unempathetic and unaware, empathetic but unaccountable, fearful guilt, insensitive and afraid, and informed empathy and guilt. The last group is most likely to produce antiracists, given the high empathetic reaction, high levels of racial awareness and cultural sensitivity, and high likelihood of interracial friendships. This cluster is also the least commonly found.

Kathleen Kordesh teamed up with Lisa Spainerman and Helen Neville (cocreator of the CoBRAS scale discussed in previous chapters) to look more closely at students in this "informed empathy and guilt" group. They compared their interview results to interviews held with students drawn from the other cluster groups. Overall, they found that the antiracist group had a more nuanced and complex understanding of racism and a commitment to action for social justice. Much like Linder's work, Kordesh and colleagues found that the antiracist participants often felt like helpless outsiders.

Empathy, especially in the case of racism, is not about being soft. When translated into action, empathy carries with it experiences of disillusion and isolation and the pain of witnessing members of one's moral community face injustice. This, too, is what is asked of people of color when they are marginalized: anticipate the other's perspective, fight through your isolation. For White people to experience this alike goes beyond idle posturing to the heart of the left's most honest path to effectively combat racism.

## GUILT AND FRAGILITY

The widespread antiracist movement in 2020 predictably produced negative reactions from racial conservatives and other White Americans (e.g., Brown 2021; Glaser 2020; Zhao 2021). Any discussion of this backlash would be lacking without two words: White fragility.

In 2018, educator and consultant Robin DiAngelo published a book, entitled *White Fragility*, about the defensiveness of White people when challenged about racism. The book is rooted in stories about the behavior she observed among White participants in her over two decades of experience leading diversity seminars. DiAngelo terms the anger (usually from men) and tears (usually from women) in response to challenges in these meetings as "White fragility."

Though DiAngelo's work has been held up as all that is wrong (e.g., Bejan 2020; Cooper 2020; Levitz 2021b; McWhorter 2020) with "woke ideology," to the extent such a thing exists, it should be noted that the book is not intended to be self-congratulatory. She holds herself and fellow White liberals accountable for causing daily pain to Black people. White liberals are more likely to interact with people of color and have diverse friend groups. In those interactions, White liberals tend to get a little too comfortable in discussing race. DiAngelo's follow-up book, *Nice Racism*, addressed the ways in which White liberals unintentionally hurt people of color and perpetuate White dominance in social interactions.

DiAngelo's work, like Kendi's, has attracted conservative frustration and, occasionally, bile. The rapid-fire bills coming out of multiple states in 2021 and 2022 outlawing discussion of race or "making White people feel guilty" (Craig 2022) are a clear reaction to DiAngelo-style workplace seminars on race.

As noted earlier, conservatives express a great deal of concern about whether White people are being made to feel guilty. The conservative-liberal debate on antiracist education can be characterized as White people being told to feel bad versus White people receiving information they are not used to receiving. This illustrates the ideological disconnect within the "conversation about race," particularly when it turns to the role of White Americans.

The objection that DiAngelo idealizes the views of people of color while doubting those of White people is not without foundation. True, in DiAngelo's work and in other liberal thought, the approach to discussions about race is to trust the experiences of people of color (e.g., Christian, Seamster and Ray 2019; Heilig, Brown and Brown 2012; Taylor 1998). This is not only because of the concern among liberals that voices of color historically have been marginalized. It also is because people of color experience discriminatory systems differently than White people. Decades of data show the average American of color reports categorically different experiences within American social systems.

There is some experimental research showing that some methods of liberal antiracism can unintentionally contradict its goals. Matthew Hughey (2012) has studied how White antiracists manage their racial identity. Hughey conducted an ethnographic study, embedding himself with a White antiracist organization through fieldwork and conducting interviews and content analysis of the group's newsletter. Hughey found that the members of the group were attracted to understandings of Whiteness that stigmatized it, while their antiracist identity was stigmatized within White Americans.

The group members managed the double stigma of their White identity by showing their moral conviction against racism through their language and activism. But they were not immune to tropes of colorblind racism, such as the impulse to distinguish themselves from other White people, whom they imply are racist. In interviews they sometimes objectified people of color, such as when they bragged about having non-White friends. These assertions of authenticity and courage were attempts to manage the stigma they felt.

Do these behind-closed-doors behaviors leak out to harm people of color? Social psychologists Cydney Dupree and Susan Fisk (2019) find that White liberals may still hold stereotypical views about Black people. They conducted a series of experiments pairing White participants with a partner to study "impression management." Impression management is the adjustment of one's presentation to fit assumed expectations of one's interaction partner. For example, managing impressions of my intelligence can mean using technical terminology in discussions with colleagues. I might dial up the expanse of my vocabulary in a conversation with someone I want to impress. Or I might dial it down.

What Dupree and Fisk measured was "competence downshift," the attempt to appear less competent based on assumptions about a conversation partner. When they manipulated the race of the conversation partner, they found that White liberals in four different situations used less "competence words"—words rated high on a competence scale—with Black partners. When given the chance to rate their goals for interaction with a Black partner, White liberals reported intending to appear less competent. Throughout these studies, conservatives usually made no such shift in their approach. As the authors put it, "Ironically, those who are less explicitly antagonistic toward minorities may be more likely to display such indirect forms of bias, drawing on negative stereotypes" (601).

White liberals might be surprised to hear that their best intentions to combat racism can hurt people of color.[3] Even awareness of White privilege, which is intended to aid White people in understanding the perspectives of people of color and encourage introspection, can backfire in unforeseen ways. A group of social psychologists (Cooley, Brown-Iannuzzi, Lei and Cipolli 2019) studied how liberal beliefs about White people were affected by knowledge of White privilege. The researchers contend that the lessons of White privilege often do not delineate the important difference between White people *on average* and individual White people. This difference, when ignored, can lead to faulty assumptions about every White person.

The researchers had participants in two groups read about White privilege, then read a story about a man who was poor, was unemployed, and had served time in jail. One group's protagonist was White, and the other's was Black. Social liberals reported significantly less sympathy for the White man, yet social conservatives reported no sympathy difference. When participants did not read about White privilege first, social liberals reported higher sympathy overall for the protagonist, leading the authors to conclude that, "among social liberals, the effect of learning about White privilege is to decrease sympathy for poor White people rather than to increase sympathy for poor Black people" (Cooley et al. 2019, 2224).

For some, the increased focus on White privilege is having unintended effects: rather than increasing empathy for all people, this knowledge of the system discourages sympathy for poor White people. That is a problem that can be solved by discussing White privilege in ways that still value the humanity of White Americans. The real struggles of poor or disadvantaged White people do not need to be discounted in describing how racist systems work. Racism is an evil that is imposed beyond the other stressors and impediments of life. It benefits White people *relatively*, not *absolutely*. That doesn't make it any less wrong, nor does it mean it doesn't also hurt White people indirectly.

## ON CONSEQUENCES AND CANCELLATIONS

Empathy cuts both ways. For every example of the deep empathy of liberals for those within their moral community, we all have read of the examples of liberal rigidity toward social conservatives, the outwardly religious, and Trump supporters. When empathy is focused on one's ingroup, it often takes the form of protectiveness that results in aggression toward the group's competitors (Buffone and Poulin 2014). This is played out daily via political posts on Twitter and Facebook, and perhaps the less said about those "discussions," the better.

Which brings us, at long last, to cancel culture.

Cancellation is crowdsourcing via digital media to hold people responsible for their actions, most prominently racially insensitive behavior. When someone is caught acting in an offensive manner, people can "cancel" the offender. Canceling can be as simple as saying someone is cancelled (and not doing much about it) or as complicated as pressuring the offender's employer or sponsors to punish them.

From the perspective of the left, cancel culture is overblown and, when it does exist, it would be more appropriate to call it "consequence culture."[4] According to the political right, cancel culture is a very big deal, it is very effective, and we all should be very afraid of it. "Cancel culture" can be categorized with "woke" and "critical race theory" as terms that have become symbolized.[5] When I say symbolized, I mean that the terms have gained additional features beyond their literal meaning. In Walter Stephan and Cookie Stephan's (2000) "integrated threat theory" of prejudice, realistic threats, symbolic threats, intergroup anxiety, and negative stereotypes predict attitudes between White and Black people. Stephan and colleagues (2002) found the salience of symbolic threat led to stereotyping and discrimination.

Symbolic threats are conditions that transform differences into hostility toward an outgroup. Something becomes a symbolic threat when people believe it challenges their sense of group identity. These threats are related to perceived differences in what the other group values, their cultural essence. Ibram Kendi and Robin DiAngelo pose symbolic threats to racial conservatives. They aren't harming White people literally, but they do threaten the American assumptions of equality and colorblindness that many White people value.

Cancel culture acts as both a realistic and a symbolic threat to dominance of Whiteness. It is a realistic threat to the extent that White Americans fear aggressive reprisals such as job loss for saying or doing the "wrong thing" about race. It is a symbolic threat to some White Americans because protection of people of color upends the assumed prerogative and power of White Americans. I say all of this to note the threat to *some* White Americans. Many White Americans do not feel threatened by the consequences befalling some of cancel culture's "victims." But other Americans, not just racial conservatives, may feel threatened because they cannot make good-faith[6] statements about race without fearing, justifiably or not, excessive consequences. Some of these Americans would like to engage in the racial conversation. It is a loss to all of us if they are scared off by the symbolic omnipotence of cancel culture.

Writer Ligaya Mishan (2020) composed a thorough history of cancel culture, starting with the concept of a scapegoat, which stands in for something injurious to society. An important point she makes is that the vigilantism of online harassment is an indicator that we have lost faith in our institutions to uphold the good. It is the utter failure of the government to make significant progress on racism since the 1960s—in some cases, even rolling back previous successes such as protections in the Voting Rights Act—that has spurred some modern progressives to take the process into their own hands.

It is questionable how much power cancellations have. Musician R. Kelly, famously convicted of sexual exploitation of a child, saw staggering sales and streaming increases of his music after the verdict (Blake 2021). Comedian Dave Chappelle, who has embraced his supposed cancellation (Gardner 2021), continues to be able to set his own rates and produce widely viewed content. The one high-profile cancellation that has stuck actually cost rapper and businessman Kanye "Ye" West millions for trumpeting antisemitic beliefs in 2022. But Ye engaged in years of foolishness on race in public, with the attendant Twitter cancellations, with little damage to his bottom line.

When focused on the less powerful, though, cancel culture functions like "broken windows policing," the aggressive focus on relatively minor violations that former New York mayor Rudy Giuliani credits with reductions in violent crime during his tenure. As Mishan notes, his approach brought us the discrimination and abuse of "stop and frisk" just as cancel culture has moved from an attempt to address a greater societal ill to personalized attacks. John McWhorter is correct in *Woke Racism*, though vague about the scope, when he maligns cancel culture as costing people jobs for what are often minor reasons. Many of these violations should be grist for the mill of a racial conversation, but absent that oft-delayed goal, some frustrated racial progressives have opted for "cancelling."

Perhaps the strongest point Mishan makes is that this focus on punitiveness absolves the guilty from introspection. Remember, introspection is a central function of behavioral change. You must recognize your error so you know what you should change. Cancel culture's "victims," feeling unfairly targeted, have been put in jail without a trial. After everyone has forgotten, the punished are free to come back the same. And why not? They were never asked to consider the extent they contributed to their situation.

The focus of modern cancel culture, too, is troubling. Forcefully changing the norms on appropriate public speech surrounding race can ease the indignities visited on people of color as hate speech is further and further marginalized. But does getting someone fired for making a flippant, though offensive, remark help people of color in a meaningful way? Possibly, but just around the edges.

Imagine you are in a relationship. Your partner is a spendthrift who uses up almost all your money, and you are unable to get this person to stop. Putting all our moral weight on cancelling is the equivalent of meticulously couponing and examining your budget for ways to save a few cents. Sure, you are making a change, but you are prevented from making the most important one, and every change you do make gets harder to maintain without backslide. In the end, what have we really done here?

***

Having reviewed the Republican case for a moral mandate on racism that values humanity, how does the Democratic version compare? Again, there are two parts to the evaluation, how racism is defined and how it is addressed. The Democratic Party has embraced the conclusion of social science and the voices of people of color that racism is embedded in the American system. This definition has a rockier path to moral weight because there are no implied immoral actors; in fact, people operating within a racist system may not be hurting anyone intentionally. As a result, messaging and education become crucial elements to building an antiracist coalition. It is not surprising that Democrats are more likely to support the cultural sensitivity trainings and literature Republicans tend to distrust.

The Democrats are on more solid, moral ground in how they address racism. Their more comprehensive proposed solutions align with an empathetic view of the suffering of fellow Americans. For example, their pursuit of equitable hiring and promotion measures directly addresses a major hindrance to Americans of color. Likewise, their support for a strong social safety net assists the disproportionate number of Americans of color below the poverty line. The only weakness in their approach is that their proposals risk being agnostic, potentially antagonistic, regarding the humanity of White Americans. Other parts of their extensive antiracism program, such as debates over terminology, and overzealous offshoots, such as some "cancellations," risk breaking up an antiracist coalition before it can form.

The stated belief of the Democratic Party is that Black lives matter. By logical extension, they should believe that the lives of all the marginalized matter as well. It is this sort of "big tent" that makes the Democratic Party appealing to Americans of color, especially Black Americans. What should not be overlooked, though, is the role of the Republican Party in driving Black Americans away. *Democrats and progressives demonstrate empathy in how they address racism, yet they risk driving people of color away*, too, if the trend toward antiracist illiberalism is not honestly handled.

Overall, much like the Republicans, the Democratic case for a humanistic, moral mandate against racism is a mixed bag. Democrats do place people of color front and center. They are not rolling out the junior varsity squad to argue about "Blacks leaving the plantation" the way Republicans occasionally do. The last two Democratic presidencies featured a person of color on the ticket. The Democratic Party is poised to grow, especially as the population balance shifts away from groups that traditionally support the Republican Party, which provides more opportunities to represent voices of color.

If the Americans who support these parties are interested in a future without racism, for whatever their ideological reasons, they must be willing to communicate, listen, and value one other. Otherwise, we risk the same cycle of progress and backlash that has left us stranded, short of higher ground.

## NOTES

1. I venture that, as a linguist, McWhorter would not embrace the label "racial conservative." But his views on race, especially the criticism he reserves for the antiracist left, are of the racial conservative bent, even as he directly rejects old-fashioned racist viewpoints.

2. McWhorter (2022b) also asks those explaining systemic racism to bring their "A game," which I agree with. We should be able to back up everything we say, especially in something as important as this, which is something not every antiracist does. However, I would be highly skeptical of anyone who thinks social science research does not thoroughly bring an "A game" to documenting the operation of systemic racism and the downstream effects of racism denial.

3. This is not surprising to DiAngelo, who wrote about it in both of her books, though that theme tends to be ignored in criticism of her work.

4. A strong case can be made for this point of view. However, I will proceed in calling this phenomenon "cancel culture," if only because that is the way it is labeled in most public discourse.

5. These terms also originated among people of color, but their meanings were eventually coopted and weaponized by conservatives.

6. I say "good faith" intentionally here. I do not include people smugly "just asking questions" to avoid responsibility for their behavior. Nor do I include people using complaints about cancel culture as cover to prod and hurt others. The systems of thought underlying racial conservatism deserve to be discussed openly and exposed to honest counterpoints. That cannot be done while the equivalent of misbehaving children are demanding attention.

# Conclusion

*Must the sword devour forever? Do you not know that afterward there will be bitterness? How long before you tell the people to stop pursuing their brothers?*

—Second Book of Samuel, 2:26

Have you ever watched a balloon fly away?

I have four children, three of them at what I would consider peak balloon age. They cannot turn down a balloon (who can?), but just as importantly they want to hang on to it as long as they can. The problem is that helium balloons seem to want to get away. I've tied a lot of balloons to a lot of wrists, but I have yet to see one make it to the end of the day.

If it gets away, you have just a few moments to get it back before it's off on the skyward journey to its eventual disappearance. You can settle in and watch it fly away, which can feel both sad and peaceful. Or you can reach out to grab the string.

The moment we had in 2020 with buy-in from so many in this country to end racism is a precious balloon. It is slipping away. We must grab the string while we can.

We cannot agree on much about racism, even what its definition is, but at least we agree it is wrong, morally so. After seeing life's breath leave the earthly form of George Floyd, enough of us—Americans, together—were moved to give or march or fight after we were done crying, gasping, shaking our heads. As time drags us further away from that moment we shared, the old forces of division have reclaimed their places in our lives. The old reasons to think of this as a "we and they" thing, instead of an "everybody" thing, are sinking in. As we have seen, this is not new. This is what happens in America. It isn't because America or Americans are fundamentally bad, but it is what happens here, and if we want it to stop, it is going to take our collective Will. Not Blue Will or Red Will, Black Will or White Will, White

169

Collar Will or Blue Collar Will, Coastal Elite Will or Rural Commonsense Will. American Will.

In the first section of this book, you read about the importance of the moralization of racism to the struggle against it. You read about the century and a half of racial politics that saw the end of slavery, the rise of Southern White grievance, the weaponization of laws, and the emotional manipulation politicians used to beat back racial progress at every turn. You read about the value of an honest, moral accounting of American history, including psychological reasons many Americans oppose it. This was the legacy we have inherited.

In the second section of the book, you read about the very real impact of racism on Americans of color in almost every phase of their lives. You read about the ways a Post-Racial Lie has cloaked the ways access to American Dream has been stifled for people of color. You read about why defining *racism* is important, both psychologically and scientifically; how something that isn't old-fashioned racism yet isn't just politics is poisoning our relationships with one another. This is the challenge we face.

In the third section of the book, you read about the complicated motivations underlying voting behavior, including the damage we cause by underestimating one another's humanity. You read about how the Republican Party's approach to ending racism is undercut by the party's condoning of White nationalism. You read about the Democratic Party's struggles to coalesce on an empathetic, antiracist approach with broad appeal. This is the fork in the road.

It is obvious that racism didn't come from nowhere, it is real, and the odds are that you and everyone you know have been hurt by it. Racism impedes not only the progress of people of color, but also, for example, the economic growth of a country in desperate need of new contributors and innovation yet loath to reform the immigration process. Racism impairs—differentially, but impairs nonetheless—the mental health of Americans of color and White Americans through guilt, confusion, self-doubt, anger, depression, anxiety, fear, and the weight of unfair assumptions.

Racism affects every American because even bringing it up provokes an emotional reaction. It is not merely a problem, but a crisis of American identity.

Recalling Chapter 6's discussion of social norms, there is a norm that racism is morally wrong. However, there is no established norm for what now qualifies as racism. There was a norm as recently as the Civil Rights Era; more and more White people acknowledge that norm through the declining endorsement of Jim Crow racism. During the same time the norm grew in power, for example, the economic situation for Black Americans sputtered, Black incarceration rates skyrocketed, and the advent of the internet unleashed new, anonymous ways to spread hate. This is the same disconnect that compelled many researchers to investigate the possibility of an evolved form of racism, one that obeys the post–Jim Crow anti-racism norm but serves the purpose of maintaining the social order, with Black Americans stuck at the bottom and most other Americans of color not far above.

It is important to have the moral weight of racism because that means that people without personal stakes involved are motivated to fight against it. But it is just as important to clarify the reasons for the moral weight; otherwise, it feels to some like the goalposts have been moved. This is the double-edged sword of morality. For example, racial resentment, whether you consider it racism or not, sure seems to have a lot to do with why policies that keep hurting people of color get passed, why systems that fail us haven't been fixed, and why certain public figures are able to gain influence in this country. A light must be shined on the human costs of an immoral state of affairs.

Some of this is getting worse. Since 2014, domestic terrorism has been on the rise.[1] Most of the domestic terror attacks in the United States come from far-right, White supremacy groups, and those are the attacks most likely to be lethal (Doxsee et al. 2022). Alarmingly, this violence has been met by a rise in far-left terrorism starting in 2020. Far-left terrorism is less likely to be race-related, though reported motives include Black nationalism.

Hate crimes are on the rise against Americans of color. The democratizing of media has given lie to the idea that old-fashioned racism is a thing of the past. Individual accounts of interpersonal racism, the sort most Americans agree is immoral, are available every day on social media, and occasionally in mainstream media. Even the "easy part," reducing naked bigotry through the progress of social norms, is getting harder.

None of what was discussed in Chapters 4 and 5 is going away if we pretend it isn't a problem. Black American women aren't going to have better odds of giving birth to full-term, healthy babies. American children of color aren't going to get better educational experiences. They aren't going to be allowed to act their own age rather than being sexualized or feared. As young adults, they won't be free from the relentless nicks and cuts of being treated as an interloper instead of a person. As older adults, they won't pass down to their children a lifetime of saved wealth. The cycle will continue.

Americans of color can't be fully free of racism's shadow until we confront it. White Americans will benefit from decreased politicization of the social safety net and immigration; they will be freed from irrational fears of fellow Americans who look differently from themselves. The stranglehold racism has on the American Dream must, and can, be broken.

\*\*\*

When I started training to be a counseling psychologist, back in my first year of graduate school, I didn't know anything.

I mean, I knew some psychology, and I had a vague concept of what therapy was. But I didn't know the first thing about how to do what I was there to do. There were many days when I woke up and planned on just sitting silently in that counseling office, in that chair, halfway across the room from another person in another chair while they talked about their troubles. Best to keep my fool mouth shut, let them vent, and run out the clock.

The first important thing I learned, and I had to keep relearning and haven't stopped learning since, was how to *listen*. Technique aside, theory aside, I needed to learn how to listen all over again.

It is often said that listening is more than waiting for your turn in a conversation. That is patience. Patience, too, is nice. But my patience alone can't help you. Listening is going past the words the person is saying to reach the message. If you listen well enough, you show you can be trusted. If you show you can be trusted, the other person might even open up enough to give you what you need to understand. To make it to this point, you must be real.

In beginning counseling courses, I talk to the students about "first date behavior." This is your polished-up, best-foot-forward version of yourself. You're trying to impress. That behavior might get you somewhere, like on a second date, if that is what you are looking for. If you are looking for a relationship—for understanding—sooner or later you are going to have to start being real. Otherwise, you face the prospect of having to keep up an act while you wonder if you're in a relationship with someone who doesn't like you for who you are. Can you trust that relationship?

From the counseling perspective, listening helps us develop a relationship with the client. It was not until I learned to listen, instead of trying to show what I knew or panicking over whether I knew anything at all, that I began to connect with the person sitting in the other chair. That connection, the rapport between client and therapist, is one of the most valuable resources we have in therapy. Rapport is built on trust: the client believes I will continue to listen, that I want to understand, that what I say holds weight because it is informed, and that I am there to help. Connection helps a client come back after an awkward or painful session. The connection is the pathway to progress.

How much of our discussion about race in this country is about listening? If we don't listen, we don't develop trust, and we can't understand. The fact of the matter is that we talk a lot about ending racism, and the Will is there to do so, but we are a mess about how to do it. Not surprisingly, some of us want to share, but we don't trust we will be heard. Of course, many of us want to skip to the end. That doesn't work.

This is the process for behavioral change, built on almost a century of counseling psychology research, ratified by a powerful civil rights movement whose echoes reverberate to this day. If we want voting patterns to change, if we want politicians who help instead of making the racial discourse worse, if we want the American system to be fair, if we want everyone to have an equal shot at the American dream, we start with trust and shared humanity.

The preceding chapters have produced the following nine conclusions:

First, *we are better equipped to fight racism when we are supported by a moral mandate* and *empathy can lead to this moral inclusion*. As demonstrated by research in social and counseling psychology and in recent history, this approach is the most likely to get us to higher ground.

Second, *throughout American history, racial discrimination has evolved side by side with politics content to ignore it or eager to use it to gain power*. Politics designed to maximize White resentment and gain votes represents a significant obstacle blocking meaningful progress on racism.

Third, *less gatekeeping and more honesty about American history humanizes and strengthens our shared story*. Anxiety over Critical Race Theory is another manipulation to divide Americans and claim power. The truth about America offers opportunities for White students to bond with students of color over the present and future, rather than the past.

Fourth and fifth, *racism is still real, and it is dangerous in many ways to Americans of color*. Though we have made progress in stigmatizing and moralizing racist hate, *a Post-Racial Lie covers American systems' reproduction of real disadvantages for people of color*. These realities are the human cost to racism in America.

Sixth, *a certain set of beliefs, which we categorize as modern racism, leads to support for policies that disadvantage Americans of color*. The work of those studying modern racism provides both insight into the humanity of those opposing progress and opportunities to build the mutual trust necessary for an antiracist coalition.

Seventh, *the racialization and polarization of American politics have wounded our prospects of coalescing against racism*. Ignoring or magnifying America's racial problems can pull us further apart. When polarized, we are less likely to look within and to engage empathetically, both required to reach higher ground.

Eighth, and ninth, *both American political parties have flaws in how they approach racism*: Republicans for their racism denial in pursuit of White votes and Democrats for their tendency to devalue collaboration with less-progressive Americans. Neither have a monopoly on moral weight in their approach to racism.

These conclusions, supported by research and history, can be condensed into our path to higher ground. Namely,

- We share a moral community.
- Racism, individual and systemic, violates this community.
- Moral conviction motivates Americans to take meaningful action.

- Thus, our efforts to fight racism must hold moral weight.

If we are to grab the string of the balloon, if we are to reach higher ground, we need people involved who are moved by these conclusions. Building that coalition starts with common understanding. Understanding is rooted in a basic observation: the other person is a human being with dignity. My intent in the discussion of specific political interpretations of racism and proposed solutions in this book was to engage with those ideas on their merit, including their psychological appeal. Tolerating difference, but not engaging with it, has led to the problem encountered by many on the left when trying to open a dialogue about race with conservatives (Lawson 2021).

It is going to take a team effort to move us toward higher ground. This means we will need to be comfortable with a big tent encompassing multiple points of view. One way we can start the work is to embrace what philosopher Mary Parker Follet called Integrative Democracy. Follet introduced her idea in the early twentieth century for management purposes, but social scientist Graham Wright (2019) has proposed applying it to breaking through our political polarization.

Integrative Democracy is designed to eliminate the win-lose scenarios we often see in American politics. To ensure cooperation, the opposite sides cannot bring their own solutions to the discussion. They bring their problems, their needs, and their views. Then both sides, as an integrative group, work toward a new and creative solution that satisfies each side's core desire. Persuasion is not the point. We retain our desires; we just let go of the preferred method for achieving them.

Dunking on someone on Twitter is not a core desire. Owning the libs is not a core desire. These are distractions that have become so endemic that they look like strategies. They are signs that alert us to a sickness without indicating how it can be healed. Some of the solutions to racism from both left and right have nothing to do with creating a more equal society, addressing the persistent disparities experienced by Americans of color, or moving us closer to making the American Dream something every American has a realistic shot of attaining.

Integrative Democracy is built from three main steps. The first is to bring differences into the open. This is important because honesty about differences is more productive than pretending we all want the same thing. Wright notes that mass media already does a decent job of this.

The second step is to disaggregate wholes so the pieces of each side's goal can be dealt with. Sometimes solutions are rejected because there is one part, a poison pill, that prevents the other side from considering it at all. Disaggregation also involves separating the substance from the symbol, which is the meaning the desire has accumulated beyond its usefulness.

During the first two stages, both sides can begin rethinking their original stances, especially what is most important to them. By the time they reach the third stage, they can use those reevaluated and reprioritized proposals to contribute to a creative solution. In a creative solution, both sides get their core desire satisfied; it just might not be in the way they had expected.

The shabby state of "race relations" in this country means that there won't be a lot of trust and respect in that room, at first. Disrespect is contagious and counterproductive, no matter how much you disagree with what the other side represents. A set of common rules encouraging straightforward communication and discouraging disengagement, like those suggested by April Lawson's (2021) Braver Angels Debate or those operational in the Civilized Conversation group in my hometown, could be a start. Participants should be reminded that the group works best when people are open because that is the only path to a solution that will work for everyone.

When I saw Graham Wright (2022) speak at a recent conference, he applied Integrative Democracy to the aims of Critical Race Theory. As I wrote about in Chapter 3, CRT's aims are often symbolized by politicians on the right and rejected by many White Americans. But if we break apart CRT's aims into the core desires—that America be a just place for everyone, that all children can be raised in a country that recognizes their autonomy and dignity, that laws be written and enforced in a fair manner—there are elements of it that can align with the goals of those on the right, especially those feeling protective of history or law enforcement.

To take just one side of a thorny issue, let's consider the progressive suggestion of defunding the police. This is an idea born from frustration with police mistreatment and killings of innocent or unarmed Black Americans. But defunding is nowhere near a popular idea. Not just among White Americans, but among many Americans of color who need the protection and services the police are intended to provide. So, we start at, what is the goal of defunding?

There are likely to be many answers to that question. To get at them, we may need to disaggregate defunding. Defunding police is not a core desire; it is a solution to a larger, societal problem. Let's examine the desire underlying the quest for defunding, stripped of its symbolic meaning. Similarly, we should want to know more about those opposed to defunding the police. Aside from the symbols, such as "Blue Lives Matter," what do defunding opponents really want?

The major advantage of Integrative Democracy is that both sides are invested in the outcome. There is no resentment over "losing" because each side's desire is represented in the solution. This adds to the legitimacy of the outcome: the solution transcends any one side's ideas. Trying creative solutions would counteract the radicalization problem plaguing both parties, in which policy goals are increasingly reflective of its most devoted and radical members, ensuring the ideas are anathema to at least half the country.

All these elements increase trust in future collaborations. And any collaboration is better than what is occurring right now, with one side marching and the other fuming.

\*\*\*

For all the talk about tribalism in the United States, we should remind ourselves that, though the political parties may be devolving into tribes (Clark, Liu, Winegard and Ditto 2019; Marietta and Barker 2019; Mason 2018), recent research shows that race does not need to be tribal. Cidgem Sirin, Nicholas Valentino, and José Villalobos (2021) have studied what they call "group empathy," the ability to relate to the people in a different racial group and care about their welfare. They find, in a wide variety of situations and in both the United States and Great Britain, that a strong sense of group identity usually leads to *higher* levels of outgroup empathy. For example, Black Americans were more strenuously opposed to a wall on the southern US border than even Latinos, and this is after accounting for political ideology.

The one exception, unfortunately, is the largest racial group in the United States. Increased group identity among White Americans decreases the likelihood of empathizing with people of color. If there is anything that should assuage those White Americans threatened by demographic change, it is that there is nothing biological preventing them from building connections to the rising Americans of color in their communities. But this logic must clear the hurdle of centuries of fear and loathing woven into the fabric of White identity in the United States. As they put it, "empathy for outgroups might be a key tool for reducing conflicts" (Sirin et al. 2021, 237). Given the temperature of most political debate in America, it is likely many are ready to try something new.

The good news from the group empathy studies is that not all groups hate one another, even when they are supposedly in competition. For example, the Black people whose economic stability is most precarious and should be most threatened by immigration are strongly empathetic to American Latinos. Latinos, some of whom share physical features with Arab Americans, are likely to be victimized by spillover racism and the effects of domestic terrorism. They still empathize with Muslims and Arab Americans targeted by zealous anti-terrorism. These examples are not limited to passive sympathy for the plight of other groups. In study after study, Sirin and colleagues found that those high on group empathy were willing to (and, in some experiments, did) sign up for political action on an outgroup member's behalf.

Perhaps the most interesting part for the prospects of real movement against racism is that, even though White Americans lagged Americans of color on all these measures, Americans of color still showed a basic level of empathy for their White countrymen. Their group empathy often matched the level of empathy White Americans had for their ingroup. Furthermore, race is not set in stone. We've seen how Italian, Irish, and Hungarian immigrants became "American" in the previous century.

Empathy, as I have written throughout this book, is a building block for honest and meaningful relationships that lead to real change. Empathy is powerful in therapy; similarly, there are many ways it is adaptive in society (Sirin et al. 2021). But just as I had to learn how to empathize with people I just met during my training, many of us may need to learn how to build empathy for those we don't yet understand. There, too, group empathy research shows promise.

Sirin and colleagues show in a series of studies that group empathy can be built through educational experiences such as games and simulations, and community engagement through service learning. The opportunities are there to build the crucial empathy and trust that can move the conversation on race forward.

The path to higher ground includes expanding our moral community. According to work by Márton Hadarics and Anna Kende (2019), exclusion from a moral community—which has operated like the tribalism we see in our politics—can lead to discrimination and violence. As they note (266) regarding outgroup threats, "moral exclusion of that group can be an effective tool to stop the frustration. However, this is done at the expense of the group's treatment."

Expanding our moral communities to include people who do not look like us is more than being nice or empathetic. It is courageous: it shows our will to extend principles of morality where others will not. Hanna Szekeres and colleagues (Szekeres, Halperin, Kende and Saguy 2019) found that seeing racism morally leads to action when participants feel they will lose integrity by not acting. The immorality of racism, as discussed throughout this book, is obvious. Racism dehumanizes and unjustly victimizes our fellow human beings, it debases those who espouse it, and it impairs the functioning of our society. Research, history, shows us that moral conviction against racism can help us reach higher ground.

\*\*\*

I opened Chapter 1 of this book quoting the second Judeo-Christian creation story to explain the unique moral weight accorded racism in the United States of America. That moral weight is a precious resource that encourages us to root out hate in our midst and pursue a social vision that values every human being equally.

That resource, like most others, can be depleted. When the definition of racism exceeds public understanding or what is racist becomes too subjective, we risk losing the forceful response the label contains. Yet limiting our understanding of racism, perhaps conveniently for some, demotivates us to act even when moral violations are occurring (Szekeres et al. 2019).

The moral weight of racism draws from the value of humanity: it is beyond the pale to treat fellow human beings as less than human. We can push the modern racial project forward by reengaging with a concept of shared humanity, undergirded by a strong moral mandate to pursue a solution that benefits all Americans. This moral mandate is a corollary to the Golden Rule: approach race, racial issues, and racial politics in a way that values others the way you want to be valued.

As Heather McGhee (2021) demonstrates through her interviews and historical examples, fighting racism does not need to be a zero-sum game. No matter what your level of motivation, something can be done. The guiding light, though, is not strictly a liberal view or a conservative view. It is neither Dr. Kendi nor Dr. King, neither Donald J. Trump nor Booker T. Washington. The guiding light is what would materially improve the lives of poor and discriminated-against people of color in this country. The work may take different forms for each of us.

For those on the left, there is an abundance of resources for pursuing your moral conviction against racism in texts like *How to Be an Antiracist, Why Are All the Black Kids Sitting Together in the Cafeteria?* and *So You Want to Talk About Race?* These solutions should be pursued in the name of justice, of course, but also in the name of shared humanity. Your path should include leaving liberal spaces and comfort zones. It also means moving beyond symbolic gestures to take actions that materially reduce discrimination and inequality.

For those on the right, you do not need to abandon your conservatism to follow this guiding light. Many public policies that help poor people of color benefit all poor people. Your path could mean donating time and resources to charities that prioritize racial equality. It could be pushing Republican candidates to commit to opportunity zones. It should include rethinking the aspects of conservatism that contribute to our impasse, splitting voting tickets when necessary to avoid supporting race-baiting candidates.

For the social scientists like myself, we need to study racism from the perspective of helping people of color. We need to continue investigating how differences in how Americans define racism impact our society. We need to help those who fight racism clearly communicate the stakes, so the conversation is not derailed by self-serving politicians or fearmongers. When we study human behavior, we must continue to include and listen to the voices of those affected by racism.

For those who just want to navigate the craziness, you can try breaking the cycle of local sorting, online echo chambers, and cable news to reach out to new people. New hires at work, new people in the neighborhood, new spaces online, new faithful at your place of worship, new experiences. When deciding which political candidates deserve your vote, you should consider in your equation whether they are alleviating or feeding the racial polarization in this country.

For everyone, remember how our emotions influence our political decisions. Whenever you read political news that gives you a negative emotional reaction—whether it's fear, anger, or anxiety—consider a few things. First, slow down and allow yourself to experience that reaction. Think about why you might be experiencing this feeling. Ask yourself some questions. *Why might someone want me to be afraid/angry/anxious? Am I okay with how I'm feeling? What would a vote based on this feeling mean, and could it hurt my fellow human beings?* Finally, *have I fallen into a pattern where I seek a daily dose of this negativity, and if so, how is it serving me?*

For those who see my suggestions and think this is not enough, I understand. But look at the power of the big tent, the way the New Deal was able to bring together a multifaceted coalition of Americans to win a war and beat a Depression. That coalition led to the Voting Rights Act and the Civil Rights Act. It can be re-created so long as people are welcomed for what they are willing to do. This problem is too big for us to derail it with purity tests.

Yes, people of color, especially Black people, often feel they can't trust White people about racism. It cuts too close to the bone. Why be vulnerable and put your trust in people who aren't fully committed? There definitely are some people who are about themselves rather than the cause, and when those people are White, it can feel like a betrayal. That pattern has a history, and it is why Americans of color often view White allyship with a jaundiced eye.

Just like we can't allow a bad relationship to sour us on love itself, we cannot allow the mistakes or selfishness of a few to close us off to a common goal. We need each other to force lasting action on racism. Building a movement bit by bit may seem small, but decades of research show us that a foot in the door[2] can be productive in securing larger commitments.

Action on racism cannot be limited by one's comfort. These aren't ingredients that all can be bought at Whole Foods, or at Walmart. We can reach out to the people who disagree with us simply by saying, "Help me understand." We all recognize change will take something big. The last few years have shown us that we can't let it become small again.

No matter what you think about its extent, it is undeniable that racism has influenced our history and our politics. That racism causes daily pain to its victims in many facets of life cannot be ignored or explained away. That racism cannot be solved by living within one silo of American thought becomes more apparent as this great nation tears itself apart through the temptation of political polarization.

I closed the introduction of this book using the metaphor of a wave, with the American people as the wind who power the wave of action against racism. Not only our sense of shared humanity but our integrity is endangered by the false security of a calm sea, the deceptive relief of a receding tide. The history, politics, and psychology of racism show us that this is a uniquely human but solvable problem. There are reasons to be satisfied, passive, it is true. Yet the moral weight of this problem insists that we push that wave of racial reckoning forward, the wave tipping, crashing, spilling across the sand, rushing forward to touch all that awaits.

## NOTES

1. There are extensive data, testimony, and reports on changes over the years available on the website for the Center for Strategic and International Studies (csis.org).

2. The foot-in-the-door phenomenon refers to the higher likelihood of acceding to a large request after first granting a smaller request (Burger 1999; Cacioppo and Freberg 2013; Freedman and Fraser 1966). Once a person has granted the smaller request, they feel bound by their prior behavior and a commitment to honor the relationship with the other person. This is the same technique used by email lists, reward programs, and service apps.

# Bibliography

Abernathy, Gary. 2017. "In Trump Country, Russia Just Isn't Big News. Here's Why." *Washington Post*, July 21. https://www.washingtonpost.com/opinions/in-trump -country-russia-just-isnt-big-news-heres-why/2017/07/21/8514f49e-6cc3-11e7 -9c15-177740635e83_story.html.

Abernathy, Scott F. 2005. *School Choice and the Future of American Democracy.* Ann Arbor, MI: University of Michigan.

Abramowitz, Alan and Jennifer McCoy. 2019. "United States: Racial Resentment, Negative Partisanship, and Polarization in Trump's America." *The Annals of the American Academy of Political & Social Science*, 681: 137–56.

Act.tv. 2019. "Systemic Racism Explained." *YouTube*, April 16, Educational video, 4:23. https://www.youtube.com/watch?v=YrHIQIO_bdQ.

Adorno, Theodor W., Else Frenkel-Brunswik, Daniel Levinson and Nevitt Sanford. 1950. *The Authoritarian Personality.* New York, NY: Harper & Row.

Alamillo, Rudy. 2019. "Hispanics Para Trump? Denial of Racism and Hispanic Support for Trump." *Du Bois Review*, 16 (2): 457–87.

Alexander, Michelle. 2012. *The New Jim Crow: Mass Incarceration in the Age of Colorblindness.* New York, NY: The New Press.

Alfano, Mark. 2016. *Moral Psychology: An Introduction.* Cambridge, UK: Polity Press.

Andrasfay, Theresa and Noreen Goldman. 2020. "Intergenerational Change in Birthweight: Effects of Foreign-Born Status and Race/Ethnicity." *Epidemology*, 31 (5): 649–58.

Anti-Defamation League. 2021. *Online Hate and Harassment: The American Experience 2021.* adl.org/media/16033/download.

Anti-Defamation League. 2022. *"The Great Replacement": An Explainer.* https:// www.adl.org/resources/backgrounders/the-great-replacement-an-explainer.

Awad, Germine H., Kevin Cokley and Joseph Ravitch. 2005. "Attitudes Toward Affirmative Action: A Comparison of Color-Blind versus Modern Racist Attitudes." *Journal of Applied Social Psychology*, 35 (7): 1384–99.

Azerrad, David. 2022. "Race-Based Idolatry." *American Mind.org*, August 29. https: //americanmind.org/features/rule-not-by-lies/race-based-idolatry/.

Bacon, Perry. 2017. "The Obamacare Fight is about Way More Than Health Care." *FiveThirtyEight,* March 23. https://fivethirtyeight.com/features/the-obamacare -fight-is-about-way-more-than-health-care/.

Badger, Emily, Claire C. Miller, Adam Pearce and Joshua Quealy. 2018. "Extensive Data Shows Punishing Reach of Racism for Black Boys." *New York Times*, March 19. Retrieved from https://www.nytimes.com/interactive/2018/03/19/upshot/race -class-white-and-black-men.html.

Badolato, Gia M., Meleah D. Boyle, Robert McCarter, April M. Zeoli, William Terrill and Monika K. Goyal. 2020. Racial and ethnic disparities in firearm-related pediatric deaths related to legal intervention. *Pediatrics*, 146 (6): 1–3.

Bailey, Greg. 2016. "This Presidential Speech on Race Shocked the Nation . . . in 1921." *Narratively.com*, October 26. https://narratively.com/this-presidential -speech-on-race-shocked-the-nation-in-1921/.

Baker, Paxton K. 2020. "Why Saying 'All Lives Matter' Misses the Big Picture." *CNN*, June 23. https://www.cnn.com/2020/06/23/opinions/all-lives-matter-misses -the-big-picture-baker/index.html.

Baptiste, Nathalie. 2019. "Democrats Say They Want to End Mass Incarceration. There's No Way They'll Do What's Needed to Get There." *Mother Jones*, September 20. https://www.motherjones.com/crime-justice/2019/09/democrats-say -they-want-to-end-mass-incarceration-why-dont-they-address-the-real-solution/.

Banks, Antione J. 2014. *Anger and Racial Politics.* New York, NY: Cambridge University Press.

Banks, Antoine J. and Melissa A. Bell. 2013. "Racialized Campaign Ads: The Emotional Content in Implicit Racial Appeals Primes White Racial Attitudes." *Public Opinion Quarterly*, 77 (2): 549–60.

Baron, James N. and William T. Biebly. 1980. "Bringing the Firms Back in: Stratification, Segmentation, and the Organization of Work." *American Sociological Review* 45: 737–65.

Barr, Luke. 2021. "Hate Crimes Against Asian Americans Rose 76% in 2020 Amid Pandemic, FBI Says." *ABC News*, October 25. https://abcnews.go.com/US/hate -crimes-asians-rose-76-2020-amid-pandemic/story?id=80746198asdfasf.

Bates, Karen G. 2017. "Stand Your Ground Laws Complicate Matters for Black Gun Owners." *NPR.org*, February. https://www.npr.org/sections/codeswitch/2017/02/27 /517109271/stand-your-ground-laws-complicate-matters-for-black-gun-owners.

Bayne, Bijan C. 2022. "How 'Woke' Became the Least Woke Word in U.S. English." *Washington Post*, February 2. https://www.washingtonpost.com/opinions/2022/02 /02/black-history-woke-appropriation-misuse/.

Bayram, Seyma. 2021. "Ohio's Black Leaders Sound Alarms Over New Stand Your Ground Law Effective Today." *Akron Beacon Journal*, April 6. https://www .beaconjournal.com/story/news/2021/04/06/ohios-black-leaders-sound-alarms -over-new-stand-your-ground-law/7089980002/.

Beauchamp, Zachary. 2019. "Tucker Carlson's Claim that White Supremacy Is a 'Hoax' Is False—But Revealing." *Vox*, August 7. https://www.vox.com/policy-and -politics/2019/8/7/20757366/tucker-carlson-white-supremacy-hoax-el-paso.

Beck, Aaron. T., A. John Rush, Brian F. Shaw and Gary Emery. 1979. *Cognitive Therapy of Depression*. New York: Guilford Press.

Bejan, Raluca. 2020. "Robin DiAngelo's 'White Fragility' Ignores the Differences Within Whiteness." *TheConversation.com*, August 27. https://theconversation.com /robin-diangelos-white-fragility-ignores-the-differences-within-whiteness-143728.

Bell, Derrick A. 1995. "David C. Baum Memorial Lecture: Who's Afraid of Critical Race Theory?" *University of Illinois Law Review*, 1995: 893–910.

Bellamy, Claretta. 2021. "Support for Black Lives Matter Movement is Declining, According to New Poll." *NBC News*, November 16. https://www.nbcnews.com/ news/nbcblk/support-black-lives-matter-movement-declining-according-new-poll -rcna5746.

Bennett, Dylan and Hannah Walker. 2018. "Cracking the Racial Code: Black Threat, White Rights, and the Lexicon of American Politics. *American Journal of Economics & Sociology*, 77 (3/4): 689–727.

Best, Paul. 2021. "George Floyd: What to Know." *Fox News.com*, March 25. https:// www.foxnews.com/us/george-floyd-what-to-know.

Bilewicz, Michal and Wiktor Soral. 2020. "Hate Speech Epidemic. The Dynamic Effects of Derogatory Language on Intergroup Relations and Political Radicalization." *Political Psychology*, 41 (S1): 3–33.

Bischoff, Bill. 2020. "Two Years After the Tax Cuts and Jobs Act, Who Are the Winners and the Losers?" *Market Watch*, February 28, 2020. https://www .marketwatch.com/story/two-years-after-the-tax-cuts-and-jobs-act-who-are-the -winners-and-the-losers-2020-02-11.

Bishop, Bill. 2008. *The Big Sort: Why Clustering of Like-Minded America Is Tearing Us Apart*. Boston, MA: Mariner Books.

Black Lives Matter. 2021. "8 Years Strong." July 13. https://blacklivesmatter.com/8 -years-strong/.

Blackmon, Douglas. 2008. *Slavery by Another Name*. New York: Anchor Books.

Blake, Aaron. 2018. "The Alleged Trump N-word Tape is Suddenly Less Hypothetical." *Washington Post*, August 14. https://www.washingtonpost.com/politics/2018/08/14 /alleged-trump-n-word-tape-is-suddenly-less-hypothetical/.

Blake, Emily. 2021. "R. Kelly's Sales Soared 500 Percent After Guilty Verdicts." *Rolling Stone*, October 8. https://www.rollingstone.com/music/music-news/r -kellys-sales-streams-guilty-verdict-1239159/.

Bloom, Pazit B. N. 2013. "The Public's Compass: Moral Conviction and Political Attitudes." *American Politics Research*, 41 (6): 937–64.

Bloom, Peter. 2016. "Trump and the Triumph of Hopeful Nihilism." *The Conversation.com*, November 9. https://theconversation.com/trump-and-the -triumph-of-hopeful-nihilism-68534.

Blow, Charles M. 2021. "Gwen Ifill Was Right About 'Missing White Woman Syndrome.'" *New York Times*, September 23. https://www.nytimes.com/2021/09 /22/opinion/petito-missing-person-cases.html.

Blumer, Herbert. 1958. "Race Prejudice as a Sense of Group Position." *The Pacific Sociological Review*, 1 (1): 3–7.

Bobo, Lawrence. 1999. "Prejudice as Group Position: Microfoundations of a Sociological Approach to Racism and Race Relations." *Journal of Social Issues*, 55 (3): 445–72.

Bobo, Lawrence. 2018. "Race as a Complex Adaptive System." *DuBois Review*, 15 (2): 211–15.

Bobo, Lawrence, James R. Kluegel and Ryan A. Smith. 1996. "Laissez-Faire Racism: The Crystallization of a 'Kindler, Gentler' Anti-Black Ideology." In *Racial Attitudes in the 1990s: Continuity and Change*, Steven A. Tuch and Jack K. Martin (Eds.), 15–44. Westport, CT: Praeger.

Bonilla-Silva, Eduardo. 2001. *White Supremacy and Racism in the Post-Civil Rights Era.* Boulder, CO: Lynne Rienner Publishers.

Bonilla-Silva, Eduardo. 2014. *Racism without Racists: Color-Blind Racism and the Persistence of Racial Inequality in America.* Lanham, MD: Rowman & Littlefield Publishers.

Bonilla-Silva, Eduardo. 2015. "The Structure of Racism in Color-Blind, 'Post-racial' America." *American Behavioral Scientist*, 59 (11): 1358–76.

Bonilla-Silva, Eduardo. 2018. *Racism Without Racists: Colorblind Racism and the Persistence of Racial Inequality in America.* Lanham, MD: Rowman & Littlefield.

Bonn, Gregory. 2015. "Primary Process Emotion, Identity, and Culture: Cultural Identification's Roots in Basic Motivation." *Frontiers in Psychology*, 6: 218.

Borges, Ron. 2022. "Existence of Rooney Rule Proves Damning to NFL's Argument Against Brian Flores." *Sports Illustrated*, February 7. https://www.si.com/nfl/talkoffame/nfl/flores-lawsuit-challenges-rooney-rule-fraud.

Bouie, Jamelle. 2016. "There's No Such Thing as a Good Trump Voter." *Slate*, November 15. https://slate.com/news-and-politics/2016/11/there-is-no-such-thing-as-a-good-trump-voter.html.

Boyon, Nicholas. 2019. "A 90% Favorability Rating for Martin Luther King, Jr. on His 90th Birthday." *Ipsos.com*, January 18. https://www.ipsos.com/en-us/news-polls/90-favorability-rating-martin-luther-king-jr-2019-01-18.

Braddock, Jomills H. and Alex R. Piquero. 2022. "What the Case of Fired Dolphins Coach Brian Flores Says About the NFL Today." *Tampa Bay Times*, February 5. https://www.tampabay.com/opinion/2022/02/05/what-the-case-of-fired-dolphins-coach-brian-flores-says-about-the-nfl-today-column/.

Brader, Ted. 2006. *Campaigning for Hearts and Minds: How Emotional Appeals in Political Ads Work.* Chicago: The University of Chicago Press.

Brandt, Mark J., Daniel C. Wisneski and Linda J. Skitka. 2015. "Moralization and the 2012 U.S. Presidential Election Campaign." *Journal of Social and Political Psychology*, 3 (2): 211–37.

Bray, Susan and Richard S. Balkin. 2013. "Master's-level Students' Beliefs Concerning the Causes of Poverty, Implicit Racial Attitudes, and Multicultural Competency." *Journal of Professional Counseling: Practice, Theory, and Research*, 40 (2): 33–44.

Brinson, Jesse A. 2011. "Using Moral Exclusion Theory as a Framework for Redefining Racism in Counselor Education." *Journal of Construction & Testing*, 15 (1): 4–9.

Brondolo, Elizabeth, Wan Ng, Kristy-Lee J. Pierre and Robert Lane. 2016. "Racism and Mental Health: Examining the Link Between Racism and Depression from a Social Cognitive Perspective." In The Cost of Racism for People of Color: Contextualizing Experiences of Discrimination, ed. Alvin N. Alvarez, Christopher T. H. Liang and Helen A. Neville, 109–32. Washington, DC: American Psychological Association.

Broockman, David and Joshua Kalla. 2016. "Durably Reducing Transphobia: A Field Experiment on Door-to-Door Canvassing." *Science*, 352 (6282): 220–24.

Brooks, David. 2022. "Seven Lessons Democrats Need to Learn—Fast." *New York Times*, April 28. https://www.nytimes.com/2022/04/28/opinion/seven-lessons -democrats-need-to-learn-fast.html.

Brown, Jessica A. 2016a. "Running on Fear: Immigration, Race and Crime Framings in Contemporary GOP Presidential Debate Discourse." *Critical Criminology*, 24: 315–31.

Brown, Jessica A. 2016b. "The New 'Southern Strategy': Immigration, Race, and 'Welfare Dependency' in Contemporary US Republican Political Discourse." *Geopolitics, History, and International Relations*, 8 (2): 22–41.

Brown, John A. 2016. "The New 'Southern Strategy': Immigration, Race, and 'Welfare Dependency' in Contemporary US Republican Political Discourse." *Geopolitics, History, and International Relations*, 8 (2): 22–41.

Brown, Lee. 2021. "Disney Reportedly Scrubs Woke Anti-Racism Training After Backlash." *New York Post*, May 13. https://nypost.com/2021/05/13/disney-scrubs -anti-racism-training-after-backlash-report/.

Brown, Tony N. 2008. "Race, Racism, and Mental Health: Elaboration of Critical Race Theory's Contribution to the Sociology of Mental Health." *Contemporary Justice Review*, 11 (1): 53–62.

Brugal, Sommer. 2022. "DeSantis Signs 'Stop Woke Act' into Law, Touts 'Education, Not Indoctrination.'" *Miami Herald*, April 23. https://www.miamiherald.com/news /local/education/article260665822.html.

Bryant, Nick. 2015. "America's 50-Year Journey from Bloody Sunday in Selma." *BBC News*, March 7. https://www.bbc.com/news/magazine-31759338.

Bryant-Davis, Thema and Carlota Ocampo (2005). "Racist Incident-Based Trauma." *The Counseling Psychologist*, 33 (4): 479–500.

Buffone, Anneke E. and Michael J. Poulin. 2014. "Empathy, Target Distress, and Neurohormone Genes Interact to Predict Aggression for Others—Even Without Provocation." *Personality and Social Psychology*, 40: 1406–22.

Bureau of Labor Statistics. 2021. "Labor Force Characteristics by Race and Ethnicity, 2020." November. https://www.bls.gov/opub/reports/race-and-ethnicity /2020/home.htm.

Burger, Jerry M. 1999. "The Foot-in-the-Door Compliance Procedure: A Multiple-Process Analysis and Review." *Personality and Social Psychology Review*, 3 (4): 303–25.

Burkard, Alan and Sarah Knox. 2004. "Effect of Therapist Color-Blindness on Empathy and Attributions in Cross-Cultural Counseling." *Journal of Counseling Psychology*, 51 (4): 387–97.

Bynum, Victoria, James M. McPherson, James Oakes, Sean Wilentz and Gordon S. Wood. 2019. Letter to the editors, *New York Times Magazine*, December 4. https://www.cbs17.com/wp-content/uploads/sites/29/2021/07/NYT-1619-Letter-Bennet.pdf.

Cacioppo, John T. and Laura A. Freberg. 2013. *Discovering Psychology.* Belmont, CA: Wadsworth Cengage Learning.

Calderone, Michael. 2009. "Fox's Beck: Obama Is "a Racist." *Politico*, July 28. https://www.politico.com/blogs/michaelcalderone/0709/Foxs_Beck_Obama_is_a_racist.html.

Capatides, Christina. 2020. "Why Saying 'All Lives Matter' Communicates to Black People That Their Lives Don't." *CBS News*, July 8. https://www.cbsnews.com/news/all-lives-matter-black-lives-matter/.

Caputo, Marc and Sabrina Rodriguez. 2021. "Democrats Fall Flat with 'Latinx' Language." *Politico*, December 6, 2021. https://www.politico.com/news/2021/12/06/hispanic-voters-latinx-term-523776.

Carbado, Devon W. and Daria Roithmayr. 2014. "Critical Race Theory Meets Social Science." *Annual Review of Law and Social Science*, 10: 149–67.

Carlson, Tucker. 2021. "Everything the Media Didn't Tell You about the Death of George Floyd." *Fox News.com*, March 11. https://www.foxnews.com/opinion/tucker-carlson-george-floyd-death-what-media-didnt-tell-you.

Carmichael, Stokely and Charles V. Hamilton. 1967. *Black Power: Politics of Liberation in America.* New York: Random House.

Carmines, Edward G., Paul M. Sniderman and Beth C. Easter. 2011. "On the Meaning, Measurement, and Implications of Racial Resentment." *The Annals of the American Academy of Political and Social Science*, 634 (2): 98–116.

Carney, Riley K. and Ryan D. Enos. 2015. "Conservatism and Fairness in Contemporary Politics: Unpacking the Psychological Underpinnings of Modern Racism. Paper presented at the Midwest Political Science Association Annual Conference, Chicago, IL, April.

Carter, Niambi M. and Efrén O. Pérez. 2016. "Race and Nation: How Racial Hierarchy Shapes National Attachments." *Political Psychology*, 37 (4): 497–513.

Casas, J. Manuel. 2005. "Race and Racism: The Efforts of Counseling Psychology to Understand and Address the Issues Associated with These Terms." The Counseling Psychologist, 33 (4): 501–12.

Casselman, Ben. 2017. "The Trump Job Market Looks a Lot Like the Obama Job Market." *FiveThirtyEight.com*, July 7. https://fivethirtyeight.com/features/the-trump-job-market-looks-a-lot-like-the-obama-job-market/.

Chait, Jonathan. 2020. "Is the Anti-Racism Training Industry Just Peddling White Supremacy?" *New York Magazine*, July 16. https://nymag.com/intelligencer/2020/07/antiracism-training-white-fragility-robin-diangelo-ibram-kendi.html.

Chambers, John R., Barry R. Schlenker and Brian Collisson. 2012. "Ideology and Prejudice: The Role of Value Conflicts." *Psychological Science*, 24 (2): 140–9.

Chang, Alisa, Audie Cornish, Mary L. Kelly and Ari Shapiro. 2016. "Decades-old Housing Discrimination Case Plagues Donald Trump." *All Things Considered* (radio program transcript), September 29. https://www.npr.org/2016/09/29 /495955920/donald-trump-plagued-by-decades-old-housing-discrimination-case.

Chavez, Leo R. 2001. *Covering Immigration: Popular Images and the Politics of a Nation.* Berkeley, CA: University of California Press.

Chavez, Manuel, Scott Whiteford and Jennifer Hoewe. 2010. "Reporting on Immigration: A Content Analysis of Major U.S. Newspapers' Coverage of Mexican Immigration." *Norteamérica*, 5 (2): 111–25.

Cherry, Robert. 2019. "The Problem with Trying to Measure 'Racial Resentment.'" *National Review*, January 24. https://www.nationalreview.com/2019/01/measuring -racial-resentment-problems/.

Christian, Michelle, Louis Seamster and Victor Ray. 2019. "New Directions in Critical Race Theory and Sociology: Racism, White Supremacy, and Resistance." *American Behavioral Scientist*, 63 (13): 1731–40.

Cillizza, Chris. 2021. "Democrats Have a Major Problem with Hispanic Voters." *CNN*, December 9, 2021. https://www.cnn.com/2021/12/09/politics/biden-hispanic -voters-democrats-problem/index.html.

Clark, Cory J., Brittany S. Liu, Bo M. Winegard and Peter H. Ditto. 2019. "Tribalism Is Human Nature." *Current Directions in Psychological Science*, 28 (6): 587–92.

Cobb, James C. 2018. "Even Though He Is Revered Today, MLK Was Widely Disliked by the American Public When He Was Killed." *Smithsonian Magazine*, April 4. https://www.smithsonianmag.com/history/why-martin-luther-king-had-75 -percent-disapproval-rating-year-he-died-180968664/.

Cohen, Rebecca. 2020. "Framework for Understanding Structural Racism: The Cult of Purity." *Journal of Ecumenical Studies*, 55 (1): 46–62.

Cole Wright, Jennifer, Jerry Cullum and Nicholas Schwab. 2008. "The Cognitive and Affective Dimensions of Moral Conviction: Implications for Attitudinal and Behavioral Measures of Interpersonal Intolerance." *Personality and Social Psychology Bulletin*, 34 (11): 1461–76.

Cooley, Erin, Jazmin L. Brown-Iannuzzi, Ryan F. Lei and William Cipolli III. 2019. "Complex Intersections of Race and Class: Among Social Liberals, Learning about White Privilege Reduces Sympathy, Increases Blame, and Decreases External Attributions for White People Struggling with Poverty." Journal of Experimental Psychology: General, 148 (12): 2218–28.

Congressional Research Service. 2019. *The Economic Effects of the 2017 Tax Revision: Preliminary Observations.* June 7, 2019. https://crsreports.congress.gov /product/pdf/R/R45736.

Converse, Philip E., Aage R. Clausen and Warren E. Miller. 1965. "Electoral Myth and Reality: The 1964 Election." *The American Political Science Review*, 59 (2): 321–36.

Cook, Lindsey. 2015. "U.S. Education: Still Separate and Unequal. *U.S. News & World Report*, January 28. https://www.usnews.com/news/blogs/data-mine/2015 /01/28/us-education-still-separate-and-unequal.

Cooley, Charles H. 1902. *Human Nature and Social Order.* New York, NY: Scribner's.

Cooper, Ryan. 2020. "The Limits of White Fragility's Anti-Racism." *The Week*, June 24. https://theweek.com/articles/921623/limits-white-fragilitys-antiracism.

Cooper, Ryan. 2021. "Why Are Conservatives Throwing a Tantrum About Anti-Racism? The George Floyd Protests." *TheWeek.com*, June 24. https://theweek .com/politics/1001865/critical-race-theory-george-floyd-protests.

Cornielle, Olivier, Vincent Y. Yzerbyt, Anouk Rogier and Geneviève Buidin. 2001. "Threat and the Group Attribution Error: When Threat Elicits Judgments of Extremity and Homogeneity." *Personality and Social Psychology Bulletin*, 27 (4): 437–46.

Courtney, Shaun. 2020. "Systemic Flaws or Bad Apples? Parties Split on Police Overhaul." *Bloomberg News*, June 10. https://about.bgov.com/news/systemic -flaws-or-bad-apples-parties-split-on-police-overhaul/.

Cox, Daniel, Rachel Lienesch and Robert P. Jones. 2017. "Beyond Economics: Fears of Cultural Displacement Pushed the White Working Class to Trump." *Public Religion Research Institute: The Atlantic*. https://www.prri.org/research/white -working-class-attitudes-economy-trade-immigration-election-donald-trump/.

Craig, Maureen A. and Jennifer A. Richeson. 2014a. "On the Precipice of a 'Majority-Minority' America: Perceived Status Threat from the Racial Demographic Shift Affects White Americans' Political Ideology." *Psychological Science*, 25 (6): 1189–97.

Craig, Maureen A. and Jennifer A. Richeson. 2014b. "More Diverse yet Less Tolerant? How the Increasingly Diverse Racial Landscape Affects White Americans' Racial Attitudes." *Personality and Social Psychology Bulletin*, 40 (6): 750–61.

Craig, Maureen A. and Jennifer A. Richeson. 2018. "Majority No More? The Influence of Neighborhood Racial Diversity and Salient National Population Changes on Whites' Perceptions of Racial Discrimination." *RSF: The Russell Sage Foundation Journal of the Social Sciences*, 4 (5): 141–57.

Craig, Tim. 2022. "Florida Legislature Passes Bill That Limits How Schools and Workplaces Teach About Race and Racism." *Washington Post*, March 10. https:// www.washingtonpost.com/nation/2022/03/10/florida-legislature-passes-anti-woke -bill/.

Cramer, Katherine. 2020. "Understanding the Role of Racism in Contemporary US Public Opinion." *Annual Review of Political Science*, 23: 153–69.

Cummings, William. 2018. "Here is a List of People Who Have Come to Roseanne Barr's Defense." *USA Today*, May 30, 2018. https://www.usatoday.com/story/news /politics/onpolitics/2018/05/30/people-defending-roseanne-barr/656999002/.

Daily Wire. 2021. "Ben Shapiro DEBUNKS Viral 'Systemic Racism Explained' Video." *Facebook*, June 26, 2021. Daily Wire Profile. https://www.facebook.com /DailyWire/videos/ben-shapiro-debunks-viral-systemic-racism-explained-video /217440616900804/.

Danzer, Graham, Sarah M. Rieger, Sarah Schubmehl and Doug Cort. 2016. "White Psychologists and African Americans' Historical Trauma: Implications for Practice." *Journal of Aggression, Maltreatment, & Trauma*, 25 (4): 351–70.

David, Richard and James Collins. 2007. "Disparities in Infant Mortality: What's Genetics Got to Do With It?" *American Journal of Public Health*, 97 (7): 1191–97.

Decety, Jean and Thalia Wheatley. 2015. *The Moral Brain: A Multidisciplinary Perspective*. Cambridge, MA: MIT Press.

De Cristofaro, Valeria, Valerio Pellegrini, Mauro Giacomantonio, Stefano Livi and Martijn van Zomeren. 2021. "Can Moral Convictions Against Gender Inequality Overpower System Justification Effects? Examining the Interaction Between Moral Conviction and System Justification." *British Journal of Social Psychology*, 60: 1279–302.

Del Real, Jose A. 2020. "'Latinx' Hasn't Even Caught on Among Latinos. It Never Will." *Washington Post*, December 18. https://www.washingtonpost.com/outlook /latinx-latinos-unpopular-gender-term/2020/12/18/bf177c5c-3b41-11eb-9276 -ae0ca72729be_story.html.

Del Real, Jose A. and Shawn Sullivan. 2016. "'Jew-S-A!' Chant Is Latest Reminder of White Supremacist Support for Trump." *Washington Post*, October 30. https: //www.washingtonpost.com/politics/trump-campaign-manager-condemns-rally -supporter-who-chanted-jew-s-a/2016/10/30/.

De Luca, Vanessa. 2021. "Black Students Stage Protests and Walkouts in Response to Racism and Bullying in Schools." *The Root*, December 5. https://www.theroot.com /black-students-stage-protests-and-walkouts-in-response-1848163639.

Demby, Gene. 2020. "Why Now, White People?" June 16, in *Code Switch*, podcast transcript, National Public Radio. https://www.npr.org/transcripts/878963732.

Demby, Gene and Shareen Marisol Meraii. 2019. "The Original Blexit." In *Code Switch*, podcast transcript, National Public Radio, September 25. https://www.npr .org/transcripts/763957341.

Democratic National Committee. 2020. "2020 Democratic Party Platform." August 18. https://democrats.org/where-we-stand/party-platform/.

DeSante, Christopher D. 2013. "Working Twice as Hard to Get Half as Far: Race, Work Ethic, and America's Deserving Poor." *American Journal of Political Science*, 57 (2): 342–56.

DeSante, Christopher D., and Candice W. Smith. 2018. *Fear, Institutionalized Racism, and Empathy (FIRE): A Holistic Measure of White Americans' 21st Century Racial Attitudes*. Paper presented at the American Political Science Association Annual Conference, Boston, MA, August 31.

Ditto, Peter H and Brittany S. Liu. 2016. "Moral Coherence and Political Conflict." In *Social Psychology of Political Polarization*, ed. Piercarlo Valdesolo and Jesse Graham, 102–22. New York, NY: Routledge; Dovidio, John F. and Samuel F. Gaertner. 2004. "Aversive racism." In *Advances in Experimental Social Psychology (Vol. 36)*, Mark Zanna (Ed.), 1–52. San Diego, CA: Elsevier Academic.

Doescher, Tim. 2022. "Heritage Explains: Woke Corporate Capitalism." *The Heritage Foundation*, April 11. https://www.heritage.org/progressivism/heritage-explains/ woke-corporate-capitalism.

Douthat, Ross. 2018. "The Rise of Woke Capital." *New York Times*, February 28. https://www.nytimes.com/2018/02/28/opinion/corporate-america-activism.html.

Douthat, Ross. 2021. "The Excesses of Antiracist Education." *New York Times*, July 3. https://www.nytimes.com/2021/07/03/opinion/antiracist-education-history.html.

Drakulich, Joshua, Joshua H. Wozniak, John Hagan and Devon Johnson. 2020. "Race and Policing in the 2016 Presidential Election: Black Lives Matter, the Police, and Dog Whistle Politics." *Criminology*, 58 (2): 370–402.

Downs, Anthony. 1957. "An Economic Theory of Political Action in a Democracy." *Journal of Political Economy*, 65 (2): 135–50.

Doxsee, Catrina, Seth G. Jones, Jared Thompson, Grace Hwang and Kateryna Halstead. 2022. "Pushed to Extremes: Domestic Terrorism Amid Polarization and Protest." *Center for Strategic and International Studies*, May 17. https://www.csis .org/analysis/pushed-extremes-domestic-terrorism-amid-polarization-and-protest.

Drakulich, Joshua, Joshua H. Wozniak, John Hagan and Devon Johnson. 2020. "Race and Policing in the 2016 Presidential Election: Black Lives Matter, the Police, and Dog Whistle Politics." *Criminology*, 58 (2): 370–402.

Dubey, Akash D. 2020. "The Resurgence of Cyber Racism During the COVID-19 Pandemic and its Aftereffects: Analysis of Sentiments and Emotions in Tweets." *JMIR Public Health and Surveillance*, 6 (4): e19833.

Du Bois, W. E. B. 1903. *The Souls of Black Folk: Essays and Sketches*. Chicago, IL: A. C. McClurg & Co.

Dupree, Cydney H. and Susan T. Fiske. 2019. "Self-presentation in Interracial Settings: The Competence Downshift by White Liberals." *Journal of Personality and Social Psychology*, 117 (3): 579–604.

Dutton, Donald G. and Aron, Arthur P. 1974. "Some Evidence for Heightened Sexual Attraction under Conditions of High Anxiety." *Journal of Personality and Social Psychology*, 30 (4): 510–17.

Ecarma, Caleb. 2021. "Conservative Media is Amplifying the Critical Race Theory Opposition." *Vanity Fair*, June 22. https://www.vanityfair.com/news/2021/06/ conservative-media-critical-race-theory-opposition.

Edwards, Frank, Hedwig Lee and Michael Esposito. 2019. "Risk of Being Killed by Police Use of Force in the United States by Age, Race-Ethnicity, and Sex." *Proceedings of the National Academy of Sciences*, 116 (34): 16793–98.

Edwards, Griffin S. and Stephen Rushin. 2018. "The Effect of President Trump's Election on Hate Crimes." SSRN, January 14. http://dx.doi.org/10.2139/ssrn .3102652.

Effron, Daniel A., Dale T. Miller and Benoit Monin. 2012. "Inventing Racist Roads Not Taken: The Licensing Effect of Immoral Counterfactual Behaviors." *Journal of Personality and Social Psychology*, 103 (6): 916–32.

Ehrlichman, J. (1982). *Witness to power: The Nixon years*. New York: Simon and Schuster.

Eisenberg, Nancy, Richard A. Fabes, Paul A. Miller, Jim Fultz, Rita Shell, Robin Mathy and Ray R. Reno. 1989. "Relation of Sympathy and Personal Distress to Prosocial Behavior: A Multimethod Study. *Journal of Personality and Social Psychology*, 57 (1): 55–66.

Enders, Adam M. and Jamil S. Scott. 2019. "The Increasing Racialization of American Electoral Politics, 1988–2016." *American Politics Research*, 47 (2): 275–303.

Enten, Harry. 2022. "Americans See Martin Luther King, Jr. As a Hero Now, But That Wasn't the Case During His Lifetime." *CNN.com*, January 17. https://www .cnn.com/2022/01/17/politics/mlk-polling-analysis/index.html.

Fagan, Jeffrey A. and Alexis D. Campbell. 2020. "Race and Reasonableness in Police Killings." *Boston University Law Review*, 100: 951–1016.

Farhi, Paul. 2022. "Conservative Media Is Familiar with Buffalo Suspect's Alleged 'Theory.'" *Washington Post*, May 15. https://www.washingtonpost.com/media /2022/05/15/buffalo-suspect-great-replacement-theory-conservative-media/.

Federal Bureau of Investigation. 2021. *2019 Hate Crime Statistics*. https://ucr.fbi.gov /hate-crime/2019/tables/table-1.xls.

Feinberg, Ayal, Regina Branton and Valerie Martinez-Ebers. 2019. "Counties That Hosted a 2016 Trump Rally Saw a 226 Percent Increase in Hate Crimes." *Washington Post*, March 22. https://www.washingtonpost.com/politics/2019/03/22 /trumps-rhetoric-does-inspire-more-hate-crimes/.

Feola, Michael. 2021. "'You Will Not Replace Us': The Melancholic Nationalism of Whiteness." *Political Theory*, 49 (4): 528–53.

Feola, Michael. 2022. "How 'Great Replacement' Theory Led to the Buffalo Mass Shooting." *Washington Post*, May 25. https://www.washingtonpost.com/politics /2022/05/25/buffalo-race-war-invasion-violence/.

Fernandez, Celestino and Lawrence Pedroza. 1982. "The Border Patrol and News Media Coverage of Undocumented Mexican Immigration During the 1970s: A Quantitative Content Analysis in the Sociology of Knowledge." *California Sociologist*, 5 (2): 1–26.

Fleming, Crystal M., Miche'le Lamont and Jessica S. Welburn. 2012. "African Americans Respond to Stigmatization: The Meanings and Salience of Confronting, Deflecting Conflict, Educating the Ignorant and 'Managing the Self.'" *Ethnic and Racial Studies*, 35 (3): 400–17.

Foner, Eric. 2014. *Reconstruction: America's Unfinished Revolution, 1863–1877*. New York: Harper.

Forman, Tyrone A. and Amanda E. Lewis. 2006. "Racial Apathy and Hurricane Katrina." *Du Bois Review*, 3 (1): 175–202.

Fortin, Jacey. 2021. "Critical Race Theory: A Brief History." *New York Times*, July 27. https://www.nytimes.com/article/what-is-critical-race-theory.html.

Fowler, Matthew, Vladimir E. Medenica and Cathy J. Cohen. 2017. "Why 41 Percent of White Millennials Voted for Trump." *Washington Post*, December 15, 2017. https://www.washingtonpost.com/news/monkey-cage/wp/2017/12/15/racial -resentment-is-why-41-percent-of-white-millennials-voted-for-trump-in-2016/.

Frankenberg, Erica. 2019. "What School Segregation Looks Like in the US Today, in 4 Charts." *The Conversation.com*, July 19. https://theconversation.com/what -school-segregation-looks-like-in-the-us-today-in-4-charts-120061.

Freedman, Johnathan L. and Scott C. Fraser. 1966. "Compliance Without Pressure: The Foot-in-the-Door Technique." *Journal of Personality and Social Psychology*, 4 (2): 195–202.

Friedersdorf, Conor. 2020. "Anti-Racist Arguments are Tearing People Apart." *The Atlantic*, August 20. https://www.theatlantic.com/ideas/archive/2020/08/meta -arguments-about-anti-racism/615424/.

Gaertner, Samuel F. and John F. Dovidio. 2004. "Aversive Racism." In *Advances in Experimental Social Psychology (Vol. 36)*, Mark Zanna (Ed.), 1–52. San Diego, CA: Elsevier Academic.

Gainous, Jason. 2012. "The New 'New Racism' Thesis: Limited Government Values and Race-Conscious Policy Attitudes." *Journal of Black Studies*, 43 (3): 251–73.

Gale, William G. and Claire Haldeman. 2021. *The Tax Cuts and Jobs Act: Searching for Supply-Side Effects.* Economic Studies at Brookings, June 28. https://www.brookings.edu/wp-content/uploads/2021/07/20210628_TPC_GaleHaldeman_TCJASupplySideEffectsReport_FINAL.pdf.

García, Emma. 2020. "Schools Are Still Segregated, and Black Children Are Paying a Price." *Economic Policy Institute*, February 12. https://www.epi.org/publication/schools-are-still-segregated-and-black-children-are-paying-a-price/.

Gardner, Chris. 2021. "Dave Chappelle Gets Standing Ovation Amid Netflix Special Controversy: 'If This Is What Being Canceled Is, I Love It.'" *The Hollywood Reporter*, October 8. https://www.hollywoodreporter.com/news/general-news/dave-chappelle-netflix-special-critics-cancel-culture-1235028197/.

Garrett, Kristin N. and Alexa Bankert. 2020. "The Moral Roots of Partisan Division: How Moral Conviction Heightens Affective Polarization." *British Journal of Political Science*, 50 (2): 621–40.

Geller, Amanda, Jeffrey Fagan, Tom Tyler and Bruce G. Link. 2014. "Aggressive Policing and the Mental Health of Young Urban Men." *American Journal of Public Health*, 104 (12): 2321–27.

Georgeac, Oriane A. M., Aneeta Rattan and Daniel A. Effron. 2018. "An Exploratory Investigation of Americans' Expression of Gender Bias Before and After the 2016 Presidential Election." *Social Psychological and Personality Science*, 10 (5): 342–62.

Gertz, Matt. 2021. "The Feedback Loop the Conservative Movement is Using Against 'Critical Race Theory.'" *Media Matters*, June 23. https://www.mediamatters.org/fox-news/feedback-loop-conservative-movement-using-against-critical-race-theory.

Ghosh, Palash. 2021. "A Year after George Floyd Killing, Fewer Americans Support Black Lives Matter Movement, Poll Finds." *Forbes*, May 25. https://www.forbes.com/sites/palashghosh/2021/05/25/a-year-after-george-floyd-killing-fewer-americans-support-black-lives-matter-movement-poll-finds/?sh=5ac699db53a2.

Gillespie, Andra. 2022. "Virginia's New Lieutenant Governor is a Black Republican Woman. That Identity is More Common Than You May Think." *Washington Post*, January 21. https://www.washingtonpost.com/politics/2022/01/21/winsome-sears-black-republicans/.

Gilliam, Franklin D. and Shanto Iyengar. 2000. "The Influence of Local Television News on the Viewing Public." *American Journal of Political Science*, 44 (3): 560–73.

Giscombé, Cheryl L. and Marci Lobel. 2005. "Explaining Disproportionately High Rates of Adverse Birth Outcomes Among African Americans: The Impact of Stress, Racism, and Related Factors in Pregnancy." *Psychological Bulletin*, 131 (5): 662–83.

Glaser, April. 2020. "Current and Ex-employees Allege Google Drastically Rolled Back Diversity and Inclusion Programs." *NBC News*, May 13. https://www

.nbcnews.com/news/us-news/current-ex-employees-allege-google-drastically -rolled-back-diversity-inclusion-n1206181.

Glasgow, Joshua. 2009. "Racism as Disrespect." *Ethics*, 120: 64–93.

Glick, Peter. 2019. "Gender, Sexism, and the Election: Did Sexism Help Trump More Than It Hurt Clinton?" *Politics, Groups, and Identities*, 7 (3): 713–23.

Gonyea, Don. 2017. "Majority of White Americans Say They Believe Whites Face Discrimination." *NPR.org*, October 24. https://www.npr.org/2017/10/24 /559604836/majority-of-white-americans-think-theyre-discriminated-against.

Gonzalez, Mike. 2021. "Marxism Underpins Black Lives Matter Agenda." *Heritage.org*, September 8. https://www.heritage.org/progressivism/commentary/ marxism-underpins-black-lives-matter-agenda.

Goodridge, T. P. 2016. "Black Lives Matter Timeline." https://www.sps186.org/ downloads/basic/636414/Black%20Lives%20Matter%20Timeline%20.pdf.

Government Accountability Office. 2021. "K-12 education: Students' Experiences with Bullying, Hate Speech, Hate Crimes, and Victimization in Schools." Report to United States House of Representatives, Committee on Education and Labor. https: //www.gao.gov/assets/gao-22-104341.pdf.

Greene, Joshua. 2013. *Moral Tribes: Emotion, Reason, and the Gap Between Us and Them.* New York, NY: Penguin Press.

Griffin, Robert, Mayesha Quasem, John Sides and Michael Tesler. 2021. "Racing Apart: Partisan Shifts on Racial Attitudes over the Last Decade." *Democracy Fund Voter Study Group.* https://www.voterstudygroup.org/publication/racing-apart.

Gross, Terry. 2021. "Uncovering Who is Driving the Fight Against Critical Race Theory in Schools." *National Public Radio*, June 24 [Radio broadcast transcript]. https://www.npr.org/2021/06/24/1009839021/uncovering-who-is-driving-the-fight -against-critical-race-theory-in-schools.

Gushue, George V. and Madonna G. Constantine. 2007. "Color-Blind Racial Attitudes and White Racial Identity Attitudes in Psychology Trainees." *Professional Psychology: Research and Practice*, 38 (3): 321–28.

Hadarics, Márton. 2020. "Perceived Outgroup Characteristics as Antecedents and Consequences of Moral Exclusion." *The Social Science Journal*, 59 (1): 61–70.

Hadarics, Márton and Anna Kende. 2019. "Negative Stereotypes as Motivated Justifications for Moral Exclusion." *Journal of Social Psychology*, 159 (3): 257–69.

Haidt, Jonathan. 2001. "The Emotional Dog and Its Rational Tail: A Social Intuitionist Approach to Moral Judgment." *Psychological Review*, 108 (4): 814–34.

Haidt, Jonathan. 2012. *The Righteous Mind: Why Good People Are Divided by Politics and Religion.* New York, NY: Vintage Books.

Haley, Hillary, & Jim Sidanius. 2006. "The Positive and Negative Framing of Affirmative Action: A Group Dominance Perspective." *Personality and Social Psychology Bulletin*, 32 (5): 656–68.

Haltinner, Kristin. 2016. "Individual Responsibility, Culture, or State Organized Enslavement? How Tea Party Activists Frame Racial Inequality." *Race & Class Inequalities*, 59 (2): 395–418.

Hanci, Fadil. 2019. "Hate Crimes Increase in the US Since Trump's Election." *Politics Today,* July 22. https://politicstoday.org/hate-crimes-increase-in-the-us-since-trumps-election/.

Hanson, Melanie. 2022. "College Enrollment & Student Demographic Statistics." EducationData.org, April 22. https://educationdata.org/college-enrollment-statistics.

Hanson, Victor D. 2022. "The Mythologies of Black Lives Matter." *The New Criterion*, March. https://newcriterion.com/issues/2022/3/the-mythologies-of-black-lives-matter.

Harper, S., MacLehose, R. F., & Kaufman, J. S. (2014). Trends in the Black-White lifespan expectancy gap among US states, 1990–2009. *Health Affairs*, 33(8), 1375–82.

Harriot, Michael. 2021. "Weaponizing 'Woke': A Brief History of White Definitions." *The Root*, November 12. https://www.theroot.com/weaponizing-woke-an-brief-history-of-white-definitions-1848031729.

Harriot, Michael and Brittney Cooper. 2021. "The Root Institute: Unpacking the attacks on Critical Race Theory." *The Root*, September 21. https://www.theroot.com/the-root-institute-2021-unpacking-the-attacks-on-criti-1847711634.

Harris, Leslie M. 2020. "I Helped Fact-Check The 1619 Project. The Times Ignored Me." *Politico*, March 6. https://www.politico.com/news/magazine/2020/03/06/1619-project-new-york-times-mistake-122248.

Hassan, Jennifer and Siobhán O' Grady. 2020. "Anger over George Floyd's Killing Ripples Far Beyond the United States." *Washington Post*, May 29. https://www.washingtonpost.com/world/2020/05/29/world-reacts-george-floyd-minneapolis-protests/.

Hassan, Yossi, Maya Tamir, Kea S. Brahms, J. Christopher Cohrs and Eran Halperin. 2018. "Are Liberals and Conservatives Equally Motivated to Feel Empathy Toward Others?" *Personality and Social Psychology Bulletin*, 44 (10): 1449–59.

Havercroft, Jonathan and Justin Murphy. 2018. "Is the Tea Party Libertarian, Authoritarian, or Something Else?" *Social Science Quarterly*, 99 (3): 1021–37.

Hayes, Christal, Kevin Johnson and Claire Thornton. 2022. "At Least 10 Dead, 3 Hurt in Buffalo Supermarket Shooting; Gov. Kathy Hochul Blames 'White Supremacy.'" *USA Today*, May 14. https://www.usatoday.com/story/news/nation/2022/05/14/buffalo-new-york-shooting-tops/9778322002/.

Heard-Garris, Nia J., M. Cale, L. Camaj, M.C. Hamati and T. P. Dominguez. 2018. "Transmitting Trauma: A Systematic Review of Vicarious Racism and Child Health." *Social Science & Medicine*, 199: 230–40.

Heard-Garris, Nia, Kaitlyn A. Sacotte, Tyler N. A. Winkleman, Alyssa Cohen, Patricia O. Ekwueme, Elizabeth Barnert, Mercedes Carnethon and Matthew M. Davis. 2019. "Association of Childhood History of Parental Incarceration and Juvenile Justice Involvement with Mental Health in Early Adulthood." *JAMA Network Open*, 2 (9). doi:10.1001/jamanetworkopen.2019.10465.

Heilig, Julian V., Keffrelyn D. Brown and Anthony L. Brown. 2012. "The Illusion of Inclusion: A Critical Race Theory Textual Analysis of Race and Standards." *Harvard Educational Review*, 82 (3): 403–24.

Henderson, Wade and Nancy Zirkin. 2013. *Re: Hearing on "Stand Your Ground" Laws: Civil Rights and Public Safety Implications of Expanded Use of Deadly Force.* The Leadership Conference on Civil and Human Rights, October 29. https://civilrights.org/resource/re-hearing-on-stand-your-ground-laws-civil-rights-and-public-safety-implications-of-the-expanded-use-of-deadly-force/.

Henriques, Gregg. 2011. "The Influence Matrix," in *A New Unified Theory of Psychology*, G. Henriques (ed.), 81–111. New York, NY: Springer.

Hill, Latoya and Samantha Artiga. 2021. "COVID-19 Cases and Deaths by Race/Ethnicity: Current Data and Changes Over Time." *Kaiser Family Foundation*, October 8. https://www.kff.org/racial-equity-and-health-policy/issue-brief/covid-19-cases-and-deaths-by-race-ethnicity-current-data-and-changes-over-time/.

Hill-HarrisX Poll. 2019. "Poll: Most Republicans Think White People Face Discrimination, Democrats Disagree." *The Hill*, March 8. https://thehill.com/hilltv/what-americas-thinking/433270-poll-republicans-and-democrats-differ-strongly-on-whether-white.

Hockstein, Evelyn. (@evelynpix). 2021. "The scene tonight at a raucous Loudoun County school board hearing where many came to voice opposition to critical race theory. The meeting was stopped when the crowd wouldn't quiet down and two were arrested." Tweet, June 22. https://twitter.com/evelynpix/status/1407529403169509379.

Hoffman, Timothy J. 2015. "The Civil Rights Realignment: How Race Dominates Presidential Elections." *Political Analysis*, 17 (1): 1–23.

hooks, bell. 1995. *Killing Rage: Ending Racism.* New York, NY: Holt Paperbacks.

Horowitz, Juliana M. 2021. "Support for Black Lives Matter Declined After George Floyd Protests But Has Remained Unchanged Since." *Pew Research*, September 27. https://www.pewresearch.org/fact-tank/2021/09/27/support-for-black-lives-matter-declined-after-george-floyd-protests-but-has-remained-unchanged-since/.

Horowitz, Juliana M., Anna Brown and Kiana Cox. 2019. "Race in America 2019." *Pew Research Center,* April 9. https://www.pewsocialtrends.org/2019/04/09/race-in-america-2019/.

Howard University. 2022. "Black Lives Matter Movement." *Howard University Law Library.* https://library.law.howard.edu/civilrightshistory/BLM.

Hughes, Cris E., Carla D. Hunter, Patrick T. Vargas, Michael D. Schlosser, and Ripan S. Malhi (2016). "Police Endorse Color-blind Racial Beliefs More Than Laypersons." *Race and Social Problems*, 8: 160–70.

Hughey, Matthew W. 2012. "Stigma Allure and White Antiracist Identity Management." *Social Psychology Quarterly*, 75 (3): 219–41.

Hurwitz, Jon and Mark Peffley. 2005. "Playing the Race Card in the Post-Willie Horton Era: The Impact of Racialized Code Words on Support for Punitive Crime Policy." *Public Opinion Quarterly*, 69 (1): 99–112.

Hutchings, Vincent L. and Cara Wong. 2014. "Racism, Group Position, and Attitudes about Immigration Among Blacks and Whites." *Du Bois Review*, 11 (2): 419–42.

Iati, Marisa. 2021. "What Is Critical Race Theory, and Why Do Republicans Want to Ban It in Schools?" *Washington Post*, May 29. https://www.washingtonpost.com/education/2021/05/29/critical-race-theory-bans-schools/.

Isenberg, Nancy. 2016. *White Trash: The 400-year Untold History of Class in America*. New York, NY: Penguin Books.

Itkowitz, Colby and Michael Brice-Saddler. 2019. "Trump Still Won't Apologize to the Central Park Five. Here's What He Said at the Time." *Washington Post*, June 18. https://www.washingtonpost.com/politics/trump-still-wont-apologize-to-the-central-park-five-heres-what-he-said-at-the-time/2019/06/18/.

Iyengar, Shanto, Gaurav Sood and Yphtach Lelkes. 2012. "Affect, Not Ideology: A Social Identity Perspective on Polarization." Public Opinion Quarterly 76: 405–31.

Jan, Tracy, Jena McGregor and Meghan Hoyer. 2021. "Corporate America's $50 Billion Promise." *Washington Post*, August 24. https://www.washingtonpost.com/business/interactive/2021/george-floyd-corporate-america-racial-justice/.

Jardina, Ashley. 2019. *White Identity Politics*. Cambridge, UK: Cambridge University.

Jardina, Ashley and Michael Traugott. 2019. "The Genesis of the Birther Rumor: Partisanship, Racial Attitudes, and Political Knowledge." *Journal of Race, Ethnicity, and Politics*, 4 (1): 60–80.

Jefferson, Hakeem and Michael Tesler. 2021. "Why White Voters with Racist Views Often Still Support Black Republicans." *FiveThirtyEight.com*, November 10. https://fivethirtyeight.com/features/why-racist-white-voters-often-favor-black-republicans/.

Jennings, Willie J. 2010. *The Christian Imagination: Theology and the Origins of Race*. New Haven, CT: Yale University Press.

Jones, James R. 2018. "Morality in Racialized Institutions. *The British Journal of Sociology*, 69 (3): 560–4.

Jones, Maria S., Veronica Womack, Gihane Jérémie-Brink and Danielle D. Dickens. 2021. "Gendered Racism and Mental Health among Young Adult U.S. Black Women: The Moderating Roles of Gendered Racial Identity, Centrality, and Identity Shifting." *Sex Roles*, 85: 221–31.

Jordan-Zachery, Julia S. 2021. "The Media Loves 'Missing White Women.' Black Women Are Already Missing from Public View." *Washington Post*, October 14. https://www.washingtonpost.com/politics/2021/10/14/media-loves-missing-white-women-black-women-are-already-missing-public-view/.

Jost, John T., Chadly Stern, Nicholas O. Rule and Joanna Sterling. 2017. "The Politics of Fear: Is There an Ideological Asymmetry in Existential Motivation?" *Social Cognition*, 35 (4): 324–53. Doi:http://dx.doi.org/101521soco2017354324.

Kanter, Johnathan W., Monnica T. Williams, Adam M. Kuczynski, Katherine E. Manbeck, Marlena Debreaux and Daniel C. Rosen. 2017. "A Preliminary Report on the Relationship Between Microaggressions Against Black People and Racism Among White College Students." *Race and Social Problems*, 9: 291–99.

Karikari-Yawson, Ama. 2020. *The Talk: A Black Family's Conversation about Racism and Police Brutality*. New York, NY: Milestales Publishing.

Karma, Roge. 2020. "Democrats are Running on the Most Progressive Police Reform Agenda in Modern American History." *Vox*, September 8. https://www.vox.com/21418125/biden-harris-pelosi-defund-the-police-criminal-justice-reform-2020.

Katz, A. J. 2022. "Tucker Carlson Tonight Is No. 1 in All Measurements for First Time Ever." *AdWeek*, January 3. https://www.adweek.com/tvnewser/top-cable

-news-shows-of-2021-tucker-carlson-tonight-is-no-1-in-all-categories-for-first
-time-ever/496940/.

Kendi, Ibram X. 2016. *Stamped from the Beginning: The Definitive History of Racist Ideas in America.* New York, NY: Nation Books.

Kennedy, Randall. 2011. *The Persistence of the Color Line: Racial Politics and the Obama Presidency.* New York, NY: Vintage Books.

Kessler, Jim and Robert Cotter. 2020. "If Black Lives Truly Matter, Stand Your Ground Laws Must Go." *Daily Beast*, September 4. https://www.thedailybeast.com/if-black-lives-truly-matter-stand-your-ground-laws-must-go.

Kinder, Donald R. and Lynn M. Sanders. 1996. *Divided by Color: Racial Politics and Democratic Ideals.* Chicago, IL: University of Chicago.

Kinder, Donald R. and David O. Sears. 1981. "Prejudice and Politics: Symbolic Racism Versus Racial Threats to the Good Life." *Journal of Personality and Social Psychology*, 40: 414–31.

King, Martin L. 1963. *Untitled* [Letter from a Birmingham Jail], April 16. https://www.africa.upenn.edu/Articles_Gen/Letter_Birmingham.html.

Klar, Rebecca. 2020. "National Security Adviser Blames 'A Few Bad Apples,' Says There's Not Systemic Racism in Law Enforcement." *The Hill*, May 31. https://thehill.com/homenews/administration/500328-national-security-adviser-blames-a-few-bad-apples-says-theres-not.

Klein, Ezra. 2021. "Transcript: Ezra Klein Interviews Ibram X. Kendi." *New York Times*, July 16. https://www.nytimes.com/2021/07/16/podcasts/transcript-ezra-klein-interviews-ibram-x-kendi.html.

Knuckey, Jonathan and Myunghee Kim. 2015. "Racial Resentment, Old-Fashioned Racism, and the Vote Choice of Southern and Nonsouthern Whites in the 2012 U.S. Presidential Election." *Social Science Quarterly*, 96 (4): 905–22.

Koeske, Zak. 2017. "Obama as Symbol of Hope, Possibility for Blacks, Key to Racial Legacy, Scholars Say." *Chicago Tribune*, January 13. https://www.chicagotribune.com/news/ct-sta-king-obama-legacy-st-0116-20170113-story.html.

Kordesh, Kathleen S, Lisa B. Spainerman and Helen A. Neville. 2013. "White University Students' Racial Affect: Understanding the Antiracist Type." *Journal of Diversity in Higher Education*, 6 (1): 33–50.

Krogstad, Jens Manuel. 2020. "Most Cuban American Voters Identify as Republican in 2020." *Pew Research*, October 2, 2020. https://www.pewresearch.org/fact-tank/2020/10/02/most-cuban-american-voters-identify-as-republican-in-2020/.

Krumpal, Ivar. 2013. "Determinants of Social Desirability Bias in Sensitive Surveys: A Literature Review." *Quality and Quantity*, 47: 2025–47.

Kteily, Nour S and Emile Bruneau. 2017. "Darker Demons of Our Nature: The Need to (Re)focus Attention on Blatant Forms of Dehumanization." *Current Directions in Psychological Science*, 26 (6): 487–94.

Kteily, Nour S., Gordon Hodson and Emile Bruneau. 2016. "They See Us As Less Than Human: Metadehumanization Predicts Intergroup Conflict Via Reciprocal Dehumanization." Journal of Personality and Social Psychology, 110 (3): 343–70.

Lane, Haley M., Rachel Morello-Frosch, Julian D. Marshall and Joshua S. Apte. 2022. "Historical Redlining is Associated with Present-day Air Pollution Disparities in

U.S. Cities." *Environmental Science and Technology Letters*, 9 (4): 345–50. https: //doi.org/10.1021/acs.estlett.1c01012.

Lauter, David. 2021. "Economy, COVID Drove Latino Voters Toward Trump in 2020." *Los Angeles Times*, December 17, 2021. https://www.latimes.com/politics /newsletter/2021-12-17/economy-covid-drove-latino-voters-toward-trump-2020 -essential-politics.

Lawson, April. 2021. "Building Trust Across the Political Divide: The Surprising Bridge of Conflict." *Comment Magazine*, January 21. https://comment.org/building -trust-across-the-political-divide/.

Lemon, Jason. 2020. "Half of Americans Think Trump Is Racist and Additional 13 Percent Unsure: Poll." *Newsweek*, July 16, 2020. https://www.newsweek.com/half -americans-think-trump-racist-additional-13-percent-are-unsure-poll-1518272.

Lemons, Katherine and Joshua Takano Chambers-Letson. 2014. "Rule of Law: Sharia Panic and the US Constitution in the House of Representatives." *Cultural Studies*, 28 (5–6): 1048–77.

Lent, Robert W., Steven. D. Brown and Gail Hackett. 1994. "Toward a Unifying Social Cognitive Theory of Career and Academic Interest, Choice, and Performance." *Journal of Vocational Behavior*, 45: 79–122.

Levin, Josh. 2013. "The Welfare Queen." *Slate.com*, December 19. http://www .slate.com/articles/news_and_politics/history/2013/12/linda_taylor_welfare_queen _ronald_reagan_made_her_a_notorious_american_villain.html.

Levingston, Steven. 2017. *Kennedy and King*. New York: Hachette Books.

Levitz, Eric. 2021a. "How Racist is Anti-Racism?" *New York Magazine*, July 26. https://nymag.com/intelligencer/2021/07/how-anti-racist-is-ibram-x-kendis-anti -racism.html.

Levitz, Eric. 2021b. "When Keeping It 'Woke' Gets Racist, Liberals Should Say So." *New York Magazine*, November 9. https://nymag.com/intelligencer/2021/11/ critical-race-theory-crt-schools-liberals-equity-consultants.html.

Levy, Jonathan. 2021. *Ages of American Capitalism: A History of the United States.* New York, NY: Random House.

Lin, Yu-Hsuan, Chih-Lin Chiang, Po-Hsein Lin, Li-Ren Chang, Chih-Hung Ko, Yang-Han Lee and Sheng-Hsuan Lin. 2016. "Proposed Diagnostic Criteria for Smartphone Addiction." *PloS One*, 11 (11): e0163010–e0163010.

Linder, Chris. 2015. "Navigating Guilt, Shame, and Fear of Appearing Racist: A Conceptual Model of Antiracist White Feminist Identity Development." *Journal of College Student Development*, 56 (6): 535–50.

Linder, Nicole M. and Brian A. Nosek. 2009. "Alienable Speech: Ideological Variations in the Application of Free Speech Principles." *Political Psychology*, 30 (1): 67–92.

Lockhart, P. R. 2019. "How Slavery Became America's First Big Business." *Vox*, August 16. https://www.vox.com/identities/2019/8/16/20806069/slavery-economy -capitalism-violence-cotton-edward-baptist.

Lodge, Milton and Charles S. Taber. 2013. *The Rationalizing Voter.* New York, NY: Cambridge University Press.

Logan, Erin B. 2020. "'A Man's Man': Why Some Black Men Are Drawn to Trump's Toxic Masculinity." *Los Angeles Times*, October 28. https://www.latimes.com/opinion/story/2020-10-28/la-ol-black-trump-voters-men.

Long, Cindy. 2016. "Study: Access to School Library Resources Forms Along Racial Lines." *National Education Association News*, November 2. https://www.nea.org/advocating-for-change/new-from-nea/study-access-school-library-resources-forms-along-racial-lines.

Long, Heather. 2020. "The Trump vs. Obama Economy—in 16 Charts." *Washington Post*, September 5. https://www.washingtonpost.com/business/2020/09/05/trump-obama-economy/.

Lotto, David. 2016. "The South Has Risen Again: Thoughts on the Tea Party and the Recent Rise of Right-Wing Racism." *The Journal of Psychohistory*, 43 (3): 156–166.

Love, Bettina L. and Brandelyn Tosolt. 2010. "Reality or Rhetoric? Barack Obama and Post-Racial America." *Race, Gender, and Class*, 17 (3/4): 19–37.

Lukianoff, Greg and Jonathan Haidt. 2018. *The Coddling of the American Mind.* New York, NY: Penguin Press.

Lumpkin, Lauren and Susan Svrluga. 2022. "Fear, Anxiety Follow Third Wave of Bomb Threats Targeting HBCUs." *Washington Post*, February 2. https://www.washingtonpost.com/opinions/2022/02/02/black-history-woke-appropriation-misuse/.

MacKuen, Michael, George E. Marcus, W. Russell Neuman and Luke Keele. 2007. "The Third Way: The Theory of Affective Intelligence and American Democracy." In *The Affect Effect*, W. Russell Neuman, George E. Marcus, Ann N. Crigler and Michael MacKuen (eds), 124–51. Chicago, IL: University of Chicago.

Madison, Lucy. 2011. "On Bus Tour, Obama Embraces 'Obamacare,' Says, 'I Do Care.'" *CBS News*, August 15. https://www.cbsnews.com/news/on-bus-tour-obama-embraces-obamacare-says-i-do-care/.

Major, Brenda, Alison Blodorn and Gregory M. Blascovich. 2018. "The Threat of Increasing Diversity: Why Many White Americans Support Trump in the 2016 Presidential Election." *Group Processes and Intergroup Relations*, 21 (6): 931–40.

Marable, Manning. 2007. *Race, Reform, and Rebellion: The Second Reconstruction and Beyond in Black America, 1945–2006.* Jackson, MS: University of Mississippi Press.

Marietta, Morgan and David C. Barker. 2019. *One Nation, Two Realities: Dueling Facts in American Democracy.* New York, NY: Oxford University Press.

Mason, Lilliana. 2018. *Uncivil Agreement: How Politics Became Our Identity.* Chicago, IL: University of Chicago Press.

Maxwell, Angie and T. Wayne Parent. 2012. "The Obama Trigger: Presidential Approval and Tea Party Membership." *Social Science Quarterly*, 93 (5): 1384–401.

Mayorga-Gallo, Sarah. 2019. "The White-Centering Logic of Diversity Ideology." *American Behavioral Scientist*, 63 (13): 1789–809.

McArdle, Megan. 2021. "The Debate over 'Latinx' Highlights a Broader Problem for Democrats." *Washington Post*, December 10. https://www.washingtonpost.com/opinions/2021/12/10/debate-over-latinx-highlights-broader-problem-democrats/.

McCarthy, Andrew C. 2020. "Systemic Racism? Make Them Prove it." *National Review*, September 19. https://www.nationalreview.com/2020/09/systemic-racism-criminal-justice-system-make-critics-prove-charge/.

McCarthy, Tom. 2015. "Here's Why Donald Trump Won't Win the Republican Presidential Nomination." *The Guardian*, August 22. https://www.theguardian.com/us-news/2015/aug/22/donald-trump-wont-win-republican-presidential-nomination.

McClintock, Andrew S., Timothy Anderson, Candace L. Patterson and Edgar H. Wing. 2018. "Early Psychotherapeutic Empathy, Alliance, and Client Outcome: Preliminary Evidence of Indirect Effects." *Journal of Clinical Psychology*, 74 (6): 839–48.

McElwee, Sean. 2016. "Yep, Race Really Did Trump Economics: A Data Dive on His Supporters Reveals Deep Racial Animosity." *Salon*, November 13. https://www.salon.com/2016/11/13/yep-race-really-did-trump-economics-a-data-diveon-his-supporters-reveals-deep-racial-animosity/.

McGhee, Heather. 2021. *The Sum of Us: What Racism Costs Everyone and How We Can Prosper Together.* New York, NY: One World.

McWhorter, John. 2020. "The Dehumanizing Condescension of White Fragility." *The Atlantic*, July 15. https://www.theatlantic.com/ideas/archive/2020/07/dehumanizing-condescension-white-fragility/614146/.

McWhorter, John. 2021. *Woke Racism.* New York, NY: Portfolio/Penguin.

McWhorter, John. 2022a. "When 'Racism' Is Not Really Racism." *New York Times*, November 15. https://www.nytimes.com/2022/11/15/opinion/racism-systemic-structural.html.

McWhorter, John. 2022b. "'Racism' Without Racists." *New York Times*, November 22. https://www.nytimes.com/2022/11/22/opinion/racism-racists-systemic.html.

Media Matters Staff. 2021. "Tucker Carlson: 'Nonwhite people' are 'cheering the extinction of white people.'" *MediaMatters.org*, August 13. https://www.mediamatters.org/tucker-carlson/tucker-carlson-nonwhite-people-are-cheering-extinction-white-people.

Medina, Jennifer. 2020. "The Macho Appeal of Donald Trump." *Washington Post*, October 14. https://www.nytimes.com/2020/10/14/us/politics/trump-macho-appeal.html.

Meier, August. 1956. "The Negro and the Democratic Party, 1875–1915." *Phylon*, 17 (2): 173–91.

Merritt, Anna C., Daniel A. Effron, Steven Fein, Kenneth K. Savitsky, Daniel M. Tuller, and Benoit Monin. 2012. "The Strategic Pursuit of Moral Credentials." *Journal of Experimental Social Psychology*, 48: 774–77.

Meyer, Oanh L. and Nolan Zane. 2013. "The Influence of Race and Ethnicity in Clients' Experiences of Mental Health Treatment." *Journal of Community Psychology*, 41 (7): 884–901.

Michel, Casey. 2021. "Fox News Star Tucker Carlson's 'Great Replacement' Segment Used a New Frame for an Old Fear." *NBC News*, April 12, 2021. https://www.nbcnews.com/think/opinion/tucker-carlson-s-great-replacement-fox-news-segment-uses-newer-ncna1263880.

Miller, Steven V. 2018. *Economic anxiety or racial resentment? An evaluation of attitudes toward immigration in the U.S. from 1992 to 2016.* (Working Paper) http://svmiller.com/research/economic-anxiety-racial-resentment-immigration-1992-2016/.

Mishan, Ligaya. 2020. "The Long and Tortured History of Cancel Culture." *The New York Times Style Magazine*, December 3. https://www.nytimes/com/2020/12/03/t-magazine/cancel-culture-history.html.

Moore, Wendy L. and Joyce M. Bell. 2019. "The Limits of Community: Deconstructing the White Framing of Racist Speech in Universities." *American Behavioral Scientist*, 63 (13): 1760–75.

Moyer, Justin W., Jenny Starrs and Sarah Larimer. 2016. "Trump Supporter Charged After Sucker-Punching Protester at North Carolina Rally." *Washington Post*, March 11. https://www.washingtonpost.com/news/morning-mix/wp/2016/03/10/trump-protester-sucker-punched-at-north-carolina-rally-videos-show/.

MSNBC. "Biden Campaign Releases New Ad Aimed at Black Voters." YouTube. September 3, 2020. News video, 0:13 to 1:13. https://www.youtube.com/watch?v=rPBswTmpxm8.

Muhammad, Khalil G. 2010. *The Condemnation of Blackness.* Cambridge, MA: Harvard University Press.

Mullen, Elizabeth and Janice Nadler. 2008. "Moral Spillovers: The Effect of Moral Violations on Deviant Behavior." *Journal of Experimental Social Psychology*, 44: 1239–45.

Muravchick, Stephanie and Jon A. Shields. 2020. "Why Trump Made Gains Among Minority Men Against Biden." *Fortune*, November 6. https://fortune.com/2020/11/06/trump-support-black-latino-men-rappers/.

Mutz, Diana C. 2018. "Status Threat, Not Economic Hardship, Explains the 2016 Presidential Vote." *Proceedings of the National Academy of Sciences*, 115 (19): 4330–39.

Napier, Jaime L. and Tom R. Tyler. 2008. "Does Moral Conviction Really Override Concerns About Procedural Justice? A Reexamination of the Value Protection Model." *Social Justice Research*, 21: 509–28.

National Research Council. 2014. *The Growth of Incarceration in the United States: Exploring Causes and Consequences.* https://nap.nationalacademies.org/read/18613/chapter/1.

Nelson, Thomas E. and Donald R. Kinder. 1996. "Issue Frames and Group-Centrism in American Public Opinion." *Journal of Politics*, 58: 1055–78.

Neuman, W. R., George E. Marcus, Ann N. Crigler and Michael MacKuen. 2007. *The Affect Effect*, 124–51. Chicago, IL: University of Chicago.

Neville, Helen A., Roderick L. Lilly, Georgia Duran, Richard M. Lee and LaVonne Browne. 2000. "Construction and Initial Validation of the Color-Blind Racial Attitudes Scale (CoBRAS)." *Journal of Counseling Psychology*, 47 (1): 59–70.

Neville, Helen A., Lisa Spainerman and Bao-Tran Doan. 2006. "Exploring the Association Between Color-Blind Racial Ideology and Multicultural Counseling Competencies." *Cultural Diversity and Ethnic Minority Psychology*, 12 (2): 275–90.

Nisbet, Erik, Ronald Ostman and James Shanahan. 2008. "Shaping the Islamic Threat: The Influence of Ideology, Religiosity, and Media Use on Public Opinion toward Islam and Muslim Americans." In *Muslims in Western Politics*, Abdulkader Sinno (Ed.), 161–99. Bloomington, IN: University of Indiana Press.

Norton, Michael I. and Samuel R. Sommers. 2011. "Whites See Racism as a Zero-Sum Game That They Are Now Losing." *Perspectives on Psychological Science*, 6 (3): 215–18.

NPR Staff. 2021. "Understanding the 2020 Electorate: AP VoteCast Survey." *National Public Radio*, May 21, 2021. https://www.npr.org/2020/11/03/929478378/understanding-the-2020-electorate-ap-votecast-survey.

Obama, Barack H. 2006. *The Audacity of Hope: Thoughts on Reclaiming the American Dream.* New York, NY: Crown Publishers.

Obama, Barack H. 2020. *A Promised Land.* New York, NY: Crown Publishers.

Opotow, Susan. 1991. "Adolescent Peer Conflicts: Implications for Students and for Schools." *Education and Urban Society*, 23: 416–41.

Opotow, Susan. 1995. "Drawing the Line: Social Categorization, Moral Exclusion, and the Scope of Justice," in *Conflict, Cooperation, and Justice*, B. B. Bunker and J. Z. Rubin (eds.), 347–69. San Francisco: Jossey-Bass.

Opotow, Susan, Janet Gerson and Sarah Woodside. 2005. "From Moral Exclusion to Moral Inclusion: Theory for Teaching Peace." *Theory into Practice*, 44 (4): 303–18.

Ostfeld, Mara and Michelle Garcia. 2020. "Black Men Shift Slightly Toward Trump in Record Numbers, Polls Show." *NBC News*, November 4, 2020. https://www.nbcnews.com/news/nbcblk/black-men-drifted-democrats-toward-trump-record-numbers-polls-show-n1246447.

Outten, H. Robert, Michael T. Schmitt, Daniel A. Miller and Amber L. Garcia. 2012. "Feeling Threatened About the Future: Whites' Emotional Reactions to Anticipated Ethnic Demographic Changes." *Personality and Social Psychology Bulletin*, 38 (1): 14–25.

Pager, Devah and Hana Shepherd. 2008. "The Sociology of Discrimination: Racial Discrimination in Employment, Housing, Credit, and Consumer Markets." *Annual Review of Sociology*, 34: 181–209.

Panova, Tayana and Xavier Carbonell. 2018. "Is Smartphone Addiction Really an Addiction?" *Journal of Behavioral Addictions*, 7 (2): 252–59.

Passini, Stefano and Paola Villano. 2018. "Justice and Immigration: The Effect of Moral Exclusion." *International Journal of Psychological Research*, 11 (1): 42–9.

Paul, Joshua. 2019. "'Not Black and White, but Black and Red': Anti-Identity Identity Politics and #AllLivesMatter." *Ethnicities*, 19 (1): 3–19.

Pearce, Joseph. 2020. "What is 'Systemic Racism'?" *The Imaginative Conservative*, July 12. https://theimaginativeconservative.org/2020/07/what-systemic-racism-joseph-pearce.html.

Peckel, Linda. 2017. "Criteria for Identification of Smartphone Addiction." *Psychiatryadvisor.com,* July 27. https://www.psychiatryadvisor.com/home/topics/addiction/criteria-for-identification-of-smartphone-addiction/.

Peffley, Mark and Jon Hurwitz. 1998. "Whites' Stereotypes of Blacks: Sources and Political Consequences." In *Perception and prejudice: Race and politics in the United States*, Jon Hurwitz and Mark Peffley (Eds.), 58–99. New Haven, CT: Yale University Press.

Pereira, Ivan. 2022. "NFL Commissioner Addresses Issues with Diversity Following Brian Flores Lawsuit: ESPN." *ABC News*, February 5. https://abcnews.go.com /US/nfl-commissioner-addresses-issues-diversity-brian-flores-lawsuit/story?id =82693472.

Pérez, Efrén O. 2016. *Unspoken Politics: Implicit Attitudes and Political Thinking.* New York, NY: Cambridge University Press.

Perry, Andre M., Jonathan Rothwell and David Harshbarger. (2018). The devaluation of assets in Black neighborhoods. Brookings Institute. https://www.brookings.edu/ research/devaluation-of-assets-in-black-neighborhoods/.

Pew Research. 2009. Dissecting the 2008 Electorate: Voter Demographics Report. https://www.pewresearch.org/hispanic/2009/04/30/dissecting-the-2008-electorate -most-diverse-in-us-history/.

Pew Research. 2014. *Political polarization in the American public*, June 4. https: //www.pewresearch.org/politics/2014/06/12/political-polarization-in-the-american -public/.

Pfeifer, Michael J. 2009. "The Origins of Postbellum Lynching: Collective Violence in Reconstruction Louisiana." *Louisiana History*, 50 (2): 189–201.

Phelan, Julie E., & Laurie A. Rudman. 2011. "System Justification Beliefs, Affirmative Action, and Resistance to Equal Opportunity Organizations." *Social Congition*, 29 (3): 376–90.

Piazza, James A. 2020. "Politician Hate Speech and Domestic Terrorism." *International Interactions*, 46 (3): 431–53.

Pieterse, Alex L., Nathan R. Todd, Helen A. Neville and Robert T. Carter. 2012. "Perceived Racism and Mental Health Among Black American Adults: A Meta-Analytic Review." *Journal of Counseling Psychology*, 59 (1): 1–9.

Pilecki, Andrew. 2017. "Moral Exclusion," in *The Wiley-Blackwell Encyclopedia of Social Theory*, B.S. Turner (Ed.). https://doi.org/10.1002/9781118430873.est0796.

Porter, Eduardo. 2016. "Where Were Trump's Votes? Where the Jobs Weren't." *New York Times*, December 13. https://www.nytimes.com/2016/12/13/business/ economy/jobs-economy-voters.html.

Porter, Eduardo. 2020. *American Poison.* New York: Alfred A. Knopf.

Porter, Tom. 2021. "Tucker Carlson Stressed about Biden's War on White Supremacy and Sean Hannity Renewed Attacks on Hunter in a First Wave of Fox News Attacks on the New Administration." *Business Insider*, January 21. https://www .businessinsider.com/fox-news-carlson-hannity-attack-biden-inauguration-day -2021-1.

Potter, David. 1978. *The Impending Crisis: America Before the Civil War.* New York, NY: Harper Perennial.

Pratto, Felicia, James H. Liu, Shana Levin, Jim Sidanius, Margaret Shih, Hagit Bachrach and Peter Hegarty. 2000. "Social Dominance Orientation and the

Legitimization of Inequality Across Cultures." *Journal of Cross-Cultural Psychology*, 31 (3): 369–409.

Prowse, Gwen, Vesla M. Weaver and Tracy L. Mears. 2019. "The State from Below: Distorted Responsiveness in Policed Communities." *Urban Affairs Review*, 1–49.

Public Broadcasting System. 2016. *Birmingham and the Children's March*, April 26. https://www.pbs.org/wnet/religionandethics/2013/04/26/april-26-2013-birmingham-and-the-childrens-march/16051/.

Pyke, Karen D. 2010. "What Is Internalized Racial Oppression and Why Don't We Study It? Acknowledging Racism's Hidden Injuries." *Sociological Perspectives*, 53 (4): 551–72.

Quinton, Sophie. 2021. "Republicans Respond to Black Lives Matter with Anti-Protest Bills." *Pew Trusts.org*, February 4. https://www.pewtrusts.org/en/research-and-analysis/blogs/stateline/2021/02/04/republicans-respond-to-black-lives-matter-with-anti-protest-bills.

Rabinowitz, Joshua L., David O. Sears, Jim Sidanius and Jon A. Krosnik. 2009. "Why Do White Americans Oppose Race-Targeted Policies? Clarifying the Impact of Symbolic Racism." *Political Psychology*, 30 (5): 805–28.

Raimondo, Justin. 2016. "Do You Suffer from Trump Derangement Syndrome?" *Los Angeles Times*, December 27. https://www.latimes.com/opinion/op-ed/la-oe-raimondo-trump-derangement-syndrome-20161226-story.html.

Ramirez, Chris. 2020. "Black Conservatives in New Mexico Decry BLM, Systemic Racism." *KOB 4 News*, July 29. https://www.kob.com/new-mexico-news/black-conservatives-in-new-mexico-decry-blm-systemic-racism/5810806/.

Reid, Jason. 2022. "Miami's Firing of Brian Flores Is Latest Blow to NFL's Poor Record of Inclusive Hiring." *Andscape.com*, January 11. https://theundefeated.com/features/miamis-firing-of-brian-flores-is-latest-blow-to-nfls-poor-record-of-inclusive-hiring/.

Reny, Tyler, Loren Collingwood and Ali A. Valenzuela. 2019. "Vote Switching in the 2016 Election: How Racial and Immigration Attitudes, Not Economics, Explain Shifts in White Voting." *Public Opinion Quarterly*, 83 (1): 91–113.

Reuters. 2022. "Disney CEO, Asked if Company is 'Too Woke,' Says It Will Cater to Audience." October 26. https://www.reuters.com/business/media-telecom/disney-ceo-asked-if-company-is-too-woke-says-it-will-cater-audience-2022-10-26/.

Rhodes, Jesse, Raymond La Raja, Tatishe Nteta and Alexander Theodoridis. 2022. "Martin Luther King Jr. Was Right. Racism and Opposition to Democracy Are Linked, Our Research Finds. *Washington Post*, January 17. https://www.washingtonpost.com/politics/2022/01/17/mlk-racism-democracy-opinion/.

Riddle, Travis and Stacey Sinclair. 2019. "Racial Disparities in School-Based Disciplinary Actions Are Associated with County-Level Rates of Racial Bias." *PNAS*, 116 (17): 8255–60.

Rigeur, Leah Wright. 2016. *The Loneliness of the Black Republican.* Princeton, NJ: Princeton University.

Robenalt, James D. 2020. "The Republican President Who Called for Racial justice in America after Tulsa Massacre." *Washington Post*, June 21. https://www

.washingtonpost.com/history/2020/06/21/warren-harding-tulsa-race-massacre-trump/.

Robinson, Ishena. 2022. "How Woke Went from 'Black' to 'Bad.'" *Legal Defense Fund,* August 26. https://www.naacpldf.org/woke-black-bad/.

Rodriguez, Adrianna. 2019. "Fox News Host Tucker Carlson Says White Supremacy Is 'Not a Real Problem in America.'" *USA Today,* August 7. https://www.usatoday.com/story/news/politics/2019/08/07/fox-host-tucker-carlson-white-supremacy-not-real-problem-america/1941585001/.

Roediger, David (2005). *Working Toward Whiteness.* New York, NY: Basic Books.

Roman, John K. 2013. *Race, Justifiable Homicide, and Stand Your Ground Laws: Analysis of FBI Supplementary Homicide Report Data.* Urban Institute, July. https://www.urban.org/sites/default/files/publication/23856/412873-Race-Justifiable-Homicide-and-Stand-Your-Ground-Laws.PDF.

Roper Center for Public Opinion Research. "How Groups Voted in 2012." January 10, 2013. https://ropercenter.cornell.edu/how-groups-voted-2012.

Rosen, Sherwin. 1988. "The Value of Changes in Life Expectancy." *Journal of Risk and Uncertainty,* 1 (3): 285–304.

Rosenberg, Kenneth D., Rani A. Desai and Jianli Kan. 2002. "Why Do Foreign-Born Blacks Have Lower Infant Mortality than Native-Born Blacks? New Directions in African-American Infant Mortality Research." *Journal of the National Medical Association,* 94 (9): 770–78.

Rosenzweig, Saul. 1936. "Some Implicit Common Factors in Diverse Methods of Psychotherapy." American Journal of Orthopsychiatry, 6 (3): 412–15.

Rothstein, Richard. 2017. *The Color of Law.* New York: Liveright Publishing.

Rothwell, Jonathan T. and Pablo Diego-Rosell. 2016. *Explaining Nationalist Political Views: The Case of Donald Trump* (working paper). http://dx.doi.org/10.2139/ssrn.2822059.

Rubin, Simon. 1981. "A Two-Track Model of Bereavement: Theory and Research." *American Journal of Orthopsychiatry,* 51 (1): 101–09.

Rubin, Simon S. 1984. "Mourning Distinct from Melancholia: The Resolution of Bereavement." *British Journal of Medical Psychology,* 57: 339–45.

Rubin, Simon S. 1999. "The Two-Track Model of Bereavement: Overview, Retrospect and Prospect." *Death Studies,* 23 (8): 681–714.

Rubin, Simon S., Eliezer Witzum and Ruth Malkinson. 2017. "Bereavement and Traumatic Bereavement: Working Within the Two-Track Model of Bereavement." *Journal of Rational-Emotional Cognitive-Behavioral Therapy,* 35: 78–87.

Rufo, Christopher. 2021. "Ibram X. Kendi Is the False Prophet of a Dangerous and Lucrative Faith." *New York Post,* July 22. https://nypost.com/2021/07/22/ibram-x-kendi-is-the-false-prophet-of-a-dangerous-and-lucrative-faith/.

Russonello, Giovanni and Patricia Mazzei. 2021. "Trump's Latino Support Was More Widespread than Thought, Report Finds." *New York Times,* October 8. https://www.nytimes.com/2021/04/02/us/politics/trump-latino-voters-2020.html.

Ryan, Timothy J. 2014. "Reconsidering Moral Issues in Politics." *The Journal of Politics,* 76 (2): 380–97.

Sabes, Adam. 2022. "Students Rip 'Woke' Colleges for Halloween 'Offensive' Costume Warnings: 'Don't Think That's Their Place.'" *Fox News*, October 28. https://www.foxnews.com/us/students-rip-woke-colleges-halloween-cultural-appropriation-messages.

Said, Edward W. 1997. *Covering Islam: How the Media and the Experts Determine How We See the Rest of the World.* New York: Vintage Books.

Samuels, Alex and Neil Lewis. 2022. "How White Victimhood Fuels Republican Politics." *FiveThirtyEight,* March 21. https://fivethirtyeight.com/features/how-white-victimhood-fuels-republican-politics/.

Santiago-Rivera, Azara, Hector Y. Adames, Nayeli Y. Chavez-Dueñas and Gregory Benson-Flórez. 2016. "The Impact of Racism on Communities of Color: Historical Contexts and Contemporary Issues." In *The Cost of Racism for People of Color: Contextualizing Experiences of Discrimination,* Alvin N. Alvarez, Christopher T. H. Liang and Helen A. Neville (Eds.), 229–45. Washington, DC: APA Books.

Sargent, Greg. 2017. "Why Did Trump Win? New Research by Democrats Offers a Worrisome Answer." *Washington Post*, May 1. https://www.washingtonpost.com/blogs/plum-line/wp/2017/05/01/why-did-trump-win-new-research-by-democrats-offers-a-worrisome-answer/.

Saucier, Donald A and Audrey J. Cawman. 2004. "Civil Unions in Vermont: Political Attitudes, Religious Fundamentalism, and Sexual Prejudice." *Journal of Homosexuality*, 48 (1): 1–18.

Saul, Josh. 2016. "Why Did Donald Trump Win? Just Visit Luzerne County, Pennsylvania." *Newsweek*, December 5. http://www.newsweek.com.

Saunders, Doug. 2016. "Economic Victims Didn't Elect Trump. The Well-Off and Segregated Did." *TheGlobeandMail.com,* November 9. https://www.theglobeandmail.com/news/world/us-politics/the-average-trump-supporter-is-not-an-economic-loser/article32746323/.

Saunders, George. 2016. "Trump Days: Who Are All These Trump Supporters?" *The New Yorker*, July. https://www.newyorker.com/magazine/2016/07/11/george-saunders-goes-to-trump-rallies.

Schaffner, Brian F., Matthew MacWilliams and Tatishe Nteta. 2018. "Understanding White Polarization in the 2016 Vote for President: The Sobering Role of Racism and Sexism." *Political Science Quarterly*, 133 (1): 9–34.

Schickler, Eric. 2016. *Racial Realignment: The Transformation of American Liberalism, 1932–1965.* Princeton, NJ: Princeton Press.

Schiller, Brad. 2016. "Why Did Trump Win? The Economy, Stupid." *Los Angeles Times*, November 9. http://www.latimes.com/opinion/op-ed/la-oe-schiller-trump-victory-economy-20161109-story.html.

Schoen, Douglas E. and Zoe Young. 2021. "Democrats Must Face the Reality of Their Latino Voter Problem." *The Hill*, December 26. https://thehill.com/opinion/campaign/587231-democrats-must-face-the-reality-of-their-latino-voter-problem?rl=1.

Schuman, Howard. 2000. "The Perils of Correlation, the Lure of Labels, and the Beauty of Negative Results." In *Racialized Politics: The Debate About Racism in America*, David O. Sears, Jim Sidanius and Lawrence Bobo (Eds.), 302–21. Chicago, IL: University of Chicago Press.

Scott, Tim. 2021. "Senator Scott Praises Opportunity Zones' Positive Impact at House Committee Meeting." News release, November 16. https://www.scott.senate .gov/media-center/press-releases/senator-scott-praises-opportunity-zones-positive -impact-at-house-committee-hearing.

Sears, David O. and P. J. Henry. 2003. "The Origins of Symbolic Racism." *Journal of Personality and Social Psychology*, 85 (2): 259–75.

Sears, David O. and P. J. Henry. 2005. "Over Thirty Years Later: A Contemporary Look at Symbolic Racism and Its Critics." In *Advances in Experimental Social Psychology*, Mark Zanna (Ed.), 95–150. New York: Academic Press.

Sears, David O., John J. Hetts, Jim Sidanius and Lawrence Bobo, L. 2000. "Race in American Politics." In *Racialized Politics*, David O. Sears, Jim Sidanius and Lawrence Bobo (Eds.), 1–43. Chicago, IL: Chicago Press.

Sears, David O. and Donald R. Kinder. 1971. "Racial Tensions and Voting in Los Angeles." In *Los Angeles: Viability and Prospects for Metropolitan Leadership*, Werner Z. Hirsch (Ed.), 51–88. New York, NY: Praeger.

Sears, David O., Jim Sidanius and Lawrence Bobo. 2000. *Racialized Politics.* Chicago, IL: Chicago University.

Serwer, Adam. 2011. "Debunking the Right's Crackpot Sharia Panic." *Washington Post*, March 31. https://www.washingtonpost.com/blogs/plum-line/post/debunking -the-rights-crackpot-sharia-panic/2011/03/04/AFMFYr9B_blog.html.

Settle, Jaime E., Christopher T. Dawes, Nicholas A. Christakis and James H. Fowler. 2010. "Friendships Moderate an Association Between a Dopamine Gene Variant and Political Ideology." *The Journal of Politics*, 72 (4): 1189–98.

Shapira, Ian. 2022. "VMI Alumni Push to Reverse Diversity Reforms, Invoking Critical Race Theory." *Washington Post*, April 16. https://www.washingtonpost .com/dc-md-va/2022/04/16/vmi-critical-race-theory-equity/.

Shapiro, Ben. 2009. "Rap Is Crap." *Breitbart.com*, March 29. https://www.breitbart .com/entertainment/2009/03/29/rap-is-crap/.

Shapiro, Ben. 2021a. "No, the Derek Chauvin Trial Isn't a Referendum on American Racism." *Pontiac Daily Leader*, March 31. https://www.pontiacdailyleader.com /story/opinion/2021/03/31/ben-shapiro-column-looks-trial-officer-floyd-case /4822048001/.

Shapiro, Ben. 2021b. "Debate: Ben Shapiro vs. Leftists on Systemic Racism." YouTube. September 1, 2021. *The Ben Shapiro Show*, clip, 0:53. https://www .youtube.com/watch?v=CYm6V7a8Gnk.

Shear, Michael D. 2011. "With Document, Obama Seeks to End 'Birther' Issue." *New York Times*, April 27. https://www.nytimes.com/2011/04/28/us/politics/28obama .html.

Sherif, Muzafer, O. J. Harvey, B. Jack White, William R. Hood and Carolyn W. Sherif. 1961. Intergroup Conflict and Cooperation: The Robbers Cave Experiment (Vol. 10). Norman, OK: University Book Exchange.

Sidanius, Jim, Seymour Feshbach, Shana Levin and Felicia Pratto. 1997. "The Interface Between Ethnic and National Attachment: Ethnic Pluralism or Ethnic Dominance?" *Public Opinion Quarterly*, 61: 102–33.

Sidanius, Jim, Felicia Pratto and Lawrence Bobo. 1996. "Racism, Conservatism, Affirmative Action, and Intellectual Sophistication: A Matter of Principled Conservatism or Group Dominance." *Journal of Personality and Social Psychology*, 70 (3): 476–90.

Sidanius, Jim, Pam Singh, John J. Hetts and Chris Federico. 2000. "It's Not Affirmative Action, It's the Blacks." In *Racialized Politics*, David O. Sears, Jim Sidanius and Lawrence Bobo (Eds.), 191–235. Chicago, IL: Chicago Press.

Sides, John, Chris Tausanovitch and Lynn Vavrek. 2022. *The Bitter End: The 2020 Presidential Campaign and the Challenge to American Democracy.* Princeton, NJ: Princeton University Press.

Sides, John, Michael Tesler and Lynn Vavreck. 2016. "The Electoral Landscape of 2016." *The Annals of the American Academy of Political and Social Science*, 667: 50–71.

Sides, John, Michael Tesler and Lynn Vavreck. 2017. "How Trump Lost and Won." *Journal of Democracy*, 28 (2): 34–44.

Silverstein, Jake. 2019. "We Respond to the Historians Who Critiqued the 1619 Project." *New York Times Magazine*, December 20. https://www.nytimes.com/2019/12/20/magazine/we-respond-to-the-historians-who-critiqued-the-1619-project.html.

Simmons, Alicia D. and Lawrence D. Bobo. 2019. "Understanding 'No Special Favors': A Quantitative and Qualitative Mapping of the Meaning of Responses to the Racial Resentment Scale." *Du Bois Review*, 15 (2): 323–52.

Sirin, Cidgin, Nicholas A. Valentino and José D. Villalobos. 2021. *Seeing Us in Them: Social Divisions and the Politics of Group Empathy.* Cambridge, UK: Cambridge University Press.

Skitka, Linda J. and G. Scott Morgan. 2014. "The Social and Political Implications of Moral Conviction." *Political Psychology*, 35 (S1): 95–110.

Skitka, Linda. J. and Daniel C. Wisneski. 2011. "Moral Conviction and Emotion." *Emotion Review*, 3 (3): 328–30.

Slocum, Fred. 2001. "White Racial Attitudes and Implicit Racial Appeals: An Experimental Study of 'Race Coding' in Political Discourse." *Politics & Policy*, 29 (4): 651–69.

Smith, David. 2020. "Trump Blames Racism in Policing on 'Bad Apples' during Visit to Kenosha." *The Guardian*, September 2. https://www.theguardian.com/us-news/2020/sep/01/donald-trump-division-kenosha-protests-jacob-blake.

Smith, Tom W. 1987. "That Which We Call Welfare by Any Other Name Would Smell Sweeter: An Analysis of the Impact of Question Wording on Response Patterns." *Public Opinion Quarterly*, 51: 75–83.

Sniderman, Paul, Richard A. Brody and Philip E. Tetlock. 1991. *Reasoning and Choice: Explorations in Political Psychology.* Cambridge, UK: Cambridge University Press.

Sniderman, Paul M., Gretchen C. Crosby and William G. Howell. 2000. "The Politics of Race. In *Racialized Politics: The Debate About Racism in America*, David O. Sears, Jim Sidanius and Lawrence Bobo (Eds.), 236–79. Chicago, IL: University of Chicago Press.

Sniderman, Paul and Thomas Piazza. 1993. *The Scar of Race*. Cambridge, MA: Harvard University Press.

Sniderman, Paul M. and Philip E. Tetlock. 1986. "Reflections on American Racism." *Journal of Social Issues*, 42 (2): 173–87.

Snyder, C. R. and Julia D. Taylor. 2000. "Hope as a Common Factor Across Psychotherapy Approaches: A Lesson from the Dodo's Verdict," in *Handbook of Hope*, C. R. Snyder (ed.). San Diego, CA: Academic Press, 89–108.

Snyder, Jeffery A. 2021. "Why Ibram Kendi's Antiracism is so Flawed." *Heterodox Academy*, February 23. https://heterodoxacademy.org/blog/why-ibram-kendis-antiracism-is-so-flawed/.

Sorokowska, Agnieszka, Piotr Sorokowski, Peter Hilpert and Katarzyna Cantarero. 2017. "Preferred Interpersonal Distances: A Global Comparison." *Journal of Cross-Cultural Psychology*, 48 (4): 577–92.

Southern Poverty Law Center. 2020. *"Stand Your Ground" Kills: How These NRA-Backed Laws Promote Racist Violence*. https://www.splcenter.org/sites/default/files/_stand_your_ground_kills_-_how_these_nra-backed_laws_promote_racist_violence_1.pdf.

Spainerman, Lisa B. and Mary J. Heppner. 2004. "Psychosocial Costs of Racism to Whites Scale (PCRW): Construction and Initial Validation." *Journal of Counseling Psychology*, 51 (2): 249–62.

Spainerman, Lisa B., V. Paul Poteat, Amanda M. Beer and Patrick I. Armstrong. 2006. "Psychosocial Costs of Racism to Whites: Exploring Patterns Through Cluster Analysis." *Journal of Counseling Psychology*, 53 (4), 434–41.

Spohr, Dominic. 2017. "Fake News and Ideological Polarization: Filter Bubbles and Selective Exposure on Social Media." *Business Information Review*, 34 (3): 150–60.

St. Amour, Madeline. 2020. "Report: College Access Remains Inequitable." *Inside Higher Ed*, July 21. https://www.insidehighered.com/news/2020/07/21/inequity-college-access-continues-black-latinx-students-report-finds.

Stampp, Kenneth M. 1989. The Peculiar Institution. New York, NY: Alfred A. Knopf.

Stark, Tobias H., Floor van Maaren, Jon A. Krosnik and Gaurav Sood. 2019. "The Impact of Social Desirability on Whites' Endorsement of Racial Stereotypes: A Comparison Between Oral and ACASI Reports in a National Survey. *Sociological Methods & Research*, 51 (2): 605–31. Doi:10.1177/0049124119875959.

Staub, Ervin. 2005. "The Origins and Evolution of Hate." In *The Psychology of Hate*, Robert J. Sternberg (Ed), 51–66. Washington, D.C.: American Psychological Association.

Stein, Howard F. and Seth Allcorn. 2018. "A Fateful Convergence: Animosity Toward Obamacare, Hatred of Obama, the Rise of Donald Trump, and Overt Racism in America." *The Journal of Psychohistory*, 45 (4): 234–43.

Steinberg, Stephen. 2001. *The Ethnic Myth: Race, Ethnicity, and Class in America.* Boston, MA: Beacon Press.

Stelter, Brian. 2019. "Tucker Carlson Wrongly Tells His Viewers the Country's White Supremacy Problem 'Is a Hoax.'" *CNN*, August 7. https://www.cnn.com/2019/08/07/media/tucker-carlson-white-supremacy-reliable-sources/index.html.

Stephan, Walter G., Kurt A. Boniecki, Oscar Ybarra, Ann Bettencourt, Kelly S. Ervin, Linda A. Jackson, Penny S. McNatt and C. L. Renfro. 2002. "The Role of Threats in the Racial Attitudes of Blacks and Whites." *Personality and Social Psychology Bulletin*, 28 (9): 1242–54.

Stephan, Walter G. and Cookie W. Stephan. 2000. "An Integrated Threat Theory of Prejudice," in *Reducing Prejudice and Discrimination*, Stuart Oskamp (ed), 23–45. New York, NY: Taylor & Francis.

Stephens-Dougan, LaFleur. 2020. *Race to the Bottom: How Racial Appeals Work in American Politics.* Chicago, IL: University of Chicago Press.

Sternberg, Robert J. 2005. "Understanding and Combating Hate." In *The Psychology of Hate*, Robert J. Sternberg (Ed.), 37–50. Washington, D.C.: American Psychological Association.

Stevens, Francis L. and Katherine Taber. 2021. "The Neuroscience of Empathy and Compassion in Pro-Social Behavior." *Neuropsychology*, 159: 1–10.

Stewart, David O. 2009. *Impeached: The Trial of President Andrew Johnson and the Fight for Lincoln's Legacy.* New York, NY: Simon & Schuster.

Stroebe, Margaret, Henk Schut and Kathrin Boerner. 2017. "Cautioning Health-Care Professionals: Bereaved Persons Are Misguided Through the Stages of Grief." *Journal of Death and Dying*, 74 (4): 455–71.

Struyk, Ryan. 2017. "By the Numbers: 7 Charts that Explain Hate Groups in the United States." *CNN.com*, August 15. https://www.cnn.com/2017/08/14/politics/charts-explain-us-hate-groups/index.html.

Sue, Derald W. 1998. "In Search of Cultural Competence in Psychotherapy and Counseling." American Psychologist, 53 (4): 440–48.

Sue, Derald W. 2010. *Microaggressions in Everyday Life.* New York, NY: Wiley.

Sue, Derald W., Christina M. Capodilupo, Gina C. Torino, Jennifer M. Bucceri, Aisha M. B. Holder, Kevin Nadal and Marta Esquilin. 2007. "Racial Microaggressions in Everyday Life: Implications for Clinical Practice." American Psychologist, 62 (4): 271–86.

Sullivan, Margaret. 2022. "A Racist Theory May Have Driven the Buffalo Tragedy. The Murdochs Thrive on It." *Washington Post*, May 17. https://www.washingtonpost.com/media/2022/05/17/fox-murdoch-tucker-replacement-theory-buffalo-shooting/.

Sustar, Lee. 2013. "Marxism and Right-Wing Populism: The Case of the Tea Party." *New Labor Forum*, 22 (1): 58–65.

Swain, Randall D. 2018. "Negative Black Stereotypes, Support for Excessive Use of Police Force, and Voter Preference for Donald Trump during the 2016 Presidential Primary Election Cycle." *Journal of African American Studies*, 22 (1): 109–24.

Swan, Jonathan. 2021. "Exclusive: Fresh Data Reveal How Trump Made Inroads with Latinos." *Axios*, April 2. https://www.axios.com/trump-data-latino-support-49a0f0ed-b244-4b27-86b3-ee022e21f8c1.html.

Sweney, Mark. 2008. "Fox News Anchor Taken Off Air After Obama 'Terrorist Fist Jab' Gaffe." *The Guardian*, June 13. https://www.theguardian.com/media/2008/jun/13/television.barackobama.

Szekeres, Hanna, Eran Halperin, Anna Kende and Tamar Saguy. 2019. "The Effect of Moral Loss and Gain Mindset on Confronting Racism." Journal of Experimental Social Psychology, 84: Article 103833.

Tagar, Michal R., G. Scott Morgan, Eran Halperin and Linda J. Skitka. 2014. "When Ideology Matters: Moral Conviction and the Association Between Ideology and Policy Preferences in the Israeli-Palestinian Conflict." *European Journal of Social Psychology*, 44: 117–25.

Tanner, Courtney. 2021. "Community Mourns Utah 10-year-old Who Died by Suicide After Her Mom Says She Was Bullied for Being Black and Autistic." *Salt Lake Tribune*, November 9. https://www.sltrib.com/news/education/2021/11/09/community-mourns-utah/.

Taylor, Edward. 1998. "A Primer on Critical Race Theory: Who Are the Critical Race Theorists and What Are They Saying?" *The Journal of Blacks in Higher Education*, 19 (1): 122–27.

Taylor, Jamila. 2019. "Racism, Inequality, and Health Care for African Americans. *The Century Foundation*, December 19. https://tcf.org/content/report/racism-inequality-health-care-african-americans/?session=1.

Tesler, Michael. 2016a. *Post-Racial or Most Racial? Race and Politics in the Obama Era.* Chicago, IL: University of Chicago.

Tesler, Michael. 2016b. "Economic Anxiety Isn't Driving Racial Resentment. Racial Resentment is Driving Economic Anxiety." *Washington Post*, August 22. https://www.washingtonpost.com/news/monkey-cage/wp/2016/08/22/economic-anxiety-isnt-driving-racial-resentment-racial-resentment-is-driving-economic-anxiety/?utm_term=.026c406f09ef.

Tesler, Michael. 2016c. "Analysis: Views about Race Mattered More in Electing Trump than in Electing Obama." *Washington Post*, November 22. https://www.washingtonpost.com/news/monkey-cage/wp/2016/11/22/peoples-views-about-race-mattered-more-in-electing-trump-than-in-electing-obama/.

Tesler, Michael. 2020. "Support for Black Lives Matter Surged During Protests But Is Waning Among White Americans." *FiveThirtyEight*, August 19. https://fivethirtyeight.com/features/support-for-black-lives-matter-surged-during-protests-but-is-waning-among-white-americans/.

*The Economist*. 2021. "The Threat from the Illiberal Left." September 4. https://www.economist.com/leaders/2021/09/04/the-threat-from-the-illiberal-left.

The Tax Policy Center. 2021. *Briefing Book: A Citizen's Guide to the Fascinating (Though Often Complex) Elements of the Federal Tax System.* Urban Institute & Brookings Institution. https://www.taxpolicycenter.org/sites/default/files/briefing-book/tpc_briefing_book_2021.pdf.

The View. 2021. "Critical Race Theory Targeted in Virginia Gov. Race." YouTube, October 20. 2:05–6:35. https://www.youtube.com/watch?v=Hdx4JsDIsWs&t=123s.

Tilley, Brian P. 2020. "'I Am the Law and Order Candidate': A Content Analysis of Donald Trump's Race-Baiting Dog Whistles in the 2016 Presidential Campaign." *Psychology*, 11: 1941–74.

Tilley, Brian P. 2021. *Not All Trump Voters are Racist? The Racial Politics of "Hold Your Nose and Vote."* Presentation given at the Midwest Political Science Association annual conference, April. Online (Scheduled for Chicago, IL).

Tilley, Brian. 2022. "Critical Humanism: Effects of Emphasizing Humanity in Critical Race Theory." Presentation at the Annual Midwest Psychological Association Conference, Chicago, IL, April 7–10.

Trent, Maria, Danielle G. Dooley and Jacqueline Dougé. 2019. "The Impact of Racism on Child and Adolescent Health." *Pediatrics*, 144 (2): 1–14. doi: 10.1542/peds.2019-1765.

Troisi, Jordan D. and Julian W. C. Wright. 2017. "Comfort Food: Nourishing Our Collective Stomachs and Our Collective Minds." *Teaching of Psychology*, 44 (1): 78–84.

Tuch, Steven A. and Michael Hughes. 2011. "Whites' Racial Policy Attitudes in the Twenty-First Century: The Continuing Significance of Racial Resentment." *The Annals of the American Academy of Political and Social Science*, 634 (1): 134–52.

Valentino, Nicholas A. 1999. "Crime News and the Priming of Racial Attitudes During Evaluations of the President." *Public Opinion Quarterly*, 63 (3): 293–320.

Van Zomeren, Martijn, Tom Postmes and Russell Spears. 2010. "On Conviction's Collective Consequences: Integrating Moral Conviction with the Social Identity Model of Collective Action." *British Journal of Social Psychology*, 51: 52–71.

Vavreck, Lynn. 2017. "A Measure of Identity? Are You Wedded to Your Party?" *New York Times*, January 31. https://www.nytimes.com/2017/01/31/upshot/are-you-married-to-your-party.html.

Victor, Daniel. 2016. "Why 'All Lives Matter' Is Such a Perilous Phrase." *New York Times*, July 15, 2016. https://www.nytimes.com/2016/07/16/us/all-lives-matter-black-lives-matter.html.

Wallace-Wells, Benjamin. 2021. "How a Conservative Activist Invented the Conflict Over Critical Race Theory." *The New Yorker*, June 18. https://www.newyorker.com/news/annals-of-inquiry/how-a-conservative-activist-invented-the-conflict-over-critical-race-theory.

Wallstein, Kevin, Tatishe M. Nteta, Lauren A. McCarthy and Melinda R. Tarsi. 2017. "Prejudice or Principled Conservatism? Racial Resentment and White Opinion Toward Paying College Athletes." *Political Research Quarterly*, 70 (1): 209–22.

Wampold, Bruce E. 2015. "How Important are the Common Factors in Psychotherapy?" *World Psychiatry*, 14 (3): 270–77.

Washington, Jesse. 2020. "Why Did Black Lives Matter Protests Attract Unprecedented White Support?" *Andscape.com,* June 18. https://theundefeated.com/features/why-did-black-lives-matter-protests-attract-unprecedented-white-support/.

Weller, Christian E. and Richard Figueroa. 2021. "Wealth Matters: The Black-White Wealth Gap Before and During the Pandemic." *Center for American Progress*, July 28. https://www.americanprogress.org/article/wealth-matters-black-white-wealth -gap-pandemic/.

Weller, Christian E. and Lily Roberts. 2021. "Eliminating the Black-White Wealth Gap Is a Generational Challenge." *Center for American Progress*, March 19. https://www.americanprogress.org/issues/economy/reports/2021/03/19/497377/ eliminating-black-white-wealth-gap-generational-challenge/.

Wells, Amy S. and Allison Roda. 2016. "The Impact of Political Context on the Questions Asked and Answered: The Evolution of Education Research on Racial Inequality." *Review of Research in Education*, 40: 62–93.

West, Keon, Katy Greenland, K. and Collette van Laar. 2021. "Implicit Racism, Colour Blindness, and Narrow Definitions of Discrimination: Why Some White People Prefer 'All Lives Matter' to 'Black Lives Matter.'" *British Journal of Social Psychology*, 60: 1136–53.

Wetts, Rachel and Robb Willer. 2018. "Privilege on the Precipice: Perceived Racial Status Threats Lead White Americans to Oppose Welfare Programs." *Social Forces*, 97 (2): 793–822.

Wilkerson, Isabel. 2010. *The Warmth of Other Suns*. New York: Vintage Books.

Wilkins, Clara L. and Cheryl R. Kaiser. 2014. "Racial Progress as Threat to the Status Hierarchy: Implications for Perceptions of Anti-White Bias." *Psychological Science*, 25 (2): 439–46.

Williams, Armstrong. 2020. "'White Privilege' is the Biggest 'White Lie' of All." *The Hill*, August 11. https://thehill.com/opinion/civil-rights/511323-white-privilege-is -the-biggest-white-lie-of-all.

Williams, Chris. 2021. "Darnella Frazier's Video of George Floyd's Death Changed Everything: 'History should remember.'" *Fox10Phoenix.com*, April 20. https: //www.fox10phoenix.com/news/darnella-fraziers-video-of-george-floyds-death -changed-everything-history-should-remember.

Williams, David R. 2018. "Stress and the Mental Health of Populations of Color: Advancing Our Understanding of Race-Related Stressors." *Journal of Health and Social Behavior*, 59 (4): 466–85.

Williamson, Vanessa and Isabella Gelfand. 2019. "Trump and Racism: What Do the Data Say?" *Brookings Institute*, August 14. https://www.brookings.edu/blog/fixgov /2019/08/14/trump-and-racism-what-do-the-data-say/.

Williamson, Vanessa, Theda Skocpol and John Coggin. 2011. "The Tea Party and the Remaking of Republican Conservatism." *Perspectives on Politics*, 9 (1): 25–43.

Winston, David. 2021. "As Democrats Go Hard Left, Hispanics Head for the Center." *RollCall.com*, June 23. https://rollcall.com/2021/06/23/as-democrats-go-hard-left -hispanics-head-to-the-center/.

Winters, Mary-Frances. 2020. *Black Fatigue: How Racism Erodes the Mind, Body, and Spirit.* Oakland, CA. Berrett-Koehler Publishers.

Wong, Julia C. 2021. "From Viral Videos to Fox News: How Rightwing Media Fueled the Critical Race Theory Panic." *The Guardian*, June 30. https://www

.theguardian.com/education/2021/jun/30/critical-race-theory-rightwing-social
-media-viral-video.

Worthington, Roger L., Rachel L. Navarro, Michael Loewy and Jeni Hart. 2008.
"Color-Blind Racial Attitudes, Social Dominance Orientation, Racial-Ethnic
Group Membership and College Students' Perceptions of Campus Climate."
*Journal of Diversity in Higher Education*, 1: 8–19.

Wright, Graham. 2019. "Integrative Democracy: Mary Parker Follett's Integration
and Deliberative Democracy." *Journal of Public Deliberation*, 15 (1): 1–25.

Wright, Graham. 2022. "Democracy and Critical Race Theory: Identifying a
Theoretical Framework for the Democratic Enactment of Antiracist Policy."
Presentation at the Midwest Political Psychology Association Annual Conference,
Chicago, IL, April 8.

Yancy, George. 2018. *Backlash: What Happens When We Talk Honestly about Racism
in America.* Lanham, MD: Rowman & Littlefield.

Yap, Wei-Jie, Bobby Cheon, Ying-Yi Hong and George I. Christopoulos. 2019.
"Cultural Attachment: From Behavior to Computational Neuroscience." *Frontiers
in Human Neuroscience*, 13: 209–26.

Yellow Horse, Aggie J., Russell Jeung, Richard Lim, Boaz Tang, Megan Im, Lauryn
Higashiyama, Layla Schweng and Mikayla Chen. 2021. *Stop AAPI Hate National
Report.* https://stopaapihate.org/wp-content/uploads/2021/08/Stop-AAPI-Hate
-National-Report-Final.pdf.

Yourish, Karen, Weiyi Cai, Larry Buchanan, Aaron Byrd, Barbara Harvey, Blacki
Migliozzi, Rumsey Taylor, Josh Williams and Michael Zandlo. 2022. "Inside the
Apocalyptic Worldview of 'Tucker Carlson Tonight.'" *New York Times*, April 30.
nytimes.com/interactive/2022/04/30/us/tucker-carlson-tonight.hml.

Zaal, Maarten P., Rim Saab, Kerry O'Brien, Carla Jeffries, Manuela Barreto and
Colette van Laar. 2017. "You're Either with Us or Against Us! Moral Conviction
Determines How the Politicized Distinguish Friend from Foe." *Group Processes &
Intergroup Relations,* 20 (4): 519–39.

Zaru, Deena. 2018. "Donald Trump's Fall from Hip-hop Grace: From Rap Icon to
Public Enemy No. 1." *ABC News*, October 11. https://abcnews.go.com/Politics/
donald-trumps-fall-hip-hop-grace-rap-icon/story?id=58411276.

Zevnik, Andreja. 2017. "Postracial Society as Social Fantasy: Black Communities
Trapped Between Racism and a Struggle for Political Recognition." *Political
Psychology*, 38 (4): 621–35.

Zhao, Christina. 2021. "Coca-Cola, Facing Backlash, Says 'Be Less White' Learning
Plan Was About Workplace Inclusion." *Newsweek*, February 21. https://www
.newsweek.com/coca-cola-facing-backlash-says-less-white-learning-plan-was
-about-workplace-inclusion-1570875.

Zinn, Howard. 2003. *A People's History of the United States.* New York, NY: Harper
Perennial.

Zwiegenhaft, Richie. 2020. "Fortune 500 CEOs, 2000–2020: Still Male, Still White."
*The Society Pages*, October 28. https://thesocietypages.org/specials/fortune-500
-ceos-2000-2020-still-male-still-white/.

# Index

replacement theory. *See* the Great
   Replacement
the Republican party, 7, 16, 34–35, 37,
   81, 86, 122, 133, 147–49;
   anti-slavery history of, 30–33;
   appeals to Americans of color, 8,
      27–28, 136–39;
   Fox News and, 48, 120, 134–36;
   neo-Nazi presence within, 17,
      134–36, 149n1, 170;
   opportunity zones and, 144, 178;
   and racial conservatism, 6, 62, 65,
      102, 110, 126–27, 134, 139–
      346, 152, 161, 165, 168n6;
   White majority within, 5, 36,
      40–41, 149;
   *See also* Black people,
      conservatism and
Roosevelt, Theodore, 34, 65, 74n6
Roosevelt, Franklin Delano, 35, 74n6
Rufo, Christopher, 48–49, 52, 56

September 11, 2001, 3, 39, 131n8
Shapiro, Ben, 62, 74n7, 139–43, 145
sharecropping. *See* South, the American
slavery:
   American, 8, 12, 25n5, 28, 30–33,
      41, 42n2, 42–43n5, 47–48,
      52–55, 57n1, 65, 69, 85,
      149–50n4, 170;
   Certificates of Freedom
      from, 121, 131;
   Christianity and, 14–15;
   imperialism and, 14–15, 57n1
social desirability, 101
social dominance theory, 51, 110, 136
social norms, 51, 84, 97–100, 104,
   108–9, 111–12, 113nn1–2, 143,
   166, 170–71
South, the American:
   Confederacy, 30–31, 121;
   convict leasing and (a.k.a.
      peonage), 32–33;
   Democratic party and (a.k.a. "the
      Solid South"), 40;

planter aristocracy, 7,
   30, 42–43n5;
   Reconstruction and, 30–32, 153;
   Redemption and, 32–33;
   sharecropping and, 32–33
Southern Christian Leadership
   Conference (SCLC), 16
Southern Strategy, 16, 40–41, 105
"Stand Your Ground" laws, 47
status threat (status anxiety),
   125–26, 135–36
status quo protection, 103, 107–9, 138,
   146–47, 158
Student Nonviolent Coordinating
   Committee (SNCC), 6, 16, 62, 113n2
systemic racism (a.k.a. racist system), 1,
   6, 21, 40, 46–47, 56, 77–78, 84–88,
   93, 112, 171;
   and American beauty
      standards, 94–95n8;
   Democrats and, 153–55, 157–58,
      160, 162–64, 166, 167n2;
   effects on education, 88–91;
   effects on career prospects, 92;
   morality and, 80, 86, 93, 173;
   Republicans and, 81,
      140–43, 146–49
"The Talk," 90–91

the Tea Party. *See* Obama, Barack
terrorism, domestic, 16, 64, 171, 176
the Tragedy of the Commons, 12
Trump, Donald, 28, 50, 74n7, 117,
   129, 133, 153;
   birtherism and, 101, 121–22;
   hate crimes and, 64–65, 125–26,
      131n11, 134–35;
   political messaging, 122–
      24, 126–28;
   "Trump Derangement
      Syndrome," 121–22;
   Trump voters, 25n9, 36, 102–3,
      123–26, 128, 136–39, 142,
      146, 154, 164
Ture, Kwame, 62, 84

# About the Author

**Brian P. Tilley** is a professor of psychology, currently serving as chair of the Counseling Psychology and Social Work Department at National University in San Diego, California. His research examines how morality impacts the views of everyday people on political issues, especially those related to race and racism. He has been an instructor of counseling psychology since 2005 and served eight years as academic program director of a Master of Arts in Counseling program.

CPSIA information can be obtained
at www.ICGtesting.com
Printed in the USA
LVHW090905240723
753027LV00079B/39